The Cost of Future Freedom

ENERGY ECONOMICS

SAMUEL M. DIX

ENERGY EDUCATION PUBLISHERS
Grand Rapids, Michigan   49506-0488

LIBRARY OF CONGRESS

CATALOG CARD NO.:   81-70046

Dix, Samuel
        The Cost of Future Freedom: Energy Economics

MI : Energy Education Publishers

248 p.

8111   810922

ISBN 0-918998-05-0
© Samuel M. Dix 1982
All rights reserved.

First printing February 1982

Energy Education Publishers
P.O. Box 6488
Grand Rapids, Michigan 49506
Telephone 616-454-8264

Table of Contents

List of Exhibits

Preface

In 1976, I completed a series of energy reports for President Ford that focused on the probable drastic decrease in supplies of oil and gas between 1990 and 2010, identifying the probable beginning of energy restraints as 1979. My forecasts which were based on geologic determination of the undiscovered resources contrasted darkly with opinions that accepted the theory of a demand-dominated economy. Although the validity of my conclusions and their implications were recognized by the President's advisers, the conclusions were not presented in the 1976 political campaign, probably because they ran contrary to those of the President's political advisers.

My reports were published in 1977 as *Energy—A Critical Decision for the United States Economy.* Since then, the country has enjoyed four years of active political debate on energy, but it is my conviction that no conclusion has been reached. Our problem with uncontrolled international credit expansion is hardly discussed. The dominant voices in the economic community continue to defend the established doctrine that ignores both energy and effective credit control.

I have spent seven years exploring this subject. My 1977 book included perspective on all sources of energy and the probable consequences of the failing supply. Today the limits of this physical supply are even more apparent and we now begin to have public awareness that all is not well, despite the assurances of political and economic leaders and periodic oil surpluses in the world market.

In this book, the critical facts relating to our country's energy dependence are analyzed in conjunction with the uncontrolled expansion of international credits. I am concerned with the validity of economic theory and its relationship to a viable social science that is compatible with the developing physical sciences. As an industrial engineer, I am not in a position to effect a new theoretical economics, but I believe that the economist who ignores the interdependence of physical energy and credit expansion does so at our country's peril.

We must gain perspective on the conflict between our political-economic ideologies and the physical resources they require. In Part One of this book the ideological problems will be discussed. Economic theory today suggests only continuation of our growth economy to the time of ultimate collapse.

In Part Two the physical evidence of the energy resources that will be available to the U.S. economy are identified resource-by-resource. No serious consideration can be given to alterations of our social-political economy until all doubts have been removed as to the quantity in each of these remaining resources.

Part Three will be concerned with the potential change, and Part Four develops my physical forecasts and supports the theoretical arguments. The critical problem today is the transition. Fear dominates consideration of change but the required change need not be socially painful. The obstacles can be overcome. We can maintain an essentially free and challenging society.

November 1981   Samuel M. Dix

ACKNOWLEDGMENT

Many persons, including my forebears and those who influenced my growing up, contributed to this writing. My grandfather, Samuel Morman, lived until I was 33, providing personal perspective on the development of our industrial nation beginning before the Civil War. My father, another industrialist, was a technocrat in the 1920s. My first book identified the many authors whose work directly contributed, but a smaller number of men and women must be especially recognized. Without them, this book and its marketing would not have succeeded.

Herman Franssen, now Chief Economist for the International Energy Agency, was the best informed person on energy in Washington between 1973 and 1980 when he left the Library of Congress Research Service for his Paris office. His original work paralleled mine and he led me to many persons and sources of information. These included Walter Levy and John Dingell. Concluding materials from his reports to Congressional committees are employed in this text. Earlier, John Henderson, now with the Canadian Geological Survey, taught me geology and Mordechai Kreinin educated me in international economics. Herman Koenig of Michigan State University kept my door open to the academic community. Betty Miller of the U.S. Geological Survey introduced me to persons and critical geological data. King Hubbert was most helpful with suggestions and early editing. President Ford's White House staff encouraged the continuation of my research and opened doors to critical offices in the administration.

Earl Cook of Texas A&M University gave me technical support with his authoritative text, *Man, Energy and Society,* and personally assisted in my research efforts. Herman Daly and Nicholas Georgescu-Roegen provided early data and personal support. Stewart Udall was most helpful in recommending my first book and encouraging my continued research. Closer to home, Gerald Elliott, for many years the chief editorial writer for the Grand Rapids *Press,* directly assisted in marketing this book. Joan Gaines and Carolyn Medendorp were my primary editors.

The following publishers permitted the reproduction of copyright data:

American Forestry Association, Washington, D.C.
American Gas Association, Washington, D.C.
American Petroleum Institute, Washington, D.C.
Bank for International Settlements, Basle, Switzerland
W. H. Freeman and Company, San Francisco
Grand Rapids Rotary
Jonathan Cape, Ltd., London, England
The New Republic, Washington, D.C.
Simon and Schuster, New York, N.Y.
The Wall Street Journal, New York, N.Y.

DEDICATION

To future generations of Americans

Part One
Future Economics

The Western world is in the early stages of an economic transition that is comparable to the Industrial Revolution of eighteenth century England. This turn of fortunes is the consequence of actual and anticipated restraints on the supply of critical physical resources. It is now clear to energy analysts that the economic rules of the last two centuries will not hold in America and the free world for very long after 1990. These economic rules contributed to and resulted from the Industrial Revolution that America grew up in (1750-1850). America became the world leader in the fulfillment of the Revolution's promise after two world wars (1920-1960).

There is little understanding of our current economic problem. The physical evidence points to the necessity of maintaining the flow of the energy resources. The consequence of their physical restriction is already visible in decade perspective, but our market economy focuses on day to day activities where supply and demand and price interact with political events. Few economists or politicians dare to recognize the reality of the physical restraints on our economy. We face the specter of radical change and we are experiencing an understandable resistance to change. This fear limits objective analysis when the answers are most needed.

How much actual change will be required? This fundamental question must be answered. We must have an economic system that controls the value of money. We must be able to conserve resources that will be needed by the generations of future managers, at least the generations that have been born. We must recognize the importance of growth and challenge and amusement in the personal lives of individuals, but the preservation of freedom poses a problem. Inevitably freedom will be curtailed if conservation becomes society's primary objective.

Fear of change and fear of freedom's loss appear to be motivating America's conservative reaction. As a nation we are walking backwards, facing our past and calling attention to the days when there were no clouds on the economic horizon. America's conservative posture in 1980 and 1981 represents a fascinating combination of realism and pure fantasy. The realism is evidenced in the reduction in the per capita consumption of goods and services. The upward trend in America's standard of living has halted and has begun to point down. It is the physical reality of the world we live in, not a temporary down turn. Any respite from this decline will be temporary.

Our fantasy is the much verbalized expectation that our economy can regain its growth. This fantasy has political and economic underpinnings. Our politicians dare not deny the promise of growth to their constituents even though there is substantial evidence that most Americans would welcome candid leaders. The promise of more every year or at least almost every year is too well established in the American political rhetoric. We have lived through devastating depressions but the dream and promise remained and, so far, we have succeeded. The promisers have done very well by their constituents and the promisers are still electable. The practical politician will not alter his formula for success until the political process demonstrates an actual reversal of voter expectancy.

The economic motivations of our fantasy are more serious. Economic theory is based on the same growth that the politicians promise, but here the finite limits of our physical world collide with growth expectancies in a most predictable way. To deny the inevitability of the ultimate victory of physical reality requires the abandonment of rationality. We are given a choice between accepting the finite limits of our planet or taking on faith the theory of an ever-expanding world economy. There is no alternative to this ultimate choice, but our political and economic leaders have proposed one. We are asked to live one day at a time. "Trust me for one more term" is the politician's platform. "Let us worry only about those things that are here and now provable without question."

The politician has little trouble finding economists to support his promise and history has been on the side of this conspiratorial combination. We have been able to avoid the crisis in the energy supply and this was the most critical problem for the Western world economy during the 1970s. We have entered the 1980s with the promise that the crisis is now a thing of the past. Rationality appears to have been defeated. But it is still possible to look at the evidence and this is what the market decision-makers in our society have been doing.

The physical evidence of our energy supply is very different from the picture drawn by our political-economic leaders. The crisis has been delayed and there is a little more time before the mathematics of reduced annual supply confronts the requirements of an expanding world population and an expanding free world economy. Price is the screen that hides the reality of the actual physical restraints on our economy. Behind the screen of increasing energy prices, energy limits and their consequences are shielded from public view. The physical evidence has not been kept secret but the capacity to interpret this evidence has been immobilized by a fascinating combination of misplaced faith in economic theory, ignorance, and charity.

Our economic system focuses on price. We judge the value of resources, corporations, and people on the basis of the prices they are able to command in the market, and the market opens each day with a new perspective, a new hope, and a new price. Nothing escapes our market perspective and its concentration on the immediate future. Even the value of money which measures all other values is price-controlled and time-restrained. There are only today and tomorrow and the rapidly retreating influence of future time in the practical politics and the practical economics of our free world. This problem faces our leaders with an almost impossible task. How can they represent a meaningful future and stay in office?

Today, Americans are divided in their loyalties, goals, and even language. We have difficulty communicating the identification of priorities. The thinking person is tempted to abandon the battle and isolate himself from the future chaos that he sees, but there must be answers. We must be able to find a way of representing our future without losing the present.

If we recognize that the solution lies in understanding the relationships between our economic system and our human value system, then we may be able to begin to communicate with each other and bridge the gap that now divides the leaders of our environmental, religious, political, and economic movements. There is a logical beginning, the acceptance of physical reality, the three-dimensional world that supports life and without which all ideologies become irrelevant.

Economics should be the integrator of physical reality with practicable theory and it can be. In point of fact, economists cannot escape the physical connection of their theory because only the increasing influence of physical reality explains the political and economic dislocations of the last two decades.

If we are to understand where the physical world is taking us, we must look at our economic origins both in historic perspective and in reviewing the books and reports that constitute our current economic literature. We must employ mathematics to project current trends in the balance between physical resource availability and the demands of a growing population. We must look carefully at the economic mechanisms for the control of credit in both the domestic and foreign markets. Finally, we must be prepared to consider change in our economic ideology. Part One concentrates on this broad perspective.

Chapter 1

Energy, Economics, and Freedom

Western civilization equates its economic system with freedom. We start with the assumption that prosperity and all that is worthwhile in our lives can be obtained by releasing man from restraints on his physical and mental activity. Man can overcome the obstacles of the natural world. The economic process begins and ends with freedom and its success is substantiated by America's two hundred year history.

Because Americans worship their economic system and its freedom, they resist analysis and questioning of their system. But question we must.

The evidence of man's dependence on the things that come out of the earth is now overwhelming. Our society and all of its successes have depended on the soils and minerals of the natural world. Exogenous energy flows activate our economic world. We have harnessed inanimate energy to serve our purposes but we have separated our physical and political-economic worlds, trusting their management to independent professions. Economics as it is understood and practiced today does not recognize the primacy of energy.

Energy economics begins with recognizing energy in all of its attributes and values. This recognition will set in motion changes that will turn economic theory upside down, and as a consequence, energy economics will necessitate a reevaluation of freedom. If we accept our dependence on limited energy resources and if we dare to question faith in miracle replacements of those resources, then we will be faced with the total inadequacy of our economic theory and the necessity for radical alteration.

Freedom will continue to represent the primary consideration in developing a new economic system, but we cannot begin and end with unlimited individual license to destroy and consume critical natural resources when these resources are in short supply and man's numbers threaten to engulf the natural world. Freedom will be limited in our new world. The task becomes the definition of the freedoms that can be preserved.

The alternative to limiting the definition of freedom is an extension of our reliance on ignorance, not knowing, riding out the last hours of the old order, pretending that nothing has occurred to upset faith in freedom's motivation of man's capacity to do all things himself.

It is difficult for men who have ruled men and the environment to conceive of a time when man cannot control his destiny, but for centuries men were not able to control their own lives as Americans have done for almost 300 years.

In America, we have been reaping a harvest we did not sow and we have been exporting the largess of our harvest to the world. The most important resource in this harvest is the fossil fuels that took an average of 300 million years to collect and store the solar energy they represent. We gave little thought to our dependence on this energy resource and we resisted recognizing the evidence of its depletion. Now the remaining critical supplies can be counted in years—no longer in decades. The limits are real and immediate. By 1990, energy limits will have begun to close off the margin of economic activity required to sustain the present form of our society.

Energy Availability Determinable

The physical availability of our critical energy supply is discernible within the degree of certainty required for decision-making. Reliable numbers and definitions have been maintained by the oil and gas trade associations and these numbers have now been confirmed by the Energy Information Administration. Prior to the creation of the EIA as an independent service to the Department of Energy, the task of finding reliable information was more difficult and it was politically popular to believe that the trade association figures were unreliable. They were reliable and they have not changed. Before 1980 a diligent person could find accurate statistics showing the status of our proved reserves. Today, it is much easier but a problem remains. The facts and figures must be interpreted in terms of future expectancy and economic implication. Little agreement can be found for these interpretations. When we leave the physical data, we enter the world of political-economic hypothesis. The line between physical projection and economic projection is as important as the line between the past and the future. Our problem lies in the combination of these two worlds of fact and opinion.

Time is the critical element in physical projection. On the basis of the quantity in the proved reserves of oil and gas and on the basis of the size of our pipelines, we can determine maximum and minimum production expectancy for a decade or more. It takes this long to find oil and gas and develop the capacity to deliver significant quantities to the places where the resource is needed. The time span is even longer for nuclear energy and electric power and the conversion of coal or shale to liquid and gaseous hydrocarbons.

We know the physical limits on the supplies of domestic oil and gas. These supplies will decline. We know the physical limits of the world supply of oil and gas. We are dependent on political forecasts to determine the quantity of oil we can expect from this world supply from year-to-year, but it is becoming obvious that these foreign supplies cannot continue to increase. Finally, we know that our economy is totally dependent on its transportation system and that it will take thirty years or more to build a system that avoids dependence on liquid hydrocarbon fuels.

Time is required to find replacements for our oil and natural gas supplies. Precise physical measures can be applied to determine the time available in the remaining oil and gas resource and we know well enough the identity of the replacements and the time required to make them available. This physical analysis tells us that we do not have enough time to develop the energy supplies that are required to maintain our present way of life.

The Cultural Problem with Energy Limits

Our cultural acceptance of energy limits is much more difficult. Everything we have been taught to believe in is threatened by an energy supply failure. Our economic theory assumes that the free market will provide the incentive for men to organize themselves and maintain the viability of our national and local communities. We have faith that our system of government will represent the will of the people. America did not become the leader of the free world by worrying about tomorrow or the cost in resources of anything the country wished to accomplish.

A crisis is a time when decision no longer can be avoided. But we have succeeded in avoiding decision and have had to accept little more than inconvenience. Energy in its critical forms has remained available. In 1981, as in 1974, our nation was nearly equally divided between persons who perceive an energy problem of gigantic proportions and those who see only political mismanagement or individuals and corporations creating problems for their selfish ends. Where do we find the truth in this confusion? The answer will be found in understanding the relationship between the physical facts of our energy supply and our cultural expectations.

Our economy has been based on expectation of an expanding energy supply. Progress has been measured in terms of extended individual freedom, privilege, and material well-being. We do not know how our society will function when there is less and less energy for the nation and for the individual.

The energy problem has been with us for so long that the public may be tired of hearing about it. We have a problem with inflation, but so does the rest of the world. Now a recession or even a depression is in process. Only a few persons relate these problems directly to energy. Most economists minimize the connection.

The inclination of our people is to question the reality of physical energy limits. America's free press cannot overcome this prejudice. The public demands confirmation of faith in America and energy limits threaten this faith. Energy limits mean reduced freedom and reduced material well-being.

As we feed our desires into the political and economic machines without regard for the realities of the world we live in, our society may hemorrhage from self-inflicted wounds. Our political-economy may be destroyed by the excesses of our ideology, expectancies, and habits.

It need not happen. America still possesses the greatest combination of natural resources, scientific capacity, and free political heritage the world has known. We can avoid the deluge if we can understand the nature of our problem. This is the challenge to America and the Western culture. If we can understand the physical facts of our energy supply and our energy dependence, then we can determine what is actually possible and which ideologies must be abandoned.

Chapter 2

Energy and Economic History

Synopsis

Our current problem in understanding and accepting energy dependence is the consequence of neglected historic perspective. Energy has always controlled economic progress, but economics and the social sciences have not been integrated with physical law. The development of fossil fuels disrupted economic theory. With the ending of the fossil fuels, the error in the theory of resource substitution will become apparent.

Economic forecasting also has failed to recognize energy reality. The employment of econometric methodologies to forecast U.S. production of liquid petroleum since 1973 provides the most concrete proof of economic forecasting failure.

E conomics controls the political and social life of America and the Western world and economists have been the priests of our society. Economic history is the key to the conflict that has developed between the natural world and our political-economic society.

Economics defines man's relationship with the environment—his source of food, shelter, and other necessities for living. Economics is man's housekeeping. Man kept house before he developed a written language. Civilization's advances proceeded from this basic relationship between man and the shelter required to sustain life. As civilization flowed and ebbed, the shelter and man's relationship to his shelter remained the constant measure of physical progress.

Paul Samuelson calls economics the queen of the social sciences in his *Economics,** the most employed text for teaching this subject. Economists have constructed an elaborate system to explain the money relationships of modern society. All activities relate to money. All goods and services have money equivalents. Money is the only measure of society's multi-faceted activity. We are dependent on money because of the complexity of our civilization while at the same time the money system has advanced the development of our complex civilization. Our political and social life, the arts and the sciences are all dependent on money and the system of money accounting which the economists explain. Economic explanation has contributed to our actual economic development. We are a money society.

*Samuelson, Paul, 1948 through 1976. *Economics.* McGraw-Hill.

Historic Perspective

Our current problem in understanding and accepting energy dependence is the consequence of neglected historic perspective. Energy has always controlled economic progress. At each stage of civilization, the source of energy defined progress, beginning with the contribution of fire to the hunting and gathering community. Then man applied his own energy and his intelligence in the selection of seed to cultivate crops which supported the earliest stable community. He multiplied the time available for leisure by trading his crops and his artifacts and his labor, taking advantage of the special benefits of the land he occupied and his natural talents. He developed money to serve his purposes before he developed a written language. Money, contracts, and what has become recognized as the law of supply and demand are the natural economics.

Early on, the human community attracted marauders who either conquered or were conquered, introducing man's exploitation of human energy in slavery. Animals were domesticated to create a second energy resource. Then the flow of rivers and the wind were harnessed, first for commerce, then for irrigation, and finally for water power. Man's discovery of the wheel and the lever and the sail contributed to employing the energy of the sun. With fire he burned wood to make charcoal and smelt metals and bake bricks and pottery and bread.

The development of civilization took more than 100,000 years. Man himself changed very little during this time. His brain had developed to its present capacity. His instincts for competition and cooperation had shaped the earliest communities. But it was the discovery of energy resources and his employment of these resources that determined his progress. After the development of a written language he left a record of his progress and he multiplied the rate of his social development. The larger human community could interrelate and contribute to the discoveries with new sources of energy and new uses in conquering the natural world and competing with other human communities.

We can measure progress in terms of energy inputs, the quantum leaps when new energy resources were employed in war, in commerce, and in spreading civilization over the discovered globe.

Until well after the discovery of America, the daily flow of solar energy was the world's main energy resource and wood was the only significant stored form. The solar cycles controlled agriculture, the source of food and animal power. They also controlled river flow and the ocean's winds. It takes years for trees to grow and man's dependence on wood for cooking, smelting, baking, and building introduced a longer cycle of dependence comparable to his own life span.

This longer cycle introduced the first conflict with natural economics, a conflict which has not been resolved in modern economics. The seven lean years described in the Book of Genesis enslaved the Hebrew people. Rome fell when the population which had become dependent on the revenues from world conquest could not be sustained by Italian agriculture. The lesson of Rome's dependence and fall was not lost on following generations. A thousand years later, the ancient world's economics of trade energized by conquest was replaced by the economics of mercantilism as modern Europe broke its feudal bonds.

Mercantilism did little to resolve the problem of economic cycles but it avoided Rome's disaster syndrome. Import dependency was discouraged in mercantile economics which demanded that exports be paid for in money, preferably gold. Under the authority of the state, import barriers were constructed and commerce restricted. The mercantile economic philosophy protected nations from developing popular appetites that would exceed productive capacity. There would be no living on the material flow of invested capital, whether this investment represented economic or military conquest. Gold must accumulate if a nation were to be counted a success. Political rulers controlled the economics of their world as well as its politics.

In 1776, the Scotsman Adam Smith introduced today's laissez-faire economics, in part based on the theory and experience of the French physiocrats. Trade would be released from restriction and the monetary accumulation would be put to use in building production and commercial enterprises. England's industrial revolution proved the efficiency of Smith's concept of the great wheel of money credits. Money spent produces purchasing power to finance and encourage production which lowers prices and stimulates purchasing. But this new release of economic power produced a counter cycle: the general glut, production slow-down, unemployment, and contracting values followed by bankruptcy.

For the 200 years after Adam Smith, economists wrestled with the new economic cycles. In 1798, Thomas Robert Malthus had identified the basic mathematical problem of exponential population growth contrasted with the arithmetic growth in the potential development of the economy's physical supports, land and raw materials. He might have mentioned the eventual exhaustion of these physical resources as man overcrowded the planet, but economists never got beyond denouncing Malthus' growth mathematics. Twenty-two years after Smith's *Wealth of Nations** introduced our current basic economic theory, the seed of its destruction had been identified by Malthus and the alienation of economics from scientific principles of objective analysis had begun.

Fifty years after Adam Smith, Karl Marx attacked laissez-faire theory with his identification of the incurable cycles of boom and bust, driving wages down and keeping labor at Malthus' starvation level. Capitalism would breed war and poverty. Marx was a better economist than Smith but he mixed his economic analysis and reform prescriptions with a call for revolutionary political change.

A hundred years after Marx, Maynard Keynes proposed the massive reinsertion of government influence to ameliorate economic cycles. Public sector economic expansion would be employed to offset contractions in the free market down-cycle. Money pumped into the economy by the government would keep people employed when business turned down. Then the government would withdraw support and scale down its debt as the cycle reversed. The value of money would be maintained by this counter-cyclical process. Depression,

*Smith, Adam, 1776. *An Inquiry into the Nature and Causes of the Wealth of Nations.*

unemployment, and deflation would be avoided all at once. Keynes deplored the economic ignorance of World War I reparations heaped on defeated Germany. How could Germany pay indemnities without productive capacity and the acceptance of her exports? The economic collapse of Germany in the 1920s and the world depression of the 1930s prepared the way for the acceptance of Keynes' economic theories. First the New Deal Democrats and finally Nixon's Republicans adopted the Keynesian theories of political influence on the economic process.

A significant variation on governmental interference with Smith's free economy was introduced after World War II by Milton Friedman who proposed control of the economy by stabilizing monetary growth. He suggested utilizing the central banking system which had developed slowly and hesitantly since the first bank of the United States was chartered in 1791, failed for renewal in 1811, was succeeded by the second bank in 1816, closed in 1836, and was finally permanently established in 1863. The government, acting through the central bank, would control the money supply to Dr. Friedman's specification.

The importance of this 200-year history is the developed monetary control of economic affairs. From 1800 to 1980, U.S. population expanded from 5,297,000 to 220,000,000, a 41.5 times increase. As recently as 1870, per capita income was estimated at $223.00 per year in 1929 dollars. In 1978, the average disposable personal income was $2,263.00 in the same dollars. There is no question about the past success of the American economic system.

The monetary theories of capitalism were adopted by the Communists and the Socialists with minor variations. The great wheel of credit worked. All systems employed the same banking rules and the same measures of progress, growth, and achievement measured in monetary terms with only relatively small differences in their perspectives on the contribution of the physical world to the support of economic activity. The political systems were radically different in the relationship of the individual to his government and to property, but these radical differences only emphasized the common material and money aspects of the systems. On the international scene, the politically-controlled Communist economy competed with the market-controlled economies of the free world. Adam Smith's laissez-faire economic theory was compromised by all, and there were differences between countries, but the compromises had become acceptable.

Economics and the social sciences have not been integrated with physical law

During the same 200 years, the social sciences emerged and achieved academic acceptance as independent disciplines. The political process softened the effect of economic law on the individual with numerous social handouts and interferences with the economic process. Throughout this time, the economies of the world grew and material wealth in the developed countries increased. Economics was successful. Few questioned why. Economists were totally concerned with their analytical methods and their use as measures of economic progress. Economists more and more became monetary specialists, occupied with a narrowly defined pursuit, even to the point of isolating economic theorists from the economic practitioners of the business world. Economics was becoming, in the view of economists, a pure science.

While economics was growing up in isolation from the influence of the physical laws and mathematics, energy's physical support of the world's economies was going through radical alterations. A revolution in energy economics developed coincident with the Industrial Revolution, the very beginning of economic theory development. Actually, two revolutions were taking place at the same time, making it difficult to identify their separate contributions.

The introduction of an economy based on coal as a source of energy provided the physical energy for the Industrial Revolution. Adam Smith's laissez-faire economics released market forces from political interference. There was never any secret about the contribution of the physical energy resource, but the world viewed its own history in terms of political and economic progress. It would have been difficult to see the significance of this historic error until the progression of energy resources became clear 200 years later. Only when oil had been substituted for coal and after natural gas and nuclear energy became important physical supports for the world economy, could the significance of energy dependence be understood.

All energy substitutions were physical, from the introduction of irrigation, river transport, the sailing ship, the waterwheel, coal, oil, gas, and finally to nuclear fission. In progressive combinations, each controlled the economy in its time. Energy supply and substitution was controlled by economic law to a very limited degree.

In economic theory, price controls the process. When a needed commodity becomes scarce, people (the market) will be willing to pay for it, otherwise they must do without. There is no limit on the price increase except necessity, the point when people *will* do without. As the price increases, people will look for a substitute commodity and will be rewarded in their search by being able to name their price for the substitute that will satisfy the need (be accepted by the market). Competition will bring the price down to its actual production cost, higher than the original product but probably not much higher. But energy cannot be called forth by economic influence when it is not available.

Economics' problem with energy is compounded by a failure of definition. Many sources of energy appear to be commodities and in some aspects they perform as commodities under the economists' expectations. But energy is not a commodity and the commodities which produce energy are not themselves energy.

Economists treat energy as a free good, a God-given substance which has no cost in the economic system. The cost of coal is represented by the rent demanded by the owner of the land on which the coal is found, the extraction and transportation labor cost, and the rewards for the capital invested in the machinery and the organization involved in marketing the coal. To the economist, coal is a commodity and its energy-producing capacity has no significance.

Contrary to the economists' view, no economic process is possible without energy. Modern society is totally dependent on exogenous energy, the energy employed by man from sources in addition to the muscle power which he himself possesses. Manual labor and manpower no longer refer to energy inputs described in these terms.

Physicists and engineers deal with energy in terms of measures of work, power, heat, and electricity, and these energy measures are all physically convertible. Economists have no translation for this physical language. To them, so long as energy is available, it can be converted from one form to another if we are willing to pay the physical cost of the conversion. So long as energy is available, all economic objectives are physically realizable. But they do not see that the reverse as also true. Without energy all processes cease, and these processes are the support of life.

The development of fossil fuels disrupted economic theory

The energy revolution of modern times began with the use of coal. Coal had been known as potential fuel for centuries, so that when wood became scarce at the very beginning of the Industrial Revolution, substitution appeared to follow the economists' prescription. It seemed to represent a substitute source of heat that was less available and more expensive than wood. But the substitution of coal and then coke for wood and charcoal developed far beyond the economists' prescription.

Coal proved to be much more than a substitute for wood. The introduction of coal permitted man to multiply the result of his labor. A miner working on a coal face could produce tens to hundreds of energy units compared with the forester or woodlot farmer whom he replaced. Many industrial innovations followed and they were credited to man's ingenuity and the benefits of capital investment. But no economic explanation took into account the developing dependence of society on the energy content of this fossil fuel and the significance of its introduction. Coal was much more than a commodity replacing wood for fuel.

The second problem with coal and economic theory was the introduction of a time cycle that exceeded the capacity of the economists' tools. Primitive man already had experienced problems with the growing cycle of trees, a cycle that exceeded his planning capacity. The depletion of forests brought the demise of some of the earliest civilizations. This same planning failure haunts economic practice today. Coal is a fossil fuel, and the oil and gas that succeeded coal also are fossil fuels. They came into existence as vegetation energized by the sun, buried, and compressed for over 200 million years, beginning 400 million years ago.

Economics, the science of human motivation and material accounting, can have little influence on the fossil fuels. Their management requires conservation over very long time horizons. Economics deals with conservation only on very short time horizons. In treating coal as a commodity and in ignoring coal's real economic contribution, economists took the first step towards weakening their claim to scientific capacity.

The next event in the energy revolution equaled the advent of coal. The discovery of oil and the development of its uses propelled the world economy into a new orbit. Coal had not become scarce or costly when oil was discovered. But to the economists, oil was simply a better, more versatile commodity that replaced coal in many of its functions.

The energy multiple in oil is almost incomprehensible. Oil could not be dealt with under free market principles and the necessity for managed control of production and price was obvious almost from the beginning. Once discovered, oil flowed from the earth under geologic pressure in virtually unlimited quantities. This physical characteristic generated competition for control of the market, not for the production of the commodity. Once under managed control, oil produced its own capital for the development of a combination of industries that took over the transportation systems of the world as well as the largest proportion of all primary energy inputs.

Natural gas was the third and last fossil fuel to follow this path. Although not as versatile as oil (it could be stored for ocean transport only as a liquid at 260° below zero Fahrenheit, an expensive process) gas had two advantages over coal and oil. First, it appeared on the economic scene in tremendous quantities, the by-product of petroleum exploration. Actually, much oil could not be produced without also taking the gas, and as such gas was a free good, requiring only the pipeline connection to a user. Second, gas could be burned as fuel or employed for chemical processing with less cost than either oil or coal. Gas energized post-World War II America and spilled energy into the free world economy. Gas appeared to be the third triumph for economic theory. As this industry picked up the slack in the slowing production of petroleum in the United States, the peaceful use of the atom was being developed and the social scientist began prophesying the dawn of a new era. Oil had already replaced coal, eliminating most of coal's atmospheric polluting characteristics. Gas was cleaner and cheaper. Nuclear power could continue the progression towards energy so abundant we would not need to meter the electricity it produced. Finally, man would be totally free of his obligation to labor. The electronic revolution was delivering automation and television and miracle computers. The U.S. dollar had replaced gold as the medium of exchange in international trade. America's capabilities were unlimited.

With the ending of the fossil fuels, the error in the theory of resource substitution becomes apparent.

Past economic progress was not in fact generated by the free market alone. Ever cheaper energy was a principal contributor, the same energy that had escaped the economists' rules at the beginning. The projected glories of nuclear energy have no more to do with economic or political decision than had the success of coal and oil and gas. Atomic power is radically different in its physical

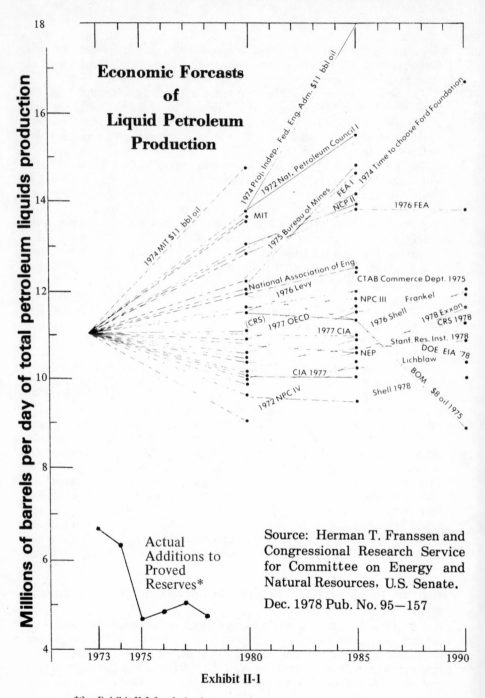

Economic Forcasts of Liquid Petroleum Production

Millions of barrels per day of total petroleum liquids production

1974 Proj. Indep. Fed. Eng. Adm. $11 bbl oil
1972 Nat. Petroleum Council I
1974 Time to choose Ford Foundation
1974 MIT $11 bbl oil
MIT
1975 Bureau of Mines
FEA I
NCP II
1976 FEA
National Association of Eng.
CTAB Commerce Dept. 1975
1976 Levy
NPC III   Frankel
1976 Shell   1978 Exxon
(CRS)   1977 OECD   CRS 1978
1977 CIA   Stanf. Res. Inst. 1978
NEP   DOE EIA '78
Lichblaw
CIA 1977   BOM
1972 NPC IV   Shell 1978 $8 oil 1975

Actual
Additions to
Proved
Reserves*

Source: Herman T. Franssen and
Congressional Research Service
for Committee on Energy and
Natural Resources, U.S. Senate.

Dec. 1978 Pub. No. 95—157

1973   1975   1980   1985   1990

Exhibit II-1

*See Exhibit II-2 for derivation.

characteristics, its source of energy. It is also different in the politics and the economics of its processing.

Nuclear fission depends on specific isotopes of uranium, a mineral resource stored in the earth in small quantities. It breaks down slowly in nature. It can be concentrated and its release of energy can be controlled to produce heat. Scientists employed nineteenth-century processes to convert nuclear heat to electric energy. Nuclear energy heats water to produce steam for electric generators. Small quantities of concentrated uranium are required, but the availability of this mineral and the cost of its processing resulted in costs that exceeded the cost of liquid and gaseous fossil fuel when their prices were controlled. As we enter the 1980s, the nuclear plant operation cost may be greater than for coal.

A second nuclear fission process employs combinations of uranium isotopes to breed a secondary fuel and greatly extends the energy producing capacity of the original ore. However, the breeder reactor is only now being perfected and the by-product fuel is plutonium which can be used to produce bombs capable of destroying civilization. Fear of plutonium and low level radiation from the nuclear process had virtually stopped the development of the nuclear energy industry in America by the end of the 1970s.

Significantly for this discussion of economics, the nuclear industry never succeeded in escaping government domination. The industry came into existence under government control to utilize knowledge developed in the production of the atomic bomb, and some 90 percent of the nuclear waste in the United States was still the result of bomb production at the end of the 1970s. The philosophic argument for the release of the industry to the private sector never succeeded. Finally, the government, responding to the demands of concerned minorities, restricted the industry to the point where its independent initiative in manufacturing nuclear process plants may be lost to foreign competition.

Economic forecasting also has failed to recognize energy reality.

Economists employ computer models that emulate market responses to changes in the supply of and demand for critical materials to forecast supply expectancy at different prices. Their forecast of energy resources has been less than successful. The conflict between economic theory and the physical facts that constitute energy reality are starkly revealed in a comparison between the oil production expectations of economists and the actual petroleum discoveries after the world price of oil was quadrupled in 1973.

The evidence is represented in a 330-page analysis by Dr. Herman Franssen,* prepared for Henry Jackson's Energy and Natural Resources Subcommittee.** A

*Dr. Franssen has been the most visible energy scientist with the Congressional Research Service. His first report, *Towards Projected Interdependence: Energy in the Coming Decade* 1975, was prepared for the Joint Committee on Atomic Energy.
**Energy: An Uncertain Future—An Analysis of U.S. and World Energy Projections Through 1990, publication #95-157, December 1978, U.S. Government Printing Office. See also other publications by Dr. Herman T. Franssen.

single chart summarizes 40 U.S. oil production forecasts. This chart is reproduced as Exhibit II-1. In 1974, the economists for the Federal Energy Administration anticipated 18 million barrels per day if prices were allowed to rise to $11 per barrel. Between 1972 and 1978, economic forecasts ranged down to only one-half this optimistic anticipation. Economists could not agree as to whether production would increase or decrease. There was agreement only on the production for the base year of approximately 11 million barrels per day of total petroleum liquids.

The record of petroleum production for the first six years is now history, but even this record requires interpretation providing opportunities for confusion. Petroleum liquids consist of crude oil, lease condensates (a liquid by-product of crude oil production) and natural gas liquids (a liquid by-product of natural gas processing). The nation cannot produce these liquid petroleum components without adding to the proved reserves and the reserves for each of these components are identified in the annual report of the American Petroleum Institute. These reserves are fixed quantities that are inventoried each year. Future production from the quantity added can be equated to the common term of million barrels per day. Between 1973 and 1978, annual additions to proved reserves decreased from 6.71 million barrels per day to 4.67. These additions to the reserve are shown graphically on Exhibit II-1 and in the table, Exhibit II-2. Obviously, the economists' fore-

Total Liquid Petroleum Additions to Reserves
Million Bbls. per Day Equiv.

	*	**	***	
	C.O.	L.C.	NGL	total
'73	5.88	.28	.55	6.71
'74	5.46	.26	.70	6.42
'75	3.61	.17	.85	4.63
'76	3.97	.18	.61	4.77
'77	3.85	.18	.96	4.99
'78	3.6	.17	.90	4.67

Exhibit II-2

casts totally failed to anticipate future petroleum supply. Even the withdrawals from proved reserves, which the industry calls production, fell below the economists' anticipations.

The failure of economists to forecast the declining supply of domestically-produced petroleum has double significance. First, the failure is so highly visible. Economists from virtually all of the public and private sector organizations who were concerned with the energy segment of the national economy have been involved. Unlimited funds were made available to many of these organizations. They cooperated in the employment of computers and computer forecast systems. All desired data were made available to them. Their information inputs included detailed reports from geologists and petroleum engineers who identified the oil fields that represent more than half of this country's proved reserves. These reports produce engineering estimates of the probable future production from each field for the ten years from 1975 to 1985 including the auditable geologic basis for these estimates. By public law, these data were made available to any economist desiring them but most economists ignored these physical facts, preferring their economic theory of price motivation on future petroleum production. These forecast data will be discussed in detail in Part Two.

*Crude Oil   **Lease condensate   ***Natural Gas Liquids

The second and most significant implication of this forecast failure is its relation to the total national economy. Liquid petroleum is not just another commodity that is traded in the market and whose availability influences its price on the market. The transportation systems of the world are dependent on liquid petroleum. If the supply fails, the world economy will collapse and most economic institutions will face devastating readjustment. American grain, Argentine beef, and Japanese machinery would be worthless if they could not be delivered to world markets. Bankers can move credit by wire and satellite communications systems, but these sophistications would lose significance in a transportation-restricted world. We forget so easily that the economy is based on materials and that the contracts that so concern our economic managers become useless if the materials cannot be delivered.

Economists seem unable to conceive of a national or global transportation-system failure. They believe that the transportation segment of the world economy will be able to afford the higher prices, continuing to distribute raw materials and finished product, while substitute energy resources and substitute transportation systems come into being because of the higher prices. In this view, there is no need for special consideration of energy commodities in our economic system. The failure of economists to forecast the liquid petroleum production in the United States is simply an embarrassment. They are not concerned with time restraints that preclude the replacement of liquid petroleum in the quantities required.

Energy economics is a problem for the future, but the time for decision is now. It is a very real problem for physical economists, engineers, and scientists who are concerned with the reality of the geological limits of continuing oil and gas flows, the technical limitations on finding equivalent sources of net energy, the material limitations of a conversion industry that could produce liquid fuel from coal and shale, and the ultimate environmental limitations on the absorption of the wastes that will be produced by this conversion industry. The physical scientist sees gigantic problems. The politician must be made aware of these problems. An energy conscious economic system must be developed.

Chapter 3
Steps Towards
Energy Economics

Synopsis

Energy is a physical science concept. Economics deals with human motivations and their consequences. Our society has great difficulty bridging the communications gap between physical science and the social disciplines. The objective of energy economics is to produce an economics that is compatible with physical science reality.

E nergy economics calls for integration of the physical reality of energy with the social influence of economics. This is a radical concept. Recognition of the necessity is progressing slowly in United States and Western world policies. Energy and economics involve two privileged worlds, each organized and dominated by its own ideology, ritual and hierarchy; each burdened with conflicting, subordinate structures. The physical world provides our sustenance. Political economic structure and cultural inheritance control our lives. We are only partially aware of the separate organizations that rule these dominions.

Energy economics develops from a simple objective. It seeks to salvage the economic structure that supports our society to the greatest extent possible within the restraints of our physical dependence on exogenous forms of energy and the limits in supply of the critical forms of this energy. Energy economics demands that we identify priorities in the relationships of social and physical science, but how is this to be accomplished? Who will judge?

Our democratic society consists of the interaction of men and procedures, accepted by a people living within physical boundaries, relating to each other and the land that supports them, and maintaining commerce with other societies on other land areas.

The market is a place where men interact and reach decision. The market reflects the accumulated intelligence of the community and is swayed by individuals' cumulative emotional reactions. The market is not a force independent of human impulses.

Our political economy is interdependent with our people as individuals and as a society. It represents the totality of our aspirations and our capacity to work together for survival. History identifies forms and procedures and history may help in anticipating future developments, but there are no inalienable rights for the individual or guarantees for his form of government.

The energy attrition now visible on the horizon of Western civilization has no identifiable precedent. Many civilizations have vanished in the course of human history but the written record spans a mere 5,000 years. We must judge most of our history on the basis of fragmentary evidence.

History discloses part of our problem of comprehending the division between the social and physical sciences today. The philosophers of the ancient world up to the nineteenth century were concerned with the solution of both physical and social problems. Men sought universal knowledge, extending the explanation for physical phenomena that had been interpreted under doctrines that were articles of faith. Religion and political control and the search for knowledge were one within the influence of a single social structure.

Modern science, first physical and later social, grew out of this simple, integrated, religious and political society by an act of separation and withdrawal. The physical sciences obtained the privilege of independent investigation of the nature of the world without regard for the opinion of the controlling, religious-political society. Within the physical sciences, the process of specialization continued with remarkable success as independent pursuits discovered the origins of life and geological processes and began formulating universal laws.

The social sciences cannot claim comparable success. Their search for universal law has made little progress in settling the philosophic arguments of their eighteenth-century progenitors. The relationship of man to his environment still is dominated by articles of faith and hope and unresolved conflict. The life issues have escaped scientific definition, but objective analysis relates energy to life support. The populations of both America and the world have gone past the point when an individual can lay claim to a significant portion of the nation's or the world's energy flow without denying life to other members of the human community. Energy in all of its forms is the primary support of life.

The reality of energy economics perspective elevates the importance of the community and, in this process, reverses American history. Man cannot live in opposition to his community in a crowded world, and we no longer have the unlimited resources and land required for individual family survival by primary agriculture. When the community is in danger, individual sacrifice must be accepted.

As the importance of community survival becomes more and more apparent, the necessity for an energy recognizing economics and the integration of our social and physical world will become more obvious and more urgent. The flow of energy must be maintained. At some point in this process, the nation will begin to think in terms of conscripting intellectual ability. We will begin to remove the barriers that inhibit the solution-finding process and its political implementation.

An intellectual revolution may be required to break down the barriers within the scientific community and within the universities. Disciplines must assume inter-disciplinary responsibility and permit meaningful investigations on their turf. Today the barriers include much of the university structure.

Our present market economics awaits market response for decision. But energy economics requires planning now for economic change we know must come. This planning must involve the economic community. A place for energy in economic theory must be found by economists. When it is found, they will name it. Until then, "energy economics" will identify the process by which physical reality is introduced into economic theory and practice.

Energy economics is not energy plus economics. It involves physical science plus social science plus all the antecedents of these sciences. Energy economics perspective requires the integration of worldly knowledge, focused on the necessity for the survival of the human community we call Western civilization. These necessities are physical. Energy economics requires the putting down or putting aside of ideologies that are in conflict with the survival of our society. Appetites, habits, prerogatives, and prejudices must change if we are to develop the conservation ethic that energy-economics implies.

How do we approach this task? What principles and methodology do we employ? How can we identify a leader and how do we test his leadership? To begin with, who controls our world today? Is it man or God or the accident of the interplay of human instincts with the natural resources of the world?

The ascendancy of our free economic system can be credited to the last explanation. Because man is concerned with the immediate present, we have accepted as law an economic value system that ignores the future. The consequence is the law of supply and demand and unlimited individual freedom. But man can neither multiply nor consume without limit and society cannot protect without limit the lives of all men without eventually exhausting all that is on the earth and in the seas. The cost of freedom will inevitably become its limitation. We can feel it now.

For many years before our preoccupation with economic competition, man fought bloody wars to decide whose interpretation of God's law was to be enforced on the people. Now, we are more inclined to place man and science on the pedestal of authority, but only a few questions are answered by this choice. What is science and how does science discover its laws? This we shall investigate.

Chapter 4

Science and Economics

Synopsis

The physical sciences developed methods to integrate the progress of disparate research within the physical science community. They have been able to reach consensus as to the relative truth of competing theoretical explanations for natural phenomena and accept revolutionary changes from generation to generation. In significant contrast, the social disciplines have been unable to escape their intimate association with political power which can tolerate neither revolution nor relative truth.

Frederick Soddy, the 1922 British Nobel laureate in chemistry, identified two critical problems in economic theory: the failure to recognize our economy's energy dependence, and the physical wealth limitation on credit expansion. Soddy's perspective can be useful in integrating the physical and social sciences, a task we must recognize.

I n searching for ways to bring energy reality into economic decision, economics' connection with science needs to be explored in greater detail.

To begin with, what is science? How does it function for the physical disciplines that it serves so well? What is the real difference between the physical and social sciences? How does each relate to the academic community? Does the science status claim help or hinder the development of the social disciplines? Can the science connection of energy assist the development of economics?

The primary characteristic of physical science is its glacial movement and momentum, its unrelenting determination to understand the natural world. Man and human society are part of that natural world and science is not barred from applying its searching, puzzle-solving procedures to human relations. Indeed, it was for this purpose that the social sciences were launched and encouraged during the last 200 years, but the social sciences have progressed little beyond their beginnings. Why? What could be different if energy economics were recognized?

Science seeks to extend human knowledge at the margin of knowledge. The body of knowledge is known and accepted. Science is not ethical or even purposeful, but science is motivated by human curiosity and guided by human organization. These are the parameters that define physical science and distinguish it from the social disciplines.

The scientific method is both evolutionary and revolutionary. Science chips away at the unknown, satisfied with progress that is insignificant to persons not involved, but science also accepts new knowledge that makes obsolete all that has preceded. Science accepts change, radical change, revolutionary change.

Our Western culture achieved its material success through science, both from the cornucopia of products and processes produced by the physical sciences and the organizations and individual initiative released by economic and political concepts. We identify science with the analysis methods applied to minerals, chemicals and dissectible life processes. The progress of material science was achieved by a marriage of mathematical and cognitive philosophy with observation, manipulation, and experimentation employing the manual arts.

Power, exercised through religious, political, or military organization, always controlled the society that supported scientific investigation. Political, military, and religious ideas and organizational prescriptions were immediately translatable in terms of power and community control. Investigations of the material world could be deferred, but when the investigations produced contributions useful to the organizations wielding power, both the products and the investigators found employment.

To a very considerable extent, the success of modern science relates to its achievement of independence from control by political power. At science's birth in the seventeenth century, that political power was exercised by the universal church. Science escaped and grew up under the protection of the Protestant Reformation assisted by the new, independent universities. The vestiges of these alliances and antagonisms exist today.

The potential development of an energy economics science is restrained by political power. That same political power restrained the development of economics even though economic theory was originally protected and encouraged by government and religion. The success of the physical sciences in achieving independence has not been matched by social science, and this is its primary problem. The social sciences are too closely coupled to the source of power.

The age-old problem in political organization is posed by the question, who shall watch the watchers? A corollary in social investigation is the question, how can we keep alive our historic perspective and protect our future development from dangerous excursions without inhibiting constructive progress? The social sciences occupy the seats of power. Can they be liberated to emulate the demonstrated progress of the physical sciences? What can we learn from physical science history that can be applied in our search to stimulate social science development?

Science grew up in medieval Europe and has maintained its image of cloistered research. Science took over the myths that explained natural phenomena to ancient civilizations, but science respected these earliest investigations and explanations, never eliminating the unknown or the mystical until a better explanation could be found. The genius of science is patience, doubt, curiosity, and a willingness to accept the new and abandon demonstrated conflict within a scientific universe that is totally interrelated.

Science's progress is dependent on the scientific community, a community without a controlling political structure; one that is both assisted and inhibited by many structures. This community is open and free. It operates through consensus over time, much longer time intervals than are apparent in historic perspective but much shorter intervals than have been achieved in philosophic investigative processes. Progress must be defined in terms of the broad acceptance of principles and laws and the elimination of contradictory explanations.

Science processes minute conceptual contributions through its structural organization. Parallel investigations in highly specialized research programs are related across the world through circuits open to the community of scientists. The key is a universal language restricted by the acceptance of current progress, the consensus of that which constitutes science at any moment in time. Scientific progress is shielded from excessive public view by the complexity of its language and the detail of discussion.

Science's great breakthroughs dominate the public image of science and these great leaps affect both the community of scientists and the broader, public understanding of our world's operation. Science's revolutions have enshrined the scientists associated with them. Copernicus, Galileo, Newton and Einstein are known to all. Dozens more have given their names to units of physical measure and historic turning points in specific physical science fields.

The revolutionary nature of science is of special interest in our search for answers to the potential development of social science. A scientific revolution totally alters our concepts and eliminates predecessor laws and explanations. Scientists do not make the law or laws. Scientists seek to find the law and, when they discover that their understanding (their current laws and explanations for broad aspects of how the natural world functions) requires too many exceptions and alterations of the stated general principles, science becomes unstable. Scientific investigation is stimulated. The unease and the discomfiture of the scientific community encourages revolution, but the scientific community does not go out to welcome revolution. Most frequently the revolution is accomplished over a generation. Pioneers of the old explanation seldom change their opinions and their disciples defend the old. Progress and acceptance grows spontaneously as science moves on and new generations take charge. This is the genius of science as demonstrated by physical sciences. This is the explanation for scientific progress. Over time, science accepts revolution. Rejected laws and conceptions fade away as their sponsors are quietly pushed out of the scientific community. (The *International Flat Earth Research Society* still exists with a Lancaster, California address, calling their publication *Truth.*) Science moves on, making old textbooks obsolete.

The revolutionary nature of science dominates. Out of public view, alterations in understandings all along the frontier of the unknown world are swept in with each new generation and the books they read. The past is buried. Only a few heros are retained to identify the major turns in scientific history.

Scientific revolutions are necessary when new discoveries become incompatible with old explanations. Astronomy cannot accept a solar-centered system as a variation of the Ptolemaic, earth-centered universe. Compromise and equivocation cannot be fitted into this science pattern. This seems obvious, but the incompatibility of lesser alterations may not be so obvious. Newton's laws of gravity and optics conflict with Einstein's theory of relativity, but the men who learned Newton's laws are still with us. It is easier for them to recognize the alteration in the general concept without understanding or attempting to apply the new mathematics. Further, mathematics and science have become too difficult for the general public, but the scientific community is free to move ahead of public opinion. New generations of men and women educated in science learn the new without equivocation or interference.

The social sciences cannot tolerate revolution. This appears to be the barrier that cannot be breached in gaining science status and in realizing the progress potential that the physical sciences have demonstrated. Obviously, the social and political power connection of the social sciences provides an explanation. Economics cannot occupy the seat of power in a community and, at the same time, accept and develop revolutionary explanations for the way the economy operates. Time is required to mature new laws and concepts and that maturing process is not compatible with public pressure. When the new laws are formulated, they cannot be introduced in opposition to established centers of power. Change in social science would introduce revolution in all its destructive attributes. Social scientists who advocate change automatically become revolutionaries. They can find only limited shelter in the university retreats. The economists who advocate revolutionary change can find no support in the practicing economic community, the world of business and banking.

Science's Historic Attempt to Rationalize Economics

In the ten years after World War I, production of electric power, fuel consumption, telephone calls, and most common measures of industrial and commercial activity more than doubled in the United States. Passenger car sales increased four times. The decade also experienced a recession and the collapse of the German economy. Manufacturing managers and engineers became aware of their influence on the economy and the nation's capacity to produce goods and services to satisfy public demand. This enthusiasm produced the Technocrats, physical scientists, engineers, and production managers who sought an economic system that would keep the wheels of industry turning and avoid the cyclical restraints introduced by the financially controlled economy.

In England, Frederick Soddy, the 1921 Nobel laureate in chemistry, set about to apply scientific analysis to economic theory. In 1926, he published *Wealth, Virtual Wealth and Debt* subtitled "The Solution of the Economic Paradox."

Little can be added to Soddy's analysis today with the benefit of the 55 intervening years. Eight years after the World War I armistice, he identified the economic causation of World War I and the inevitability of World War II if adjustments were not made in economic theory and practice. Soddy anticipated the demise of the gold standard and government intervention to mitigate cyclic economic recession (Keynesian economics). He proposed basic economic controls based on the quantity of money in circulation (Friedman's economics).

More important than Soddy's anticipations of economic changes that have occurred, he identified the major problems that are still unresolved. The limiting influence on a nation's economy is the availability of basic energy. With adequate energy supplies, virtually all economic problems can be resolved and poverty can be eliminated. Energy is the ultimate resource. Energy must be available if the free economy is to continue.

Soddy's greatest concern was the control of the economy by the banking system, the prerogatives of private bankers to expand and contract credit and thus control the nation's monetary base motivated by their own profit interests and the economic system they had created. This economic system violated physical law and ignored the capacity of science and industry to resolve production and distribution problems. An advanced nation could feed and clothe all of its citizens, eliminating poverty.

Soddy's proposals were in the scientific tradition. Economic law had been misinterpreted and revolutionary changes were required. Those changes involved the structure of the social and political society. Those changes could not be tolerated in 1926 and they could not be tolerated in 1933 when a world depression had demonstrated the prescience of his observations and when a second edition of his book was published, adding this experience to his analysis and proof. Soddy was not able to publish a third edition in 1945 when the second world war that he anticipated came to conclusion.

Today we face the necessity of a total reevaluation of the economic system Soddy criticized. Those who recognize this necessity will find insight in Soddy's analysis of our economic system fifty years ago when many of our real problems were only projectable on the basis of the economic theory of that day. The fact that political-economic changes might have been much easier then than now creates a barrier to acceptance of Soddy's recommendations, but does not limit the value of his observations. He correctly identified the primary conflicts that still exist.

The significance of Soddy's physical economics for America is the difficulty of altering our social structure to implement his concepts of credit control, but his objectives have been partly realized in Japan and have or will be undertaken in individual European economies. Although Soddy fully endorsed private property and private enterprise, he would be considered a socialist in this country, and today he would recognize the necessity for public control of the energy segment of the economy as well as public direction of resource conservation and population policy.

FREDERICK SODDY'S PHYSICAL ECONOMICS

Frederick Soddy's economics is ultimately simple and its elements are recognized in both economic theory and practice. Money is not wealth. Rather, it is the debt of a nation, an obligation to pay the possessor, and this obligation is transferable, thus serving the functional requirements of the market process. Money which entails no interest obligation can be substituted for interest obligated credit (the bank loan that expands the nation's monetary stocks) eliminating both the cost to the nation and the temptation (to the banker) to expand the monetary base. The obligation to maintain the balance between the wealth of the nation (real value) and the money stocks (which Soddy calls virtual wealth) and debt rests with the government and cannot be delegated. The value of the money (control over inflation and deflation) is realizable by exchanging money for debt (issuing and recalling government bonds). Capital formation must be both public and private with the government accepting a primary responsibility for the taxation and the sale of government bonds when it is desirable to reduce inflationary tendencies and by the direct issue of money when it is desirable to counteract deflationary economic forces. Capital is the real wealth of a nation and capital includes persons and their know-how.

Soddy's real attack is on society's organization of the decision-making process and the distribution of rewards. This organizational structure worked when the natural resources (particularly energy) appeared to be in infinite supply, supporting the deification of growth in economic theory. The market economy is not dependent on growth, but the kind of market economy associated with unrestricted laissez-faire capitalism is growth dependent. Soddy's scientific economics suggests shifting the critical decision-making process from the present capitalistic-political structure to a mandarin-political structure.

The physical efficiency perspective of Dr. Soddy conflicts peculiarly with our developed, free economy ideologies, but his concepts maintain the free market, private property, political democracy and the essential freedoms. His emphasis on the necessity for maintaining a balance between a nation's real wealth and the money-credit which reflects that wealth is difficult to deny. But Dr. Soddy would eliminate or radically curtail the authority of the power brokers who control our society today, and as a consequence, the implementation of his physical economics has not been possible.

Economic's Problem with Mathematics

Economics borrowed the banker's time-based interest payments for money rent without accepting the mathematical consequences of conservation limits. The coordinates of economic theory are supply and demand, and economics has created its own symbolism to present time-independent explanations for marketplace activity. As a consequence, economics is not predictive. The interaction of supply and demand takes place in an ever-advancing present, motivated by human decision, reaction and consensus. Predictable physical influences on the economic process are frustrated by unpredictable human inputs. Men will adjust to changing physical conditions and alter these physical conditions in effecting tomorrow's economic market. Economics is concerned with human motivation, more influenced by man's psychological nature and religious beliefs and expectancies than by physical phenomena. Historically, economics has rejected physical intrusion and economists seem to believe that human influences will always dominate the economic universe. There is little evidence in economic circles that the physical intrusion on their world must be recognized or that there are limitations on their fact-and-time-ignoring theories.

Mathematics opens a window to the future of this conflict between the physical world and our social expectations. The denial of mathematics reveals the anachronism of today's economics. Mathematics has a nature of its own. It is the interpreter of all physical phenomena including money and its relationship to both the physical and social universe. Economic theory can ignore mathematically interpreted physical fact only at the cost of losing relevance and acceptance.

Econometrics is the mathematically inclined branch of economics that has attempted to reconcile the contradictory natures of economics and mathematics. The computer has given econometric practitioners a powerful tool for their purpose but the computer can only extend the parameters and speed the computation processes of basic mathematical procedure. More and faster calculations have only revealed the depth of the basic conflict between unyielding physical fact and the expectancies of social scientists. This evidence must now be accepted but our Western culture is not ready for this acceptance.

Physical scientists have been building a world with rigid dimensions and requirements that has been irresistibly attractive in its outward appearance and the services it has been able to deliver, but our social leaders have assumed that this world could be accepted on their own terms, the terms of the economists' flexible human response to each tomorrow without a commitment to supply energy and other material resources in future years. Social scientists have assumed the privilege of ignoring physical process in projecting political control without limit. The evidence of this historic conflict is the failure of economists to forecast U.S. oil production which was discussed at the conclusion of Chapter II. Later, we will consider the problem of credit expansion and examine its implication, but first we must examine another basic problem in the economists' misuse of mathematics. This problem concerns the representation of limits in mathematical expression and their application to physical phenomena.

Uniform Exponential Growth

Mathematics employs the exponent (the numeric quantity by which a number is multiplied by itself, $10^9 = 1,000,000,000$). Logarithms are exponents and when they are employed as a scale in graphic presentation, exponential growth appears as a straight line.

Economic theory does not recognize limits or attempt to identify limits in physical phenomena. The application of infinite growth mathematics to the finite physical world compounds error in economic theory. Mathematics becomes useless when limits cannot or will not be accepted.

In its simplest terms, growth can be expressed as the time required for a population (any quantity) to double in size. Then the number of doublings can be related to a time extension. When the population is small relative to the limits of the natural world, its doubling has no significance; but when the population becomes equal to half the quantity that the world can support, then only one more doubling is possible. Suddenly, the growth of an insignificant quantity reaches a critical stage. The end of that population is now predictable.

These mathematics are very familiar to biologists who deal with the growth of living organisms that routinely multiply their numbers until their food supply is exhausted or their numbers encourage predators that reverse the growth process and develop a balance between population growths.

Economists have experienced the devastating consequence of growth at the heart of their system, credit expansion; but economists have been unwilling to interpret this phenomena as a limitation on their theory. Instead, they have employed mathematical expression to explain past credit expansion leaving open the potential misinterpretation of this historic record. They customarily present the quantity of money-credit (M1-A and similar summaries of the money supply) on a logarithmic scale where uniform exponential growth appears as a straight line with no limits on its expansion. The historic straight line implies potentially unlimited future expansion.

The truth is not quite so simple. The economies of the United States and the Western world are approaching their expansion limits. The plotting of the past money supply on an arithmetic scale more properly identifies the significance of the current development. On this scale, exponential growth demonstrates its rapidly ascending characteristic. It should be noted that the scale selection for the graphic presentation constitutes a recognition of limits as this scale selection relates to the numbers that are significant in the growth development.

The fable of the debtor king, the creditor mathematician, and the chess board demonstrates the mathematical power of doubling as well as the significance of scale selection and limits. One grain of wheat on the first square became more than all the grain in the kingdom with the final doubling on the sixty-fourth square of the board. In this fable, the mathematics was applied to multiple subtractions from a fixed universe, exactly the same situation as the subtraction of liquid petroleum in the annual "production" of oil. Each time the world's annual "production" is doubled, the sum of the withdrawals since the last doubling becomes equal to all the oil that has ever been withdrawn if the increase has been uniform.

There is very little question but that the United States has already withdrawn half the economically producible crude oil within its borders. Production peaked in November of 1972, double the production during an earlier month in 1950, a 22-year time span for the second quarter of our resources, but here the mathematical simulation of biological multiplication reverses. It is not physically possible to continue withdrawing increasing quantities of petroleum until the total resource is exhausted in another 22 years. Instead, we will withdraw less petroleum each year more nearly approaching the 113 years required to build up our petroleum "production" capacity, shortening this time span only by the economic effect of more intensive search and development for the last of the resource. Long before then, we will become dependent on the conversion of coal and oil shale for our liquid hydrocarbon supply until these resources also are exhausted.

There is no escape from these mathematical projections except the denial of the factual evidence and this is what our political-economic leaders have been doing as regards energy economics.

Chapter 5

Economics and Credit

Synopsis

Economists must control the credit system and maintain the value of money. The real wealth of America is declining. America's money stocks are expanding. Inflation is the consequence of the conflict between political expectancy and physical reality.

U.S. money stocks have been expanding at a uniform exponential rate since 1800 with variation accounting for alterations in the economic climate from decade to decade and from year to year.

T he control of credit expansion is at the heart of economic theory and practice. The nation that loses control of credit expansion destroys its economy, its political stability, and much of its social structure. International trade will be reduced to barter if the principal trading partners in the free world are unable to maintain control of the credit structure of their individual economies and the relationships with each other. The evidence that credit is moving out of control presents the most serious problem for economists. The evidence of credit difficulties multiplies the problem with energy and physical economics.

Frederick Soddy's analysis of money and credit is useful in understanding the developing credit problem. His physical science perspective lays bare the relationship of money in all its forms in its dependence on real wealth. The political and psychological dimensions of credit control may identify more accurately the art of the banker and his economic advisers, but the physical analysis cannot be denied. The multiplication of credit is limited by the dimensions of its physical support.

The Real Wealth of America is Declining

Economic theory does not explain or even recognize the decline in America's real wealth. Real wealth is not distinguished. Economics deals only with the reflection of wealth in money terms. It has no mechanism or means for identifying and counting real wealth in any terms other than money flows on a current or annual basis. These national economics reflect the accountant's profit and loss perspective.

The real wealth of a nation corresponds more closely with the accountant's balance sheet identifying assets by kind and quantity. The capital stocks of a nation are its material and service producing facilities, the natural resources that will provide the ores and energy flows in material supply, manpower in its labor force, and the know-how in its political, social, and economic structure. These physical assets can be summarized in terms of a single denominator, money, only to a limited degree.

The value of the capital stocks of America has been increasing at a decreasing rate for the last several decades. The value of America's natural resources has been decreasing since the day of its discovery and this value will continue to decrease, but here we must distinguish between real wealth in physical terms and real wealth in the economist's terms. Scarcity, the consequence of economic activity, measures the destruction of real wealth but scarcity increases the unit value of the wealth that economists measure. Thus, the remaining value of wealth may increase in economic terms when it is actually decreasing.

We cannot quantify the decline in the value of America's real wealth, but we know that the value is declining when we look around and see that the real, productive value of our farmlands and forests are barely holding their own as we harvest the annual growth. The easily obtained minerals are no longer available where they are needed. We are not keeping up with foreign competition in replacing our factories and building machinery that makes possible the future production of useful product.

In another perspective, it has become more profitable for major corporations to acquire other corporations to take advantage of the increase in their asset values which, in turn, is a consequence of ongoing inflation. While Japan's educational institutions turn out engineers and scientists who can build their country's future economy, American universities are turning out lawyers who rearrange the nation's wealth without contributing to its physical increase.

Many of these trends in economic activity can be identified and confirmed in the national accounting. There is no question about the growing dependence on imports, the declining investment in productive capital and America's increased investment in imported energy products that are consumed with only a small portion contributing to an addition to real wealth.

America's real wealth is declining and our economic system does not measure the decline. The gobbling up of the efficient small producers by often inefficient large organizations is encouraged by our tax structure. Benefits accrue to some of the equity holders, the banks, and the organizations servicing the national markets, but the nation's real wealth is decreased and the lives of many Americans are disrupted. Our economic system has been able to provide no relief from these obvious inefficiencies. Our economy is isolated from the influences that should cause economic pain and trigger constructive responses.

America's Money Stocks are Expanding

Demand for credit in America today is fueled by inflation and extended humanitarian services at all levels of its society, but the rate of expansion over the years has not changed significantly. The great concern for a reduction in monetary growth is not supported in the year-to-year perspective. Money and credit are simply expanding exponentially and the numbers are becoming very large. Pressure on the growth in money and credit is maintained as wage contracts are indexed to the rapidly expanding increase in the cost of living. Increased population and increased dollar activity require increased credit. A reversal of this expansion would induce economic hurt through the denial of customary credit to the small businesses who do not have direct access to the national and international money markets.

U.S. money stocks have been increasing at the annual rate of approximately 5.379 percent for the last 180 years. This figure is approximate for two reasons: first, the reliability of the money stock definitions and the method of determining their quantity and second, the limits of statistical precision in the interpretation of these data. Both reasons for the approximation are important in understanding the mathematical procedure, but the computed figure is very close to a true representation of economic fact, and the significance of this mathematical projection is much more important.

Our money stocks are defined as currency in circulation and the demand deposits in commercial banks upon which individuals and businesses write checks and conduct their daily business. Today, the Commerce Department of the United States defines these money stocks as M1-A. (When the deposits in thrift institutions subject to the check writing privilege are added, the Commerce Department identifies the money stock as M1-B. M2 includes savings deposits Repurchase Agreements, and Managed Money Market Fund shares. M3 extends the money stocks to include large time deposits and term Repurchase Agreements.) The recent refinements in money stocks definition have little effect on the 180-year history. Before 1867, the Commerce Department only recorded currency and this early currency reporting included both gold and gold certificates, duplicating gold's contribution to actual currency in circulation. From 1867 to 1896 the Commerce Department is dependent on the work of Milton Friedman and Ann Schwartz* in determining the quantity of money in circulation outside of banks and the quantity of demand deposits. The deposit contribution to the total in the early years was estimated by extrapolating the changing ratio of credit to currency. As we are concerned with money, not the value of money, purchasing power adjustments are not appropriate, and all of these quantities are summarized in the various Commerce Department publications, beginning with the *Historical Statistics of the United States, Colonial Times to 1957* which is a supplement to the currently published *Statistical Abstract of the United States*. At the end of July 1980, M1-A's are reported at $374 billion. This compares with an estimated $30 million in 1800.

As previously discussed, uniform exponential growth plots as a straight line on semi-log paper, but this plotting conceals the true nature of exponential growth. The consecutive doubling of a small population is hardly noticeable in a

---

*Friedman, Milton and Schwartz, Anna J., 1963. *Monetary History of the United States 1867-1960*. Princeton University Press: Princeton, New Jersey.

U.S. MONEY STOCKS, M1, 1800 TO 2020

Actual 1800 to 1980 and Computed Exponential
Growth @5.379% Per Year Compounded

Billions of Dollars

Year	Computed Money Stocks	Actual	% Difference $\left(\dfrac{Act. - Comp.}{Comp.}\right)$
1800	.03	.03	- - -
1820	.09	.10	+10%
1840	.24	.27	+13
1860	.70	.70	- - -
1867	1.00	1.30	+30 Civil War
1870	1.20	1.20	- - -
1890	3.40	3.90	+15
1900	5.70	5.80	+ 2
1910	9.60	10.00	+ 4
1920	16.00	24.00	+50 WW I
1930	27.00	25.00	- 7
1933	32.00	19.00	-40 Depression
1940	46.00	39.00	-15
1945	60.00	94.00	+57 WW II
1960	131.00	144.00	+ 9
1970	222.00	220.00	- 1
1973	259.00	260.00	+ 1
1975	288.00	281.00	- 2
1977	320.00	328.00	- 3
1979	355.00	370.00	+ 4
1980	374.00	374.00	- - -
1985	486.00		
1990	632.00		
2000	1,066.00		
2010	1,801.00		
2020	3,041.00		

Exhibit V-3

U.S. MONEY STOCKS, M1, 1800 TO 2020

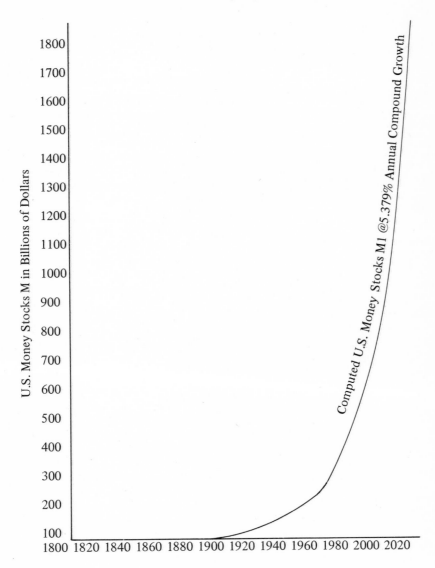

Exhibit V-3, continued

large universe, but as the population grows, the significance of the doubling increases. When the quantity is plotted against time on a uniform scale, uniform exponential growth takes the form of a boomerang as the hardly detectable increase along the horizontal, time scale transforms into an almost vertical ascent on the dollar scale, but this mathematical characteristic has significance only when the time reference and the quantity reference is relevant to social and physical fact.

The plotting of U.S. money stock quantities from 1800 to the year 2010 in Exhibit V-2 satisfies this significance requirement. The quantities for critical years are identified in the table which also demonstrates the relative accuracy of the mathematical curve conclusion to the statistical reference. The curve was computed to exactly fit the 1980 monetary stocks and the assumed 1800 stocks. Tests for accuracy are the transition years 1900 to 1910 (before the disruption of World War I) and the final decade. The United States economy moved so rapidly from the World War I disruption to the depression to World War II that no neutral time can be identified for the forty years between 1920 and 1960. Nevertheless, the differential between uniform monetary growth and recorded money stocks meets expectancy.

Money stocks were expanded 50 percent beyond uniform growth expectancy during and after World War I. The contraction of money stocks 40 percent below uniform growth is a consequence as well as a cause of the depression of the 1930s. World War II produced the 57 percent credit expansion identified in 1945 and the excess money stocks continued into the 1960s. This monetary history confirms the findings of Milton Friedman that the contraction of money stocks after the Civil War could be considered the primary cause of the depressed economy of that period and that the depression of the 1930s probably could have been mitigated if money stocks had been maintained at the level of uniform growth. Soddy reached the same conclusion employing his physical economics perspective.

The significance of this monetary history and its mathematical projection is the evidence of the irresistible expansion of the monetary stocks and the social and economic consequences of any alteration to this uniform expansion. The physical economic underpinnings are population increase and constantly advancing human expectancies originally propelled by man's imagination and our country's undeveloped natural resources. Native births have slowed, but the adult population has continued to increase as a consequence of previous births and the immigration of adult aliens. The individual productivity factor, that is dependent on resource development, has been replaced by more equitable distribution, raising per capita income. More people with higher spendable incomes require larger money stocks.

The threat to our economic future lies in the relationship of the irresistible expansion of monetary stocks relative to the real wealth of the nation. With no expansion of the real wealth, the total quantity in the monetary expansion will become effective as an inflationary influence. This inflation will be multiplied by any decrease in the actual real wealth of the nation and this decrease has already been identified.

In another perspective, the irresistible expansion of money stocks and the consistency of the expansion identifies the difficulty of attempting to control the economy by influencing the country's internal money stocks without altering our social expectancy and our political structure.

In looking to the future, the money growth rate established in the last 180 years will affect a ten times increase in the quantity of the money stocks of 1976 by the year 2020. This ten times increase exceeds any possible expansion in the real wealth of the nation. Inflation is inevitable, but the amount of inflation is not mathematically determinable. In a managed economy, credit expansion can be controlled. Social change cannot be measured in economic terms alone, but social change will be the consequence of the alteration in the balance of credit and real wealth. How will this change be managed? This is the question that must be answered if our society is to avoid chaos.

Chapter 6

The International Trade Connection of Credit

Synopsis

The Euro-dollar market employs the full faith and credit of the United States backed by the real wealth of America to support money-credits loaned by the international banking community. These credits now exceed M-1A which is the total quantity of the currencies and demand deposits circulating within the United States.

Credit expansion, led by Euro-dollar expansion, threatens the United States economy, but international trade and the free world economy depend on the U.S. dollar as presently employed. The conflict must be resolved.

Free international trade was always a basic tenet of laissez-faire economic theory, despite the evidence of social disruption in the undeveloped countries and the active restraints on trade by political movements in many developing countries. America had been moving towards free trade before World War II and accelerated the movement when, after the war, we were the only viable economy in the free world. We shipped product and spent our merchandise trade surplus on capital investments abroad. When these investments exceeded the quantity of our trade surplus, the unfavorable balance was a positive factor for the U.S. economy. We were building future income, anticipating a return on our foreign investments. We were enjoying the rewards of income generated abroad by the international corporations even though the total foreign trade contribution to the U.S. economy was relatively small.

In the late 1960s, the United States' adverse trade balances began to have significance. The economies of Europe and Japan had recovered from the War's devastation. France's de Gaulle challenged American dominance of the international market and in 1968 the international monetary arrangements based on the gold standard which had been put in place in July of 1944 began to be dismantled. On August 15, 1971, the United States closed the gold window and a new era of fluctuating exchange rates was introduced. To a considerable extent, the international bankers have been looking for a replacement for the fiction of gold's measure of currency value since that date.

The world banking system cannot return to a gold standard. Only the United States has an economy that is large enough and physically independent enough to provide the support for a world currency. Some progress has been made in developing a cooperative economic administration for the European countries, but these countries have not given up the sovereignty that is required to unify their currencies. The world bank's *drawing rights* and *basket of currencies* are nothing more than the names imply. The value of the world's currencies is dependent on the value of the real wealth of individual nations and the nation that allows its currency to be expanded beyond the ultimate value of its real wealth will lose out in the international currency trading game.

In the final analysis, all currency values are relative. The world bankers can only weigh the value of one currency over another in their confidence rating. If the system breaks down, world trade will return to barter.

Euro-Dollar Money Stocks

Euro-dollars are the dollar denominated credits originally exported as grants to foreign countries or as payments for imports including the cost of foreign investment. The Euro-dollars might have been used by persons outside of the United States to pay for U.S. exports of similar goods, but for many reasons, these dollars were not returned to the United States. Rather, they have accumulated in foreign banks, retaining their dollar denomination, and loaned to the citizens and banks of the world. In this process, they have expanded many times as these deposits are not subject to the reserve requirements of our Federal Reserve System member banks.

Euro-dollars are the same as the dollars that circulate within the United States. They can be converted into U.S. currency. They can be used for every purpose the same way as U.S. bank credits.

Euro-dollars represent the leading edge of an international community. The bankers of the world have taken unto themselves the authority to create this international credit community despite the failure of the world's politicians to give form and substance to the political community. The existence of the Euro-dollars has led other countries to allow their currencies to be employed in the same way, creating not just a Euro-dollar market, but a Euro-currency market, and this market includes the internationalized Japanese yen.

Euro-currency presents a potentially explosive credit situation. Euro-currency credits are being created without restraint and without reference to any identifiable real wealth. The creation of Euro-currency extends the theory of laissez-faire economics beyond the limits of physical reality. It sets in motion a possible world currency inflation.

This world banking situation can be related to economic politics in the United States between the chartering of the first U.S. bank in 1791 and the failure of the renewal of its charter in 1811. The states, still influenced by their previous independent colonial status, were unwilling to relinquish credit control to the national government. The state chartered banks created both their own credit media and their own currency. Without the national bank and the unifying effect of a recognized national currency, economic chaos ensued from 1811 until the second bank was chartered in 1816. This was not the end of the credit controversy in the United States, but eventually a national credit policy developed. The difference between the United States financial history and the current world financial development is the political dimension. In 1811 the U.S. had a constitution, a federal government, and the capacity to enforce uniform credit policies on the states; and the states did not have independent defense departments creating military establishments to influence political decision. The world community is only approaching a semblance of political integration and the defense related problems of the independent national states appear to be increasing.

The evidence of a potentially explosive world credit increase is growing. First, the Euro-dollar credits are expanding at more than three times the rate of growth of the currency and demand deposits within the United States. Second, the international banks are involved in a competitive race to expand the credit base upon which they operate. Third, benign neglect of international credits management appears to be the policy of the United States government and its central bank. The statistical evidence can be developed from the reports of the international banking community.

The Bank for International Settlements in Basle, Switzerland is the only source of comprehensive information on the Euro-currency market. This financial institution is providing service to the world banking community in gathering information and publishing quarterly reports that identify the Euro-currency balances held by the international banks. At the end of December 1973, Euro-currency deposits in the reporting banks of eight European countries totaled $131.4 billion. By the end of 1980 the United States supported credits deposited in European banks were counted at $548.4 billion and twelve European countries were represented in a consistent orderly reporting that had been maintained since December 1977. The bank also reported Euro-currency balances in the banks of the United States, Canada, Japan, and off-shore branches of U.S. banks.

Euro-currency is identified as the external position of the reporting banks, the deposits and loans made by these banks outside their own countries. Euro-currency deposits and loans may be made in the bank's own national currency or any of the internationalized currencies.

Two problems arise from the independence of the international banks who report their position to the Bank of International Settlements. First, duplication exists when related banks report their external positions. The Settlements Bank employs statistical procedures to eliminate this duplication. Second, the currency breakdown has been established only for the European banks. Lacking an international organization with power to enforce banking regulations on the international community, we can only estimate the total Euro-dollars that are circulating in these banks. Exhibit VI-7 uses the Settlement Bank's figures to estimate the number of Euro-dollars that our domestic economy has been supporting in the international market and projects the quantity of these dollars through the end of this century if the rate of growth established in the last three years is continued. This exercise begins with the identified dollar denominated

PROJECTION OF NET EURO-DOLLAR BALANCES

**Based on Year-end Position of Reporting World Banks
December 31, 1977 to 1980
by The Bank for International Settlements
Basle, Switzerland**

	Billions of Dollars			
	Dec. 1977	Dec. 1978	Dec. 1979	Dec. 1980
Dollar Denominated Deposits (Liabilities) of European Banks—External Balances (Exhibit A-35 column 1.)	278.8	348.6	436.6	548.4
Total Foreign and Domestic Currency in External Position of European Banks (Exhibit A-34 column 2.)	453.9	592.8	777.2	928.4
% U.S. Dollars in European Bank's External Position (Euro-Currency)	61.4%	58.8%	56.2%	59.1%
Net Euro-Currency World Reporting Banks (External Position Deposits) Corrected for Double Reporting (Exhibit #-34 column 3.)	430	540	665	810
Indicated Net Euro-Dollars	264	318	374	479
Compound Annual Growth for Three Years = 21.97%				
Computed Year End Balance at 21.97% Growth	264	322	393	479

	1985	1990	1995	2000
Projected Growth, Future Years				
Years	8	13	18	23
Euro-Dollars at Projected Growth	1,293	3,490	9,419	25,422

Exhibit VI-4

deposits in the European banks and compares these Euro-dollars with the total external position of these banks which is defined as their Euro-currency balances. Deposits constitute a bank's liabilities in balance sheet reporting. Euro-dollars range from 56 to 61% of the currencies employed in the international market by these European banks. In Euro-currency reporting by the Settlements Bank, the U.S. dollar is employed as a measure of value. Distortions are introduced when the dollar's value relative to other currencies changes, but then the reference base is consistently maintained.

Gross Euro-currency reported by the European banks increased steadily from $279 billion at the end of 1977 to $548 billion at the end of 1980. If we assume that these European banks are representative of the world banks and if we accept the correction for double reporting, we can apply the ratio of Euro-dollars to all other Euro-currencies and project the Euro-dollars component of net world credit. These are indicated on Exhibit VI-4 as increasing from $264 billion to $479 billion by the end of 1980, producing a compound annual growth for these three years of 21.9%.

The computed growth of the dollar credits that had been employed by the international banks is not comparable with the 180 year computed growth of this country's money and demand deposits discussed in Chapter Five, but the free world economy is a reflection of this credit expansion and any significant curtailment will adversely affect all measures of economic progress. More precisely, Euro-dollar expansion is actually a reflection of the expansion of the world economy. If this expansion slows down or reverses the decline in Euro-dollars will reflect the world depression.

The significance of the Euro-currency expansion is the relationship between Euro-dollars and the United States internal currency stocks. M1-A remains the primary reference base, currency plus demand deposits in this country's commercial banks.

In 1980, the Euro-currency deposits identified by the Bank for International Settlements exceeded M1-A. The assets of this country are supporting more credit in the international market than for the domestic economy. M1-A accounts for only 44 percent of the total money-credit in circulation. At this rate of expansion, American money and commercial bank accounts will

COMPARISON OF DOMESTIC AND EUROPEAN DOLLARS
Billions of Dollars

Year	U.S. Money Stocks M1-A	Euro-$ Foreign Bank Balances	Percent Domestic Money
1980	371	479	44%
1985	482	1,293	27%
1990	626	3,490	15%
1995	814	9,419	8%
2000	1,085	15,422	4%

Exhibit VI-5

represent only 27 percent by 1985. It would appear that this trend cannot be allowed to continue, and that the multiplication of Euro-dollar credits is already out of control. However most economists are not of this opinion. They know as did Frederick Soddy that money is debt and that the real economy is represented by the movement of raw materials and manufactured products. They believe that money can be expanded virtually without limit, the only consequence being inflation and the depreciation of money value. The Euro-dollar market serves the international business world which is shared by American banks and businessmen as well as foreign banks and foreign entrepreneurs. Credit in the unrestricted Euro-currency market is controlled by market demand and most economists have faith in the banking community that manages these credits.

The United States Commerce Department recognizes Euro-dollars in their money aggregate reporting, but the department counts as money stocks only the Euro-dollars that appear in money balances within the United States. The M2 Euro-dollars are identified as "overnight Euro-dollars (those issued by Caribbean branches of member banks) held by United States non-bank residents." The Commerce Department's L classification of monetary aggregates includes "other Euro-dollar holdings of U.S. non-bank residents." Euro-dollars move in and out of the international banking system to this country, but United States member banks are privileged to ignore the reserve requirements for Euro-dollar balances held by their foreign branches to maintain competition in the world money markets.

The difference between the perspective of the physical economists and the pecuniary economists—the perspective of Frederick Soddy versus today's economists and world bankers—is the physical economist's knowledge of world resource limits and the relationship between the physical world and the standard of living nation-by-nation and class-by-class.

The physical economists know the difference between money created to finance a railroad bringing agricultural products from the interior to continuously feed the world community and money created to finance oil purchases that will be consumed in a year and leave only more mouths to feed. This money generates demand without contributing to supply and without building capital stocks. The consequence is accelerating inflation.

The problem with unlimited credit expansion will become evident when the world economies are unable to adjust to the transition from abundant raw material resources to significant scarcity. From generation to generation, world population will be reduced as scarcity forces down the living standards. But we have extended the life expectancy of the human population. Physical evidence points to material resource limits that will intercept the idyllic transition that fits the pecuniary economists' requirements.

National sovereignty is proved in the independent power of a nation to make war and control the value of its currency. These powers are limited in the international community by the obvious carnage of war and by the refusal of the independent nations to accept the currency of a nation that cannot support its currency with real wealth in the marketplace. An international currency has no home, no basis for support without an international community, and there is no space on our planet to locate this community without the consent of the nations who are now in possession.

An international currency must have a physical basis for its value and that physical basis must come from the giving up of some part of every participating nation's real wealth or claim on real wealth. In the final analysis, that which must be given up is unlimited sovereignty by each nation. If the world community cannot find the means of controlling the expansion of its community credit, then faith in that community's credit will collapse.

The economist views this eventuality with equanimity. An imminent credit collapse is too great a catastrophe for the world powers to accept. It will force accommodation and the acceptance of controls over world currency expansion. The nations will give up unlimited sovereignty or the nations will retreat within their own boundaries accepting the replacement of international barter for the international credit community that exists today.

Thus, the supply of energy remains the critical factor in the economic equation. Energy is the controlling physical resource and the physical economics of energy supply and the physical costs of energy conversion will determine the economy of the future. The United States dollar has value because the United States economy still represents the greatest store of material resources and technical know-how, but the dollars will buy less material resources in the future and our standard of living will decline. However, the acceptance of this perspective in political-economic circles in the United States is growing very slowly.

Why is there so little understanding of the physical resource dependence of our free world's political-economic system? The question is difficult to answer except in terms of democracy's dependence on broad public consensus and the preoccupation of each individual with today's needs and desires. We avoid problems that can be deferred to tomorrow, or preferably, to the next generation. We all welcome an economic system which advises us that the future poses no problem if we can take care of the present.

Generally, we have faith in our country, its economic system and our leadership circle. We believe in specialization. Surely the banker can be trusted with credit problems and other public and private economic leaders must be looking after our future as they take care of their own, but there is substantial contrary evidence. The critical record will be found in the formal reports of the commissions and research organizations who have been assigned to identify the economic problems of our energy supply. These reports constitute the energy related economic literature.

Chapter 7
Energy Related
Economic Literature

Synopsis

The perspective of economists and social scientists conflicts with the physical evidence of energy resources. This conflict is reflected in the serious literature produced by government, foundation, and individual researchers during the last thirty years. The conflict takes the form of denial of the evidence presented, selection of hypotheses which arbitrarily limit the scope of potential solution, and time limits that avoid obvious conclusions. Economic theory is preserved at the expense of rational objectivity.

However, within the mass of statistical data that has been presented, sufficient factual information is available to identify the very real problems that are being generated by uninhibited population and credit increases in the face of real energy and physical resource limits.

T he major governmentally and academically supported studies of energy related economics reflect a society that is afraid to face its problems. The broadly based efforts have produced a mush of compromised conclusion. The recommendations of independent authors have been couched in careful language to avoid colleagues' criticisms. But this literature should be read. In concert, it discloses the real problems. Careful reading will force the conclusion that change is necessary.

The energy resources' debate began in the early 1950s. During the following years, the focus sharpened, but an understanding of the incompatibilities of the economists' concept of unlimited growth potential and the physical evidence of finite limits progressed not at all. Physical laws demonstrated that energy cannot be recycled. Resource limits were identified. But our society depended on growth for its freedom. The literature of the 1960s and 1970s runs in circles, presenting one argument or the other but always avoiding definitive conclusion.

Social scientists are not required to be knowledgeable as to physical science law and practice. Physical scientists are viewed as unqualified to interpret probable social response to future circumstances, whether the circumstances are physically or socially based. The public expects accommodation between the qualified proponents of these opposed perspectives, unaware of the stakes or of the limitations of individuals involved. The social scientists cannot afford to lose the debate. The physical scientists have no doubt as to the validity of their arguments. A stalemate was assured from the beginning.

In 1952, the Paley Commission, which had been appointed by the President of the United States to study possible resource limits, identified the future problem of our society by comparing projected consumption with known resource supplies for 24 commodities including each of the fossil fuels. Their report was immediately attacked by the economic community and it was quickly put aside by political scientists. The arguments against the Paley Commission findings appeared in economic literature* as recently as 1977.

The Energy Studies of the 1960s and 1970s

In the year of the Paley report, the Ford Foundation created Resources for the Future, Inc., a relatively permanent research structure that financed its own staff work and directed university grants. In 1963, this organization published *Resources for America's Future*, subtitled, *Patterns of Requirements and Availabilities 1960 to Year 2000*, identifying the authors as Hans H. Landsberg, Leonard L. Fischman and Joseph L. Fisher. This thousand-page book analyzed the adequacy of the primary resources, land, energy, and non-fuel minerals, together with the agricultural and industrial capacities of the nation to process these materials. The extensive statistical tabulations and graphs identified production and demand for numerous materials expanding exponentially to the year 2000. Finite limits for many of these resources were known at the time, but the authors of this book concluded their study with the following accommodation to accepted economic theory: "Neither a long view of the past, nor current trends, nor our most careful estimates of the future possibilities suggest any general running out of resources in this country during the remainder of this century (or, if a broad impression may serve in the absence of detailed analysis, for a long time thereafter)." Subsequently, *Resources for the Future* deluged the academic market with monographs focusing on the physical realities of resource limits but avoiding any too direct confrontation with the controllers of the market. The Ford Foundation had established its position as the principal support for resource research and this support would be focused on energy resources during the next decade.

In 1972, Dennis and Donella Meadows published *The Limits to Growth*,** a popularized interpretation of the Club of Rome research which had begun in 1968 to discuss what they identified as the "present and future predicament of man." This international, privately financed investigation was assisted by the Massachusetts Institute of Technology, represented by Carroll Wilson and Jay Forrester, professors of management and the computer capacity of M.I.T. The Club of Rome identified restraints on the continued growth of Western

*Carnesale, Albert and others, 1977. *Options for U.S. Energy Policy.* Institute for Contemporary Studies: San Francisco.
**Primary reference 25, bibliography page.

civilization with specifics as to the cause and probable time of their effect and the prediction that restraints would begin to be felt in a few decades. The Club of Rome's focus on environmental restraints stimulated the organization of environmentalists who had first been motivated by Rachel Carson's *The Sea Around Us** and *Silent Spring.*** However, the greatest reaction to *Limits to Growth* was within the economic community where opinion focused on the denial of growth limits.

In 1974, Wilson took the next step in the approach to the world's resource limits, this time concentrating on the supply and demand for energy. He put together the Workshop on Alternative Energy Strategies (WAES) with the support of America's eleven largest private foundations, including the National Science Foundation with its access to public funds. Committees were formed from the fifteen nations that use 80 percent of the world's energy, balancing economists with political and physical scientists. Wilson orchestrated the work of 75 persons to produce two massive volumes of energy supply and demand figures and commentary. They also produced a soft cover, popularized volume marketed by McGraw-Hill under the title, *Energy—Global Prospects 1985 to 2000.**** Publicity releases kept up public interest in the project's progress and its completion.

The WAES conclusion left nothing to chance or casual contradiction. It identified petroleum as the critical resource, its supply finite. Discovery additions to proved reserves and removal from these reserves were projected year-by-year. The conclusion: "Petroleum demand could exceed supply as early as 1985 if the OPEC countries maintain their present production ceilings." The WAES recommendations were also specific: energy use planning must intercept economic expansion to conserve petroleum for the transition to alternative fuels, all of which were identified, together with their probable contribution.

The WAES report may have offended the economic community. In any case, it has been largely ignored, with very little discussion of the implications of its findings since its release in the second quarter of 1977.

The Ford Foundation: Direct Contribution to our National Energy Policy

Meanwhile, the Ford Foundation had stepped back into physical resource analysis. In December of 1971, the Trustees authorized the organization of the Energy Policy Project with a supporting appropriation of $4 million. The project director was S. David Freeman, who was to become President Carter's first energy consultant, and the project had the continuing advice of a distinguished advisory board which included William Tavoulareas, the president of Mobil Oil Corporation. The Energy Policy Project moved rapidly, attempting to establish its position as the determiner of energy policy for the United States. A

---

*Carson, Rachel, 1961. *The Sea Around Us.* New York: Oxford Un. Press.
**Carson, Rachel, 1967. *Silent Spring.* Boston: Houghton Mifflin.
***Wilson, Carroll L., 1977. *Energy: Global Prospects 1985-2000.* Report of the workshop on Alternative Energy Strategy. New York: McGraw-Hill.

preliminary report, published in 1974, laid bare the conflict between the realities of the physical world and the economic, political, and social expectations of America.

The organization then edited popularized versions of its findings. *A Time to Choose** and *Exploring Energy Choices,*** which reached the public by giveaways to the nation's public libraries and Book-of-the-Month Club members. There is no evidence that these books had much public impact. The message apparently could not be simplified enough to be both acceptable and believable.

The Ford Foundation report, through its adoption by the Carter Administration, became a major contributor to the nation's energy policy. After the 1976 election, Dr. Freeman was identified as the probable choice to head the anticipated Department of Energy, but opposition to the Ford Foundation study blocked him. Political and economic America was not yet ready to submit to physical energy reality.

Tavoulareas led the opposition, employing the resources of the Mobil Oil Corporation to take issue with the would-be bureaucratic controllers of our destiny. Full-page Mobil ads appeared in 1977 and continued through the end of the 1970s. They began with carefully worded direct attacks on the developing Department of Energy and everything concerned with political interferences with private industry's control of the energy supply. Month by month this position was softened as it became evident that the oil industry would not be able to maintain the energy supplies that would be required in the 1980s. Finally the Mobil ads shifted to constructive suggestions for the resolution of our energy problem, although never abandoning protection of the industry.

Further insight into the basic problem of conflict between ideologies and physical reality was a sequel to the David Freeman vs. William Tavoulareas controversy that appeared in a series of articles by the editor of *Harper's* in 1977, running into 1978. *Harper's* editor, Lewis H. Lapham, had been brought up in the oil industry and realized the significance of the controversy. He represented in one person an investigative capacity, a reporting capacity, a publishing capacity, and a lifetime involvement in the industry and the culture it had produced. Lapham identified with the paradox that virtually all American leaders would experience: the world's physical realities conflict too radically with everything we have been taught to believe.

The Ford Foundation report and President Carter's National Energy Plan, which it influenced, took the brunt of the economic community's attack from the middle of 1977 on. The think-tanks and social science research organizations of the country divided between the supporters of resource limits and the supporters of economic growth. Economists attacking growth limits were represented on the campus of almost every university and appeared to be in

---

*The energy policy staff of the Ford Foundation 1979 *A Time to Choose America's Energy Future.* Cambridge, Mass.: Billinger.
**Energy Policy Project of the Ford Foundation, 1974. *Exploring Energy Choices.* Washington: Ford Foundation.

control of the professional economic community. This majority influence also appeared in almost every department of the government, affecting the application of economic theory whenever an opportunity arose, and demanding a hearing and an influence on the purely physical science research in the Department of Energy and in the U.S. Geological Survey.

President Carter's *National Energy Plan** employed the same basic research base as the Ford Foundation reports, attempted the same simplification of this complicated problem, and met with the same fate in the Congress of the United States. The Congressmen reflected the public dismay over the reality of our energy problem and they were unable to reach conclusion. The debate continued for all the Carter years and into the Reagan Administration. The compromise conclusions all focused on the immediate future, the next election. The significance is political. Our government has not been able to find real solutions for the energy problem.

The Harvard Business School's "Energy Future"**

After publication of the Carter Administration's National Energy Plan, two years elapsed before the energy project at the Harvard Business School published *Energy Future* late in 1979. Financed by the Energy Research and Development Administration (ERDA), a predecessor of the Department of Energy, the project had been six years in process, the work of five research men at Harvard, edited by two management professors, Robert Stobaugh and Daniel Yergin.

Energy Future is important for its recognition of the limits of this country's conventional energy resources, the fact of the growing dependence on foreign imports, and the unlikely prospects for increasing U.S. oil production by economic persuasion. However, the Harvard study foresaw continued economic expansion with conservation, assisted by solar energy (defined to include hydroelectric power, wood, and all variations of solar flow), as primary supports for the new growth economy. *Energy Future* obtained wide distribution but was attacked by economists for its failure to accept their theory of market response, as well as by physical realists who recognized the improbability of the easy transition to a conservation ethic unsupported by political dictation.

The National Research Council's CONAES report "Alternative Energy Demand Futures to 2010***

The most broadly based energy economic study of the 1970s was under the management of the National Research Council, funded by ERDA in June of 1975. It produced the Committee on Nuclear and Alternative Energy Systems (CONAES) which involved subordinate committees from all related disciplines with representatives from industry, government, and universities.

---

*Executive office of the President, Energy Policy & Planning, 1977. *The National Energy Plan.* Washington, D.C.: United States Government Printing Office.
**Primary reference 29, bibliography page.
***Primary reference 26, bibliography page.

The real question was whether the urgency for finding a solution to the nation's energy problem could overcome the barriers in the academic community. A little less than two years after the inauguration of the study, there was evidence of potential success. Eight leaders of the study were selected by the Council for the House Subcommittee on Energy and Power to assist the Congress in evaluating the Administration's energy legislation. These men, plus two others* not associated with the project, presented a timely and realistic appraisal of the nation's energy problem and the direction of solutions in a hearing before the Subcommittee on March 23, 1977.** The CONAES committee members could not speak for CONAES, as the committees had not completed their work, but told the Subcommittee that most of the CONAES participants agreed on the dimensions of the energy problem and the range of energy available to the United States' economy to the year 2010. None of the CONAES group believed that historical growth could be maintained. The two independent witnesses concurred. They indicated a probable cessation of economic growth for the last 25 years of the study (1985 to 2010). Obviously, the immediate low growth and the probable no growth future for the U.S. economy presented a shocking conclusion.

The congressional representatives could not act on this information without further confirmation. It was anticipated that the completed CONAES report would provide this confirmation within a matter of months, but this did not happen. The finished CONAES report did not appear until January 1980 and then only in a prepublication release. It presented no definite prediction as to the energy that would be available to the United States economy and no specific recommendations for a legislative program. The CONAES supply panel reported that they could not predict energy supply levels, citing political climate as the controlling influence rather than price as the motivator of supply. All evidence of physical supply restraints was ignored.

The CONAES panel on energy demand published its report under the title, *Alternative Energy Demand Future to 2010,* presenting price control scenarios to predict the range of future energy supply. Again, physical evidence was ignored as an influence on available oil and gas, the energy resource which would control economic decision for the 30 years under consideration. Significantly, the prices the supply panel chose as parameters for econometric predictions, ranged from an increase of two and four times the 1975 effective domestic energy prices to a *reduction* in energy prices representing three-quarters of the 1975 price levels. For practical purposes, this range assumed no serious problem with energy resource supplies for the next 30 years. The two co-chairmen of

*Dr. Roger Naill, who was associated with Dennis Meadows at Dartmouth College and Samuel M. Dix, whose book *Energy—A Critical Decision for the U.S. Economy* was reproduced in total as the Appendix to the Committee report.

**Published report *Long-Term Energy Policy Issues* hearing before the Subcommittee on Energy & Power of the Committee on Interstate and Foreign Commerce, House of Representatives, 95th Congress, Serial #95-15.

CONAES confirmed this interpretation by stating in their transmittal letter that "The energy problem does not arise from an overall scarcity of resources."

In 1975, the average U.S. wellhead price of crude oil (the controlling influence on consumer prices) was $7.56 per barrel. In 1979, the world price was 5.3 times this 1975 U.S. price. The highest scenario hypothesis had already been exceeded in the world market before the CONAES study was published. Without question, this would affect consumer prices in the United States before 1985, the first benchmark in the CONAES three-decade economic projection.

The CONAES report is thorough in its coverage of nuclear, coal, solar, and geothermal energy systems, and the risks of each. It effectively puts to rest the arguments delaying nuclear development, including the breeder. However, the report is deficient in both accuracy and candor in its coverage of petroleum and natural gas which have accounted for 73 percent of this nation's energy resource.

The conclusion is unavoidable. The CONAES project failed to address the nation's energy problem. To understand the significance of this conclusion, one must go back to the origin of the study and its organization.

The National Academy of Sciences is administered by the National Research Council and represents the nation's most prestigious scientific community. It is this country's agent in the organization of government-supported, broad-based research projects. Its acceptance of the energy assignment committed the nation's scientific reserves to the battle. At the same time, the dimension of the project exposed the structural weakness of the organization.

The original request to the National Academy of Sciences was for an analysis of the risks and benefits associated with alternative nuclear power sources. This was in April 1975, when physical scientists had been frustrated by environmental and ecological opposition to nuclear power, sustained by fringes of their own community. An objective study would answer the many questions that were delaying critical national decisions.

Instead of accepting the original concept, the Academy suggested that ERDA sponsor a much more comprehensive study. As a consequence, in the words of Philip Handler, chairman of the National Research Council and president of the National Academy of Sciences, "The charge to our committee was nothing less than a detailed analysis of all aspects of the nation's energy situation."* This became an assignment without precedent for the National Research Council—again in Dr. Handler's words, "a staggering challenge." However, the preoccupation with nuclear energy remained. The organization was called the Committee on Nuclear and Alternative Energy Systems (CONAES). The original objective was not ignored.

Three hundred fifty social and physical scientists, both from the academic and business community, were divided into teams and put on panels and sub-panels. Fourteen similarly representative scientists were designated "The Committee" and identified in the concluding report. Significantly, the chairmen of the four principal sub-panels, who each published independent reports, were

*Primary reference 5, bibliography page.

not identified in The Committee's concluding report. These chairmen, in turn, did not allow their eleven to fifteen supporting members to express individual opinions in sub-panel reports, nor was there identification of individuals' contributions to the many subordinate reports coordinated through this structure.

This organization structure served to speed the process, reduce public display of differences within the scientific community, and, at the same time, test these differences privately. Consensus appears to have been the primary objective. Inevitably, consensus resulted in the elimination of controversial facts and conclusions.

The project was completed a year late, overrunning its budget by $300,000, revealing the unresolved conflicts only through omission of discussion, and leaving critical questions unanswered in the concluding report. In its final form, the study represents the conclusions of a faceless committee which was dominated by the methods and ideologies of the economic discipline. This muted chorus is brought to life by the notations of the fourteen members of The Committee of whom seven presented their views and their exceptions.

The most articulate and extensive of these statements was provided by the former British economist, Kenneth Boulding, (now at Colorado University) who identified the profound uncertainties, areas of ignorance, and practical signifi- cance of the findings, while taking specific exception to many of the conclusions. Dr. Boulding's observations were concurred in by co-chairman, Harvey Brookes, professor of technology and public policy, Aiken Computation Laboratory, Harvard University. The six pages of Dr. Boulding's conclusions are more relevant than the 730 pages in the final report that preceded them and the two separately bound reports of the supply and demand panels which supported the final document.

It was Dr. Boulding's opinion that the conflicts within the scientific community should have been given much more attention. They represent the evidence for developing responsible interaction between disciplines, a problem very nearly equal to the energy problem in its need for solution.

The CONAES report provided a dismal conclusion for the decade of the 1970s. Its constructive advice is too general. Its report includes obvious error. The most critical decisions are avoided, and there is no higher authority for appeal.

The 1980s Reports

Two stepping stones to energy reality did appear in economic literature during the last half of 1980. Lester C. Thurow's *The Zero-Sum Society* reunited economics with politics in identifying the primacy of political accountability in the solution of our economic problems. President Carter's Administration produced *The Global 2000 Report to the President,* a chilling recital of the physical restraints on America's future.

The Zero-Sum Society*

Lester Thurow's *Zero-Sum Society* introduces valid suggestions for the solution of our political economic problems. A professor of economics and management at M.I.T., author and economics columnist, he demands respect from the economic community. He uses accounting language to confront our primary problems: all Americans are politically represented and enjoy equal privilege in blocking any political decision that may adversely affect their individual interests; the economies of the developed world have matured and two nations (Germany and Japan) have surpassed America in economic performance; the developing countries with resources have gained real economic power. These are the realities we must recognize.

Thurow demonstrates that the United States economy no longer is working. Our five percent annual capital investment is surpassed by Germany's 10 percent and Japan's 15 percent. We are faced with the consequence of a competitive disadvantage that has been building for 35 years. Thurow believes that the developed countries are moving ahead of America, rejecting the post-industrial world of zero economic growth. He concentrates on the necessity for reviving America's economic growth by increased investment in competitively high productive industrial capacity, but he sees no source for this investment under our present governmental structure. The task exceeds the capacity of a restricted private economy, the result of 200 years of humanitarian influence. It is not politically realistic to anticipate reversing this process. The capital can be raised by taxation, but only with political approval.

This leads to the problem of the distribution of economic benefits in our society, the sub-title of Thurow's book. Our tax structure is unequal. Our economy generates increasing disequilibrium in the distribution of income as we apply restraints on government spending and as we squeeze the money supply to control inflation. If we attempt to generate capital through private investment, this process is exacerbated, and the economically disadvantaged are able to block political decision in this direction. If we turn to the generation of capital by massive public financing, the free enterprise constituency blocks the way.

Thurow introduces the numbers in economic language. He avoids physical quantities and the identification of physical problems. He simply indicates a threefold increase in the level of capital generation to match our foreign competition. America has been employing monetary expansion to finance its current level of investment in the combination of national defense capacity, productive capacity, and social progress. The consequence is our current inflation. Thurow does not anticipate that the level of inflation which we have been experiencing can be much reduced under our present political-economic structure. His answer very simply is the necessity for change in the political structure. We must find a way to identify responsibility for political decision. A parliamentary form of government is indicated.

*Primary reference 31, bibliography page.

Always an economist, Thurow recognizes no non-renewable resources except the energy resources and in this discussion he leaves critical questions unanswered. Energy is essential to the economic growth he advocates. This he freely admits. He recognizes the tremendous capital cost of the energy conversion industry but he ignores the limits in the remaining supply of the principal resources, coal and shale; and he only touches on the social and political cost of their employment. Still, his book effectively opens the door to discussion of energy economics.

The reaction of the economic community to Dr. Thurow's book gives perspective. The *Wall Street Journal* chose George Gilder, an economics author, to write a review (June 19, 1980). Gilder recognizes the sales success of Dr. Thurow's book and accepts the accuracy of the author's economic data inputs, but he finds little agreement with the conclusion. The last paragraph of Gilder's review carries his message:

"Contrary to Mr. Thurow's belief, it is neither bountiful natural resources nor the accumulation of capital nor the guidance of government that account for the success of capitalist countries in overcoming the zero-sum equilibrium of poverty and privation. The key source of wealth in all successful centers of growth from Hong Kong to Silicon Valley, California, is the ingenuity of free individuals. They turn barren islands into thriving zones of commerce and enrichment through the gains [of commerce and enrichment through the gains] of trade, and they transform the substance of beach sand into a precious resource of mind through the miracle of semiconductor electronics. The desire of idealistic leftists to replace this unique force for progress with groups of government committees, presumably dominated by Marx-minded econometricians, seems on the surface incomprehensible except as part of a drive for power by the new class of American intellectuals. One would think, though, that a brilliant individual like Lester Thurow would do better under capitalism. Perhaps he has been demoralized by excessive taxation."

Within a year from this writing, George Gilder would become a principal spokesman for the economists responsible for President Reagan's economic policies.

The Global 2000 Report to the President*

"Global 2000" extends the United States' perspective on the relationship of energy and economics to the world community and updates the conflict between economic theory and the physical evidence of resource limits. The study employed the data banks, computer models, and expertise of federal departments. The focus of the study was the future of our civilization, with the beginning of the next century as a time reference. The study is readable, candid,

*Primary reference 4, bibliography page.

and as conclusive as possible. However, it is full of errors and omissions, highlighted in discussion between the editors and a panel of informal advisers, selected to represent critics of on-going economic theory. The perspective includes a concise history of planning attempts, both public and private, since Theodore Roosevelt. Current econometric projections are brought up to date.

"Global 2000" is the most significant single reference for historic perspective on the necessity of energy economics. It provides the state of the art in economic thinking and the state of our government's capacity to present and understand the factual information that is beginning to take control of events. The measure of progress in the developed world is money income. Population increase is the only measure for the rest of the world. The study identifies cohorts of people who march across the pages, irresistibly propelled by biological pleasure and human kindness. They swell the cities, inundating democratic processes, led on by civilizations' beacons and roadways. They cannot be stopped by cutting the generators of power and wealth. They will be born and they will strive to exist, recently four billion, ten billion by 2030 and that, the scientists say, is the limit of the earth's carrying capacity if we maintain our current concepts of human dignity. But the progression will not stop there. With optimum resource distribution and unrestricted migration, 30 billion could be supported at the subsistence level by the end of the next century.

The gap in personal income between the rich and the poor will widen as the rich continue to control the increases in their numbers and push their economic advantage. The quality of the air and the water will deteriorate. Forests in the less developed regions will decline by 40 percent by 2000, and their loss will aggravate declining water resources. After that air may begin to be affected. Agricultural land will decrease in quantity and quality. The world's deserts will have increased by 20 percent in 2000. Increased food production will be dependent on fossil fuel energy inputs as natural fertilizer is burned for heat to warm the human population and cook their food. The world will become vulnerable to natural disaster and disruption from human causes as we enter the twenty-first century.

Energy is the single most compromised segment in the "Global 2000" projections. The energy computer model employed by the study is programmed by the major variables: gross domestic product, population ranges, price assumptions, the behavior of the Organization of Petroleum Exporting Countries (OPEC), technological penetration, and conservation. These judgmental computer inputs exclude the physical data which identify the proved reserves of energy resources that are the only source of energy for the U.S. and world markets. The U.S. oil supply projected for 1990 exceeds the limits of probable physical capacity. No forecast beyond 1990 is attempted despite the availability of accurate information.

The government and non-government institutional projections for U.S. oil range between three and five times the quantity that can be substantiated by physical forecast. These are the same forecasts discussed in Chapter II, the subject of Dr. Franssen's several books. The early history is presented in the primary reference data* that preceded this writing.

There is a progression in these econometric forecasts. Each year the expectations have been lowered, introducing a little more emphasis on physical realities. Each year the influence of price on oil and gas production has been reduced. "Global 2000's" model that projects U.S. oil and gas production for 1990 employs the Project Independence Evaluation System (PIES) for the United States and the International Energy Evaluation System (IEES) for the rest of the world. In the current projection, the difference between the high GNP growth and the low growth oil production expectancy for the United States is .4 percent (9,734 barrels per day for low economic growth and 9,770 for high growth). This differential tacitly recognizes the elimination of market demand and market price influence on oil production, the fact that has been observable for most of 100 years but still is denied in economic theory.

The food projections of "Global 2000" are excessively optimistic. They assume almost ideal weather, energy prices only doubling with no physical restraints, and technological (yield) improvements that appear to exceed the extrapolation of the last seventeen years experience. With no new world trade restrictions, the study projects world grain production to increase by 78 percent by the end of the century, total food by 91 percent. An unanticipated physical energy short-fall would upset this happy expectancy. Clearly we face uncontrolled population pressures on the food supply and the problem of population momentum is spelled out in detail. The concentration of world population in the fertile age brackets guarantees increases to the levels that cannot be supported.

There is no agreement between the analysts and the econometric practitioners and their many advisers. The compromises with physical reality are half measures or less. Energy is not recognized as the driving force of our physical world. Then why is "Global 2000" important to energy economics?

The answer is the report's assistance to perspective. It fully documents our federal government's incapacity to deal with the multi-faceted problem of population growth, natural resource limits, and ideological conflict. The report lays bare the inadequacy of the social sciences to deal with their disparate political, social, and economic theorists when faced with physical realities. America's developing crisis is related to the crisis facing our western civilization.

The American Physical Economists

The only obvious link between Dr. Soddy's technocrats of the 1920s and the American economist who introduced physical perspective into economic theory in the 1970s is that neither succeeded in gaining the recognition of mainline economists.

Nicholas Georgescu-Roegen, a Vanderbilt University economist, published *The Entropy Law and the Economic Process*** in 1972, followed by a succession of articles on the same subject. Entropy is a physical concept. Specifically, it

*Reference 10, bibliography page.
**Harvard University Press 1972

measures the availability of useful energy in a heat process and thus is associated with the thermodynamic laws. Energy is required in all physical processes and physical processes are required for all economic accomplishments. Through this linkage, Roegen establishes the dependence of economics on the thermodynamic laws and these are the most stable of all the physical laws. They tell us that the energy conversion processes are irreversible and that the entire physical universe is running down. Entropy measures the running down of energy in each physical process, directly contradicting economic theory which depends on continuous expansion of the same physical processes. Thus, Roegen confronts his colleagues with irrefutable evidence that their economic theories cannot be sustained.

Herman Daly, a Louisiana State University economist, picked up Roegen's argument without emphasis on the specific laws. Unlimited economic expansion is mathematically impossible. Daly's first paper, "A Model for Steady-State Economy," was presented at the Yale University School of Forestry and Environmental Studies and published in October of 1972. Subsequently, W. H. Freeman and Company published several of Daly's books on this subject.* He attacks expansionist theory in academic terms and finds logical ways to control population increase and natural resource depletion without sacrificing our essential freedoms. Daly should be the leader of a new world order, but he is not. At Yale his steady-state economy arguments were opposed by James Tobin. In 1981, Tobin received the Nobel Prize in Economics.

The problem for the physical economists is acceptance. They have been unable to find a way to open the door for general discussion of the necessity for change in our social-economic-political order. For the present, they have joined Thorstein Veblen in providing provocative criticism of our social order. Veblen's "The Theory of the Leisure Class" offended the leaders of our society. Daly's "Steady-State Economy" is even more threatening and Daly shuns association with persons who share his critical views but might solidify a radical interpretation of his careful, academic analysis. At any rate, public discussion of steady-state economics is discouraged by almost all recognized economists, even the author of the most carefully prepared prescription.

In 1980, Jeremy Rifkin and Ted Howard published *Entropy, A New World View*.** Rifkin clothes Roegen's application of physical law to economics with historic, philosophic, and religious perspective. His book is eminently readable and his position is solidly supported. He fully develops our social dependence on the thermodynamic laws that control the physical universe. Rifkin's fact reservoir is identical to the supports of this writing, but in his broad focus he avoids discriminating between immediate and long-term time restraints.

The universe is running down on a millennia time scale. Our economic system will not survive the next two decades. The cost of future freedom represents a bill that must be paid soon and we must be able to audit the numbers that determine when it must be paid. The numbers will be presented in Section Two.

Toward a Steady-State Economy, San Francisco: W.H. Freeman and Company, 1973.
**Entropy: A New World View*, New York: The Viking Press, 1980.

Part Two

U.S. Energy
Resources

Oil and natural gas accounted for 73 percent of measured U.S. energy consumption at the beginning of 1980. The transportation sector was 99.7 percent dependent on these two fuels.

In looking at the opportunities for reduced petroleum imports, a U.S. Department of Transportation study* identified a potential saving of $320 billion in foreign expenditures by the end of the century if mileage per gallon could be stepped up to 50 for passenger cars and 35 for light trucks. The projection assumed $40 per barrel, which was the current spot market price. Most significantly, the study recognized that these mileage goals for the American industry could not be expected before 1985. Under competitive, free market influence, the American car industry has required seven years to take the first step towards producing fuel-efficient transportation and may lose 30 percent of its market to foreign competition before completing this process. Retooling costs for the next phase of this alteration are identified in excess of $100 billion. In exploratory meetings with government and industry representatives at the beginning of 1980, General Motors, Ford, and Chrysler declined to engage in discussions that would require them to abandon their full line of cars in exchange for financial assistance in retooling their industry.

The United States is committed to oil and gas consumption. Our passenger cars and light trucks represent the most rapidly depreciating and thus quickest potential turnover of all of our capital stocks. Even at that, five years are needed to start producing different cars and trucks. An alteration of our transportation system in the direction of mass transit would require far more than five years. The ultimate reduction in the consumption of gasoline and oil for transportation in the U.S. would involve relocating our population centers closer to the work place. An orderly transition out of our oil and gas dependency will take 30 to 50 years.

Although the oil and natural gas we can produce within our borders will control our destiny for the remainder of the century, the

*"Transition to the Post-1985 Motor Vehicle" by Richard R. John, U.S. Department of Transportation, Research and Special Programs Administration, Transportation System Center, Cambridge, Mass., October 31, 1979.

primary energy decisions concern the alternative resources. What are they? How can they be developed? What will they cost in human life and environmental impact? What are the physical limits in their supply?

Unavoidably, the energy picture becomes more complex. We must identify all of our present and potential sources of energy. We must resolve conflicts between the physical and political-economic segments of our society in interpreting the facts.

Editor's Note

The chapters in this part present the primary proofs for the necessity to recognize the United States' energy problem. The projection of crude oil and natural gas production for the years 1980 through 2000 is supported by details in Part Four, Derivation and Development, sections C and D. Part Two begins with the 33-year history of the proved reserves that has been kept by the American Petroleum Institute and the American Gas Association. The quantity to be expected from the undiscovered oil and gas resource was the subject of *Energy—A Critical Decision for the United States Economy** which in turn was based on U.S. Geological Survey 725 and the conclusion of corroborating geologists. Derivation and Development section B reproduces a critical summary of available resource information and the problem of public acceptance.

Within the limits of our ability to measure energy, each of the energy industries and now the Energy Information Administration maintain the record of energy production, energy reserves, and undiscovered energy resources. There is no question about these quantities and the availability of this information. There need be little question about their accuracy. In subsequent discussions, the energy information published by the E.I.A. in its *Monthly Energy Review* will be employed. Thus, the reference figures in these discussions can be constantly updated. The only exception is the American Petroleum Institute's oil and gas reserve tables taken directly from this trade association's published report. However, it should be noted that the E.I.A. has adopted these figures and will produce them in a slightly different form beginning in 1982. All of this information is available at minimal cost.

*Primary reference 10, bibliography page.

CHART I
PROVED RESERVES OF CRUDE OIL IN THE UNITED STATES, 1947-1979

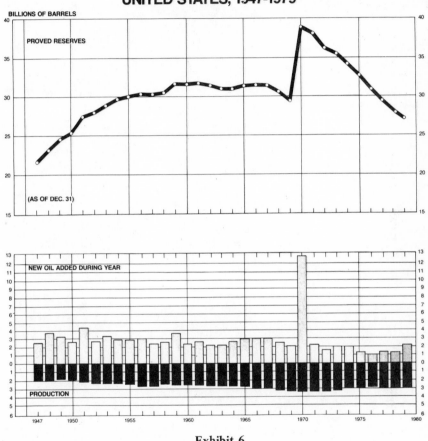

Exhibit 6

Used by permission of the copyright holder, American Petroleum Institute.

Chapter 8
Definitions

Synopsis

Common words describe our energy resources and the conversion processes that permit their employment, but these common words are often misleading. They can be manipulated to imply nearly opposite meaning. The language problem must be recognized and a common understanding of the key words must precede the introduction of the numbers that control our energy future.

66 **N**ow what is interesting about logical thought is that, once having been mastered, its rules master us. Having learned the rules of identity or transitivity, we find it impossible to disavow them. Indeed, it is much easier to lie—to distort deliberately what one hears or sees—than to forswear the veracity of a proper syllogism."*

Robert Heilbroner

The inclusion of physical energy information in economic theory and practice will be adopted when physical facts become overwhelming. Accurate information already exists on the extent of the oil and gas reserves and resources, our primary energy supply, but the accuracy of the figures is still being questioned and the obvious conclusions are still denied.

The denial rests partly on definition failures beginning with the word *energy*. The word defines physical activities that are as diverse as the constructive process of human thought (the brain functions are dependent on the energy in the food we eat) and the destructive force of a hurricane (our weather is powered by solar energy inputs).

Even the physical dimensions of energy present problems. The physicist's definitions can be useful in describing processes which are physical in nature. The British thermal unit (Btu) is the quantity of heat required to raise the temperature of a pound of water 1° Fahrenheit. Once we have entered the physicist's system his formulae will permit us to interpret Btu's in terms of mechanical power or electrical power and in other measurement systems. For most non-scientists, faith is required to accept these physical measurements. In the United States, we have been using between 70 and 80 quadrillion (a quadrillion is 1,000,000,000,000,000) Btu per year in each of the last ten years. We have come to recognize the *quad* in these terms.

*"The Dialectical Vision"—New Republic, March 1, 1980.

The definitions that cause the most trouble in identifying the fossil fuel energy that will be available for our economy are *reserves* and *resources*. Oil and gas reserves are the quantities that have been discovered and that are available for extraction (production). The oil and gas industry uses the term *proved reserves*. Petroleum engineers are able to determine the quantity of oil and gas in these reserves with remarkable precision. We will identify the accuracy of this process for crude oil measurements in Chapter X. For practical purposes, we know the extent of the proved reserve and the quantity that can be extracted from this reserve each year. The oil in our reserves can be held indefinitely for future production, but oil can be produced economically and efficiently only at the rate dictated by the geological formation. More flexibility is available in extracting natural gas and coal.

Resources are totally different from *reserves*. Resources are the undiscovered quantity of oil and gas and coal and shale, a quantity that is determined by geologists on the basis of probable discoveries. It is the undeterminable rate of discovery that introduces the uncertainty and confusion in the determination of future energy availability. We cannot *precisely* determine the quantity of the undiscovered fossil fuel resource, but we can estimate the *probable* quantity of this resource and the probable discovery both in terms of physical and economic limitations. The failure to understand and accept the meaning of probabilities causes much of the trouble in political discussions of energy availability.

Geologists determine the quantity in the undiscovered resource on the basis of surface and subterranean mapping. In the United States, more than three million wells have been drilled, providing the ultimate proof of subterranean structures to the depth explored. Seismic explorations identify subterranean structures prior to drilling. In 1978, an average of 352 crews explored 301,506 miles on-shore and over the Continental Shelves of the United States in this resource development process. The United States is the most explored area of the world and United States crews have been performing the same service over most of the free world. We also have provided instruction to the Communist world.

In 1975, the U.S. Geological Survey completed an analysis of the undiscovered oil and gas resources of the country stated in terms of a 95-percent probability of finding more than the minimum estimate and a 5-percent probability of finding more than the maximum estimate. The undiscovered oil and gas resource fairly surely lies between the numbers in this analysis. The conclusion has been confirmed by a number of independent geologists.

The record of the quantity in the proved reserve of crude oil has been kept by the industry's trade association, the American Petroleum Institute (A.P.I.), which has identified production since 1860, consistently maintaining the definition and accounting for oil in the ground—oil that has been discovered and which will be produced in the future. Other trade associations have maintained a similar record for gas, nuclear energy, and electrical energy production. The oil companies rely on this information to guide their exploration and marketing and this reliance has motivated accurate reporting.

Despite demonstrated accuracy, criticism of the energy industry, its trade associations, and the departments of the government that rely on this information has been politically de rigueur for most of this decade. Political opinion is responsible for creating the independent Energy Information Administration (E.I.A.), now taking over the reporting function. E.I.A.'s information will be more readily available to the general public, but little other improvement can be expected.

Demand and *consumption* and *production* are terms that have differing interpretations. For the economist, demand is an economic force measured in the marketplace by its effect on price. Demand causes price to rise when supply is constricted. Consumption on the other hand is a physical fact: the quantity that actually moves through the market.

The oil and gas industry uses the term *production* to define the process of removing the natural gaseous and liquid products from the ground and making them available as processed hydrocarbons. Economists anticipate production in terms of supply, the counter-force in the market syllogism with demand and price.

Description of the oil and gas that is produced can cause further problems in precise identification. The *wet gas* that comes from the well must be processed to separate out *natural gas liquids*. The *dry gas* moves through the network of the pipelines to the market. Obviously there is less energy in dry gas than in *wet gas*. The *natural gas liquids* represent a major contribution to *total petroleum liquids*. In fact, between 15 and 20 percent of our *total petroleum liquids* are this consequence of natural gas production.

Oil is an ambiguous term in energy reporting. After the natural gas industry developed (most of its growth acceleration occurred after World War II) oil usually referred to the combination of crude oil and natural gas liquids, more accurately defined as *total petroleum liquids*. In the earlier records, oil referred to crude oil only.

Physicists differentiate between energy forms in terms of the usefulness of the energy. The first law of thermodynamics identifies an irreversible process: we cannot recycle energy. The second law identifies the cost of converting energy from one form to another. Energy flows from a high temperature source to a low temperature receiver in producing mechanical or electrical forms of energy. The efficiency of the process is proportional to the temperature difference. On an average, two-thirds of the heat energy input is lost in this conversion. In the physicist's world, the potential temperature of the heat source is the critical measurement. In producing electricity, heat energy is changed to a more versatile form, electricity, and a cost must be paid.

This introduces the concept of *net energy*. Net energy is different from the physicist's identification of energy quality but it is just as important. The term *net energy* relates to the process of obtaining the energy resource, the mining of coal or the refining of uranium for example. Energy is employed in the mining process and, if more energy is required in the process than is produced, no net energy results. There must be a physical energy profit in every energy-producing process.

As we look to our future, it is the sources of energy that will be most important. The high quality, easily transportable energy that can be produced from fossil fuels will not be available. The alternative energy sources are nuclear and the solar energy complex that includes wind and hydropower. The most abundant source of solar energy results from biological processes, plants and animals which convert solar energy into wood and vegetation that can produce heat. The direct conversion of solar energy by physical processes such as photovoltaic cells or simple solar heat collectors can be demonstrated but the quantity of net energy that can be produced is small compared with our needs.

When biologically-produced energy competes with the fossil fuels, more than simple thermodynamics is involved. We must be concerned with the kind of energy used in energy production and the future availability of each kind. The energy in a bushel of corn can be determined by a single, objective measure, the Btu. But the energy cost of producing the corn can be radically different in terms of the combination of fossil fuel energy and solar energy inputs. Net solar energy may be minimal.

Agriculture today uses tremendous quantities of fossil oil and gas for fertilizer, cultivation, harvesting, crop drying, delivery, and processing. At each step, solar energy resources might be employed but this would result in a reduction in the crop quantity or a lengthening of the process time. When corn is used to produce alcohol, a substitute for gasoline, all of the fossil fuel inputs must be accounted for in determining the energy cost of the alcohol product. These costs include the fossil fuel employed in building farm machinery as well as the fossil fuels used for fuel and the energy inputs required to feed the men involved in these processes. There is no evidence today that the United States can show an energy profit in the production of alcohol from prime agricultural crops. Some energy can be produced from agricultural wastes, but the use of those wastes as fertilizer may be more important in the overall economic balance.

The alternative to using grains to produce alcohol for burning in internal combustion engines is to feed the grains to draft animals whose energy-producing capacity has been well established. Finally, the grains that are used for food to support human life provide the highest quality form of energy, but this dimension of energy quality is not identified in our physical measures.

Chapter 9
Overview of Total
U.S. Energy Supply

Synopsis

America's total energy consumption and oil dependence turned down after 1978 with the help of economic recession.

Progress towards alternatives to oil and gas has been slow and disappointing. Coal use increased but the rate of change was only half the political objective. The growth in electric power consumption slowed substantially. Hydropower declined from 1975 to 1980. Other forms of renewal energy increased, but the base is so small that this solar complex is unlikely to exceed a 2% contribution to our total energy supply at the end of this century.

The turn-down in the nuclear contribution since 1978 is the most alarming fact produced from the energy record. Foreign oil dependence has been reduced, but imported crude oil still accounted for one-third of our refinery inputs in 1980, and our reserve stocks are totally inadequate to protect the economy from any significant curtailment of the foreign supply.

E nergy supply and demand is understandable only in terms of the quantities required and the direction of change. In the first half of 1981, energy consumption turned down and an oil glut made the news headlines. The giant American economy was moving slowly away from petroleum consumption and the market price for energy company equities declined. America consumed 34.2 quads of petroleum products in 1980 compared with 34.8 in 1973. Before 1973, petroleum consumption had inreased every year except in economic depression, and the current decline is not free of this influence. The seasons and their severity affect energy consumption independently of purely economic influences. The trends are demonstrated in the Energy Information Administration's charts and tables, Exhibit IX-7.

Energy consumption by kind of resource reveals the slow progress in America's retreat from oil and gas dependence and the choice of alternatives.

It took five years after the 1973 Arab boycott for America to accept the physical evidence of petroleum limits and actually begin to reduce annual consumption. Passenger car efficiency controls the demand for petroleum.

Executive Summary

Energy Summary

Yearly

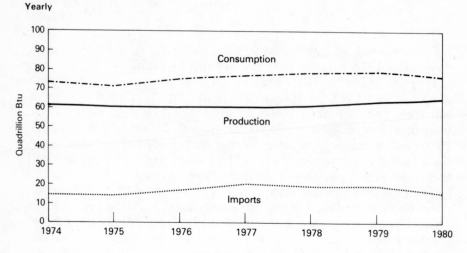

Monthly

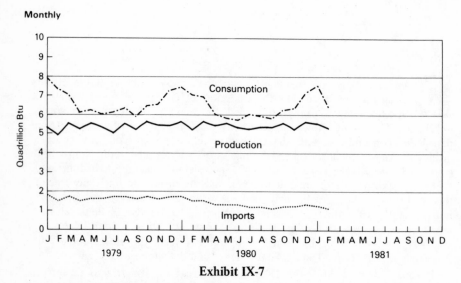

Exhibit IX-7

Source: Energy Information Administration calculations based on data appearing elsewhere in reproduced charts and tables.

Consumption of Energy by Type

	Coal[1]	Natural Gas (Dry)	Petro- leum	Hydro- electric Power[2]	Nuclear Electric Power	Net Imports of Coal Coke[3]	Other[4]	Total Energy Con- sumed
				Quadrillion (10^{15}) Btu				
1973	13.300	22.512	34.840	3.010	0.910	(0.008)	0.046	74.609
1978	13.846	20.000	37.965	3.164	2.977	0.131	0.068	78.150
1980	R15.603	20.495	R34.196	3.125	2.704	(0.037)	0.114	R76.201

R= Revised data.
Source: *Energy Information Administration calculations.

Exhibit IX-8

Passenger car efficiency deteriorated until 1973 slowly and steadily by all measures. After 1973, the improvement was hesitant. Car usage declined rapidly in recession years. Mileage efficiency slowly improved through 1979 and the pace of the improvement could be expected to increase after 1979, but the petroleum consumption record revealed no evidence of the economy's capacity to adjust to any rapid decline in petroleum availability.

Energy Indicator—U.S. Passenger Car Efficiency

	Average Fuel Consumed per Car		Average Miles Traveled per Car		Average Miles Traveled per Gallon of Fuel Consumed	
	Gallons	Index	Miles	Index	Miles	Index
1967	684	100.0	9,531	100.0	13.93	100.0
1973	763	111.5	9,992	104.8	13.10	94.0
1979	664	97.1	9,485	99.5	14.29	102.6

Source: *U.S. Department of Transportation, Federal Highway Administration, Federal Highway Statistics Division, "Highway Statistics," Table VM-1.

Exhibit IX-9

Coal has been the primary choice of the federal energy administration as an alternative to oil and gas. The Carter administration had set a goal of 5 percent per year increase in coal usage. In this century America has adequate supplies as well as the capacity to increase coal production, but the American economy cannot adjust to using more coal very rapidly. In the first of the Carter years, coal consumption continued its three-year decline, unaffected by the Arab's oil boycott despite the obvious economic influence. From 1973 to 1980, the compound annual rate of increase was 2.3 percent. As electric utilities consumed

78 percent of U.S. coal in 1979 and as all other uses of coal declined steadily, the electric industry statistics are the critical factor in projecting future coal production and consumption expectancy.

Net Electricity Production by Primary Energy Source

	Coal[1]	Petroleum[2]	Natural Gas	Nuclear	Hydro	Other[3]	Total
			Million kilowatt-hours				
1975	852,786	289,095	299,778	172,505	300,047	3,437	1,917,649
1978	975,742	365,060	305,391	276,403	280,419	3,315	2,206,331
1980	1,161,562	245,994	346,240	251,116	276,021	5,506	2,286,439

[1] Includes bituminous coal, lignite, and anthracite.
[2] Includes fuel oil No. 2, No. 4, No. 5, No. 6, crude oil, kerosene, and petroleum coke.
[3] Includes geothermal, wood, and waste.
Source: *Federal Power Commission Form 4, "Monthly Power Plant Report."

Exhibit IX-10

The source of primary energy for the production of electricity identifies the characteristics of this capital intensive industry. It is not feasible to convert natural gas and petroleum-fired power plants to coal and these three have little in common with the nuclear and hydroelectric generating facility. Natural gas is the only fuel that can be introduced with minimum cost but its employment for the production of electricity is the least desirable. Natural gas can be delivered to the residential customer without paying the three times conversion cost multiple required to produce and distribute electricity. The increased employment of natural gas can only be viewed as a failure for political-economic influence on the nation's energy use trend. The downturn in petroleum use and the upturn for coal are successes.

The decrease in hydropower's contribution to electric energy production also runs counter to generally recognized long-term public interest. Hydropower is the largest of the renewable, solar power energy contributors. The turndown reflects the scarcity of new dam sites, the vulnerability of the industry to drought years, and the necessary retirement of dams which have silted out. The reported energy production from other sources of solar energy has increased significantly, more than doubling in seven years but the contribution is very small: .06 percent of U.S. energy consumption in 1973 and .15 percent in 1980. Most of this increase represents the burning of wood and the quantity may be understated, but the actual increase cannot continue for long at the recent acceleration. Limits in wood availability already are becoming evident.

America's problem with nuclear energy is revealed in the electricity production figures. In the first five years after 1973, nuclear power generation increased 3.25 times, a remarkable growth record, the consequence of America's rapidly developing nuclear industry. We were the leaders of the free world in the design and development of nuclear power plants. By 1978 this industry was restrained by political decision affecting both our capacity to maintain our position as a supplier of nuclear plants to the world market and the continued building of new plants in the United States. Nuclear power generation after 1978 actually turned down. Behind these statistics, America had abandoned its world leadership role in this industry. To gain perspective on this turn of events, production of nuclear electricity in the international market becomes important.

This tragic turn is evidenced in the international statistics of nuclear power generation:

International
Nuclear Electricity Generation by Non-Communist Countries[1]

	Japan	France	Canada	Sweden	Switz- erland	United King- dom[3]	West Ger- many	Non- Com- munist World Ex- cluding U.S.	United States	Total Non- Com- munist World
				Billion gross kilowatt-hours						
1973	9.4	11.6	18.3	2.1	6.2	28.0	11.9	100.7	88.0	188.7
1978	53.2	30.5	32.9	23.8	8.3	36.7	35.9	263.6	292.7	556.3
1980	81.0	61.2	40.4	26.7	14.3	37.2	43.7	352.6	265.3	618.0

[1]Figures are for gross electricity generation, as opposed to net electricity generation. Net figures are generally less than gross figures by about 5 percent, which represents the energy consumed by the generating plants themselves.
[2]Less than 0.05 billion gross kilowatt-hours.
[3]The United Kingdom assesses generation at 4- or 5-week intervals, rather than by calendar month.
*Source: *Nucleonics Week.*

Exhibit IX-11

Between 1978 and 1980, France doubled its nuclear generating capacity and Japan increased theirs by more than 50 percent. France, Germany, Switzerland, and Great Britain took over the leading position in research for the development of the breeder reactor and in the delivery of nuclear power plants. Russia continued its research and development in parallel with the new European leaders.

The second most common measure of energy is the barrel of oil equivalent. Although crude oil is radically different from one producing basin to another in its physical characteristics (specific gravity, sulphur content, asphalt or paraffin base), the heat value stays fairly close to 5,800,000 Btu per barrel and a million barrels per day becomes 2.117 quadrillion Btu per year. Finally, to convert quads per year to million barrels per day, multiply by .472237 (the reciprocal).

The Energy Information Administration and most energy analysts employ this million barrel per day measure when discussing the supply of crude oil and they use the crude oil equivalent in discussing petroleum products.

Petroleum

Crude Oil

	Crude Input to Refineries	Total Domestic Production[1] [2]	Alaskan Production	Crude Oil Imports[3]	SPR* Imports	Crude Oil Exports	Primary Crude Oil Stocks[1] [3] [4]	SPR* Stocks
	Thousand barrels per day						*Thousand barrels*	
1973	12,431	9,208	198	3,244		2	†242,478	
1978	14,739	8,707	1,229	6,195	162	158	†309,421	†66,860
1980	R13,483	R8,597	R1,617	R5,177	44	284		

[1] Includes lease condensate.
[2] Includes Alaskan production.
[3] Excludes SPR. Strategic Petroleum Reserve storage began in October 1977.
[4] Beginning in January 1981, Alaskan crude oil in transit to the United States are included in Primary Crude Oil Stocks.
[5] Indicates an adjustment in reported barrels in storage.
*SPR = Strategic Petroleum Reserve.
Estimated data in italics. These are likely to be revised.
†Total as of December 31.
R = Revised data.

Exhibit IX-12

How does the total production of crude oil relate to the sources of supply and to the quantity of oil in process tanks and pipelines? At the beginning of 1981, these stocks represented less than 27 days of production and a very small portion of this quantity is actually available for consumption. Pipelines and process tanks cannot be emptied if production is to be continued. At the same time, the strategic reserves would supply our refineries for only eight days at the average rate of production in 1980.

America appears to have turned the corner on total energy consumption but the economic consequences are not yet known. Economic and political influences have reduced oil consumption in America and increased coal production. The political restraints on building nuclear electric generating plants have increased costs introducing economic discouragement. The most significant fact that develops from the overview of U.S. energy supply is the limited potential of the future solar contribution.

Chapter 10
U.S. Crude Oil
Reserves and Resources

Synopsis

The production forecast through the year 2000 based on proved reserves is confirmed by the first six year's actual production experience compared with the ten-year petroleum engineers' production forecast for the oil fields representing 52 percent of the U.S. proved reserve in 1973.

Proved reserves of crude oil within the United States have declined every year since 1971 (Derivation and Development section C). The recent record in crude oil exploration and well development has been accompanied by decreases in the quantity of oil discovered per foot of drilling. Now a downward revision is required in estimating the undiscovered crude oil resource in the United States.

Domestically produced crude oil dominates the dynamics of the future U.S. energy supply. We now know enough to be relatively precise in projecting annual production each year for the rest of this century. The projection that follows is based on extrapolation of the American Petroleum Institute's 33-year record of the reserve additions and withdrawals.*

For the years 1973 through 1984, we have totally reliable information on the expected production from each of the oil fields that, as of December 31, 1974, accounted for 52 percent of our proved crude oil reserves. This record was provided by petroleum engineers under contract with the Federal Energy Administration. A current audit of actual production establishes the accuracy of these early estimates through 1978. Thus, one can demonstrate the precision of physical estimates for these years and use this information to establish a pattern of production for the next decade. A projection for the decades that follow will be only slightly less precise.

The fossil fuels available to our economy today represent a closed system. All the resources that will ever be found are now buried in the earth and under the seas. First we must find them. Then we can remove them. Finally they can be consumed, producing heat and power and hydrocarbon products. Only these last have any salvage value. Most of the fossil fuels pass through the system once in obedience to the laws of thermodynamics and then enter the atmosphere as oxides of carbon and sulphur to be employed by future generations of animal and vegetable life.

*See Exhibit 6, page 65.

The finding of oil and gas begins with geological surveys on the surface of the earth and seismic exploration below the surface. Explosive charges are detonated remote from listening devices that record the echo response from the subterranean formations. These recordings can be interpreted to identify structures that may trap oil and gas. The same process is employed with survey ships sending sound signals below the ocean floor. The activity is reported in terms of the number of crews engaged in exploration and the number of line miles recorded and analyzed.

These activities in the United States expanded annually until 1974 and then fell back during the recession both for the number of crews employed and the line miles of exploration. Crew activity recovered in 1977 and accelerated in 1980. Geological exploration became profitable as price restraints were relaxed and finally removed for oil.

Oil and Gas Resource Development
Seismic Exploration

| | CREWS | | | MILES | | |
	Offshore	Onshore	Total	Offshore[1]	Onshore[1]	Total[1]
	Monthly average			*Annual total*		
1973	23	227	250	258,944	127,160	386,104
1974	31	274	305	341,784	158,629	500,413
1975	30	254	284	309,283	150,694	459,977
1976	25	237	262	226,303	142,926	269,229
1977	27	281	308	124,676	120,072	244,748
1978	25	327	352	174,607	135,899	310,506
1979	30	370	400	193,212	163,929	357,141
1980	37	493	530			

Sources: Society of Exploration Geophysicists, "Monthly Seismic Crew Count" and annual reports published in their bulletin, *Geophysics.*

Exhibit X-13

Exploratory drilling follows the evidence of oil and gas in the geological mapping. Exploratory wells include wells drilled in new locations (wildcats) attempting to find new fields on the basis of geological evidence and developmental wells drilled around the periphery of existing fields anticipating an extension of those fields. These developmental wells seek to produce more oil from fields that already have, been discovered and are less risky than wildcats. However, every well carries the risk of becoming a dry hole.

Drilling for production follows geological exploration. These activities responded to the obvious need for oil after the Arab boycott despite regulatory discouragements, but the quantity of oil added to the proved reserve per foot of drilling declined from 4.4 barrels in 1973 to 3.0 in 1979 as shown in Exhibit X-15 on the following page. The ratio could not be computed in 1980 as the year was lost to the publication of the reserve figures following the transfer of this activity from the American Petroleum Institute to the government's Energy Information Administration.

Oil and Gas Resource Development

	Rotary Rigs in Operation	Exploratory and Development Wells Completed[1] [2]				Total Footage of Wells Completed[1]
	Monthly average	Oil	Gas	Dry	Total	Thousand feet
1973	1,194	9,902	6,385	10,305	26,592	136,391
1974	1,475	12,784	7,240	11,674	31,698	150,551
1975	1,660	16,408	7,580	13,247	37,235	174,434
1976	1,656	17,059	9,085	13,621	39,765	181,780
1977	2,001	18,912	11,378	14,692	44,982	210,848
1978	2,259	17,775	13,064	16,218	47,057	227,110
1979	2,177	19,383	14,681	15,752	49,816	238,659
1980	2,910	R27,026	R15,730	R18,089	R60,845	R284,461

[1] These data are for well completions reported to the American Petroleum Institute during the reporting period. Excludes service wells and stratigraphic and core tests.
[2] Data reported for the first 2 months of each quarter cover 4 weeks of drilling activity, and data for the last month of the quarter cover 5 weeks of drilling activity.
R = Revised data.
Sources: *Rotary Rigs: Hughes Tool Company, "Rotary Rigs Running–By State."
*Wells: American Petroleum Institute (API), "Monthly Drilling Report" and "Quarterly Review of Drilling Statistics for the United States."

Exhibit X-14

The third step in obtaining oil involves the petroleum engineers who measure the reserves in the discovered reservoirs and determine the optimum rate of flow to produce the greatest amount of oil and gas.

Barrels Per Foot

	1973	1978	1979
1. M feet of completed wells	136,391	227,110	238,275
2. M bbls crude oil reserve additions:			
New field discoveries	116,097	199,994	239,406
New reservoirs in old fields	87,816	73,483	107,567
Extensions of existing reservoirs	390,141	366,589	368,082
Total Reserve Additions as a consequence of exploratory & development drilling	594,054	640,066	715,055
Additions per foot of oil and gas exploratory & development drilling	4.35	2.81	3.00

Sources: 1. May 1981 Monthly Energy Review, U.S. Dept. of Energy. 2. June 1980 Reserves–Vol. 34, Am. Petro. Institute.

Exhibit X-15

Finally, the stage is set for oil and gas production. "Production" begins when it is determined that the market is ready. In the context of the 100-year history of the petroleum industry, "production" is a perfectly natural term. It complements the important marketing function. Prior to 1960, oil had been in surplus almost every year. Economic control of the industry was realized by controlling the means of moving oil and marketing oil. The geologist who found the oil and the engineers who produced and refined the oil were subordinated. The industry thought in terms of creating markets and then producing oil to satisfy these markets.

After World War II, market development began to outpace world production capacity. The new balance of supply with demand occurred shortly before 1973. The critical element in the oil supply process then shifted to discovery, and that is where we are today.

We now must accept the physical evidence. Our nation's future oil supply is in fact a closed system. We know how much oil has been found (our proved reserves) and how much oil is available to be found (the remaining undiscovered resource). We now know how much we can remove from the reserve each year (future annual production). We know enough about our proved reserves and our undiscovered resources to plan future production with a high degree of accuracy.

The forecast identifying anticipated crude oil production for the years 1980 through 2000 is detailed in Derivation and Development section C, beginning with the American Petroleum Institute's record of the proved crude oil reserves year-by-year from 1946 through 1979. A primary ingredient in this forecast is the survey of the oil and gas fields which represent 52 percent of the proved reserve.* An understanding of the precision potential of this physical forecast will be significantly improved by a minimum commitment of time in studying the summary of the petroleum engineers' analysis of these fields. This summary reduces to a single line the critical information for each field including the projection of future production for the years through 1984.

The fields have been rearranged in the order of the size of reserves. The following exhibit lists the ten largest fields in the lower 48 states and the remaining fields are summarized in the four exhibits that follow. Prudhoe Bay, Alaska is the largest of the fields. It is identified separately in the final summary.

Too often, we think in terms of unidentifiable forces controlling our destiny, forces we cannot possibly understand and must accept on faith. Energy does qualify as a controlling force, but the source of crude oil production need not be a mystery. Here are the identifiable fields that have been responsible for most of the U.S. produced oil. One can note their location and the date of discovery. These are the big ones. These are all of the big ones. They tell us that these fields, which date from the beginning of this century and now account for half our remaining proved reserve, will be nearly exhausted by the year 2000 at the present rate of declining production.

*Federal Energy Administration, 1975. Final Report Oil and Gas Resources, Reserves, and Productive Capacities Volume II. Federal Energy Administration: Washington, D.C.

FIRST TEN FIELDS of lower 48 states, PROVED RESERVES and petroleum engineers estimate of ANNUAL PRODUCTION

Millions of Barrels

Field Identification	Year of Discovery	Proved Reserve 12/31/74	1973	1974	1975	1976	1977	1978	1979	1980	1981	1982	1983	1984
The East Texas Field Gregg, Rusk, and Upshur Counties	1930	1,250	75 / 76	72	71	67 / 67	66	62 / 64	62	61	59	57	55	54
Kern River, California Kern County, San Joaquin Basin	1899	1,087	28 / 28	27	28	31 / 29	30	34 / 31	32	34	35	37	38	40
Wilmington, California Long Beach Harbor, L.A. Basin	1936	886	67 / 67	65	66	59 / 65	62	48 / 57	53	48	43	39	34	30
Yates, West Texas Pecos County, S.E., Central Basin	1926	831	18 / 19	19	19	27 / 28	37	40 / 37	37	37	37	37	37	37
Midway-Sunset, California Kern & San Luis Obispo County	1901	644	35 / 35	35	35	38 / 35	35	40 / 35	35	35	34	33	32	32
Kelly-Snyder, Texas Scurry County, East Midland Basin	1908	565	72 / 71	76	73	66 / 66	60	46 / 53	46	41	35	30	25	21
Hawkins, Texas S.E. Wood County, East Texas Basin	1940	535	40 / 40	40	40	40 / 40	40	27 / 40	40	38	36	34	32	31
Wasson, Texas Gaines & Yoakum Ctys. N. Cent. Basin	1936	508	84 / 84	93	93	90 / 88	61	79 / 47	39	30	26	22	18	16
Slaughter Field, West Texas Cochran, Hockley, & Terry Ctys. N. Basin	1936	402	46 / 44	48	46	43 / 44	40	37 / 37	33	29	26	23	21	18
San Ardo, California Monterey Cty., Salinas Basin		385	13 / 13	13	15	13 / 17	18	12 / 18	18	19	20	21	22	23
		7,093	477	488	486	479	449	419	395	372	351	333	314	302

Exhibit X-16

SECOND TEN FIELDS of lower 48 states, PROVED RESERVES and petroleum engineers estimate of ANNUAL PRODUCTION

Millions of Barrels

Field Identification	Year of Discovery	12/31/74 Proved Reserve	1973	1974	1975	1976	1977	1978	1979	1980	1981	1982	1983	1984
McElroy, West Texas Crane & Upton Ctys., E. Cent. Basin	1926	266	*11* 11	13	13	*14* 14	13	*13* 12	12	11	10	10	9	8
Jay, Florida Santa Rosa & Escambia Ctys.	1970	256	*30* 30	34	34	*36* 34	34	*39* 31	29	28	27	23	16	—
Seminole Complex, Texas Gaines Cty., Central Basin	1936	239	*16* 16	21	23	*26* 23	23	*27* 23	23	19	16	14	12	10
Tom O'Connor, Texas Gulf Coast Refugio Cty., Oligocene Belt	1934	216	*28* 28	26	24	*25* 22	21	*25* 19	18	16	14	12	10	9
Caillou Island, Southernmost La. Terrebonne Parish, Onshore	1930	203	*25* 25	17	13	*13* 12	12	13	14	16	17	18	18	18
Conroe Texas Gulf Coast Montgomery Cty., Eoicene Belt	1931	201	*22* 22	22	22	*21* 22	19	*22* 16	13	11	10	8	7	6
Hastings, Texas Gulf Coast Brazoria & Galveston Ctys.	1934	182	*23* 23	28	28	*28* 28	26	*25* 24	19	15	12	10	8	6
Bay Marchand Block, Offshore La. Lafourche Parish, S. of New Orl.	1949	155	33	32	28	25	22	20	16	11	9	6	4	3
Oregon Basin, Wyoming Park County, West Big Horn Basin	1927	132	*11* 10	11	10	*12* 10	9	*11* 8	8	7	6	6	5	5
Huntington Beach, California Orange Cty., Onshore & Offshore	1920	125	*21* 21	19	16	*15* 13	11	*11* 9	7	6	5	4	3	3
		1,975	219	223	211	203	190	175	159	140	126	111	92	68

Exhibit X-17

THIRD TEN FIELDS of lower 48 states, PROVED RESERVES and petroleum engineers estimate of ANNUAL PRODUCTION

Millions of Barrels

Field Identification	Year of Discovery	12/31/74 Proved Reserve	1973	1974	1975	1976	1977	1978	1979	1980	1981	1982	1983	1984
Elk Basin, Wyoming & Montana Park County, Wyoming & Carbon County, Montana, Big Horn Basin	1914	115	*12* 12	9	8	*8* 7	6	*6* 6	5	5	5	4	4	4
Eunice, Eumont, Jalmat, & Langlie-Mattix Fields Southeastern Lea County, N. Mexico	1929	110	*10* 10	10	10	*9* 10	9	*9* 8	7	7	6	5	5	4
Grand Isle Block 43 Offshore, La. 20 Miles from Plaquemines and Jefferson Parishes		108	21	21	19	17	14	12	10	8	6	5	4	3
West Delta Block 30, Offshore, La. 8 Mi. off Plaquemines Parish		103	24	22	18	15	13	11	10	8	6	5	4	3
West Ranch Field, Gulf Coast, Tx. Jackson Cty. on shore		99	*16* 16	15	14	*13* 13	12	*11* 9	9	7	6	5	4	3
Spraberry Trend, West Texas Upton, Reagan, Irion, Martin, Midland, Glasscock Counties	1949	90	*20* 20	18	14	*18* 11	9	*16* 8	7	6	5	5	4	3
The Fairway Field, E. Texas Basin Henderson & Anderson Counties	1960	87	*17* 17	14	11	*8* 9	8	*6* 7	5	4	4	3	3	2
Cogdell Field, West Texas Scurry and Kent Counties, E. Midland Basin	1949	86	*13* 12	11	13	*11* 11	10	*7* 8	7	6	5	4	4	3
Main Pass Block 41 Offshore, La. 10 Mi. from Plaquemines Parish	1957	83	*14* 13	11	9	7	8	8	7	6	5	4	3	3
West Cote Blanche Bay, Offshore, La. St. Mary's Parish, extreme S. La.		76	*10* 10	8	8	*6* 7	7	6	6	5	5	4	4	3
		957	155	139	124	107	96	83	73	62	53	44	39	31

Exhibit X-18

FOURTH TEN FIELDS of lower 48 states, PROVED RESERVES and petroleum engineers estimate of ANNUAL PRODUCTION

Millions of Barrels

Field Identification	Year of Discovery	12/31/74 Proved Reserve	1973	1974	1975	1976	1977	1978	1979	1980	1981	1982	1983	1984
The Sooner Trend, Central Oklahoma / Garfield, Kingfisher & Logan Ctys., Anadarko Basin	1942	63	*11* / 11	10	9	*10* / 7	6	*8* / 5	5	4	3	3	3	2
Dos Cuadras, Offshore California / Santa Barbara Cty., Ventura Basin	1968	62	*17* / 17	15	14	*12* / 13	10	*10* / 8	6	5	4	3	2	1
Heidelberg Field, Mississippi / Jasper County		55	*5* / 5	5	5	*4* / 4	4	*4* / 4	4	3	3	3	2	2
Anahuac Field, Texas Gulf Coast / Chambers County, east of Houston		54	*11* / 11	9	8	*6* / 7	6	*4* / 5	4	4	3	3	2	2
Cat Canyon Field, California / Santa Barbara County, Stanta Maria B.	1908	54	*6* / 7	7	6	*6* / 6	5	*6* / 5	4	4	3	3	3	2
Timbalier Bay, Onshore, La. / Lafourche Parish		52	*9* / 9	8	6	*6* / 5	4	4	3	3	2	2	2	2
Dollarhide, West Texas & N. Mexico / Andrews Cty., Tx. & Lea Cty. N.M.		49	*7* / 7	7	6	*5* / 5	4	*4* / 4	3	3	3	2	2	2
Greater Altamont, N.E. Utah / Duchesne & Uintah Ctys., Uinta Basin		39	*14* / 14	22	21	*19* / 10	4	*12* / 2	1	1				
Bay De Chene Field, Louisiana / Jefferson & Lafourche Parishes coastline		39	*7* / 7	6	5	*4* / 4	4	3	3	3	2	2	2	2
Dune Field, West Texas / Northeast Crane Cty., E. & Cent. Basin		33	*9* / 9	7	6	*5* / 5	4	*4* / 4	3	2	2	2	1	1
		500	97	96	86	66	51	44	36	32	25	23	19	16

Exhibit X-19

FIFTH ELEVEN FIELDS of lower 48 states, PROVED RESERVES and petroleum engineers estimate of ANNUAL PRODUCTION

Millions of Barrels

Field Identification	12/31/74 Proved Reserve	1973	1974	1975	1976	1977	1978	1979	1980	1981	1982	1983	1984
South Pass Block 65, Offshore, Miss. 25 Mi. E. of Mississippi R. Mouth	29	11	10	8	6	4	3	2	2	1	1	1	--
Eugene Island Block 175, Offshore, La. 45 Mi. from Iberia Parish	24	9	8	6	4	2	3	2	1	2	1	1	--
Weeks Island, Coastal La. Iberia Parish, Weeks Bay	17	9	6	5	4	2	1	1	1	1	1	--	--
Eugene Island Block 276, Offs. La. 75 Mi. Off from St. Mary's Parish	17	6	5	4	3	3	2	1	1	1	1	1	--
Eugene Island Block 32, Offs. La. 15 Mi. from St. Mary's Parish	13	1	1	1	2	2	2	2	1	1	1	1	1
Bateman Lake Onshore La. St. Mary's Parish (pri. nat. gas)	11	2	1	1	1	1	1	1	1	1	1	1	--
Quarantine Bay, Coastline, La. Plaquemines Parish	9	4	4	3	3	1	1	1	1	1	1	1	--
Tijerina-Canales-Blucher (T-C-B) South Texas—Jim Wells and Kleberg Counties, Onsh. Gulf C.	7	7	4	2	.352	1	1	1	1	1	--	--	--
Chocolate Bayou, Texas E. Cent. Brazoria Cty., Gulf C.	3	.428	1	1	.408	1	.254	1	--	--	--	--	--
Coyanosa, West Texas Pecos Cty., Delaware Basin (pri. gas)	2	1	--	--	.338	1	.476	--	1	--	--	--	--
Bastian Bay, Onshore Louisiana Plaquemines Parish (prim. Nat. gas)	2	.439	--	--	.294	--	--	--	--	--	--	--	--
	134	52	39	31	22	18	15	12	10	7	6	4	1

Exhibit X-20

How accurate are petroleum engineers in estimating future production? How much more oil can be produced from these fields by secondary and tertiary recovery methods—methods now affordable in view of the high value of the oil produced? In response to the first question, the Dallas office of the Energy Information Administration has indicated actual production in the years 1973, 1976, and 1978. These figures appear in the italicized notations above the annual production figure for these years. Annual production is in the computer for all fields. Omission of this notation indicates that the field in question represents the combination of separate basins requiring a more difficult correlation to obtain the information from the computer.

The second question is answered in the American Petroleum Institute's report of the proved reserves for the 100 largest fields. This information is found in their annual reserves publication and reference is to Volume 34, the June 1980 report which provides information on the age of each of the fields in question. In comparing the proved reserve quantity at the end of 1978, it is obvious which of these fields experienced substantial revision (increased or decreased reserve estimate as a consequence of additions to the fields or more advanced recovery procedure or some disaster throwing off the original reserve estimate.) Generally, the fields with higher than expected production in 1978 were the fields where advanced recovery methods had been employed, made possible by higher prices. The fields without an identified date of discovery were the fields where reserves decreased. (As they were no longer among the 100 largest fields, their original discovery date could not be identified.)

In 1975 one knew with a considerable degree of accuracy how much oil would be produced from our largest fields and similar information could be obtained to complete the physical projection of a larger sample of the country's future crude oil production. The estimates are somewhat conservative, but this conservative balance has been so consistent over the years that analysts such as M. King Hubbert (the petroleum geologist who projected the 1970 peaking of U.S. oil production in 1956) have computed the expected conservative bias and made a correction for it. The correction represents a small percentage addition to the total.

Given the reliability of crude oil proved reserve statistics and the petroleum engineers' estimates of future production potential, the future United States supply of crude oil can be determined with reasonable accuracy, and one can even draw a picture of our closed system of crude oil production. The drawing on the next page is to scale, with one cubic centimeter representing 1.06 billion barrels of oil. The 2" diameter sphere (before reduction) identifies the minimum undiscovered resource of 72.73 billion barrels. The increased dimension sphere identifies 142.7 (sized just beyond the notation), the largest probable undiscovered reserve. The proved reserve is the large cylinder and annual production the smaller. All quantities are for the year 1975.

The numbers this picture presents are startling. They show the relatively large proved reserve and annual production compared to the not-very-large undiscovered resource. Is this 72.73 billion barrel remaining resource all the crude oil we can expect to find within our political boundaries, which include Alaska and the Continental Shelf? The quantity in this undiscovered resource was the subject of my first book, based primarily on U.S. Geological Survey Circular 725 and interpretation of the conclusions by the survey team that produced this report. The minimum resource estimate represents a 95-percent statistical probability of discovering this amount or more. The maximum estimate represents a 5-percent probability of exceeding the quantity indicated. In interpreting these figures, preference for a 95-percent probability of meeting the estimate is obvious and evidence today indicates that only the minimum undiscovered reserve has significance. The declining rate of discovery since 1975 will not support a larger assumption. Observe the American Petroleum Institute graph on page 65. Additions declined despite increased price.

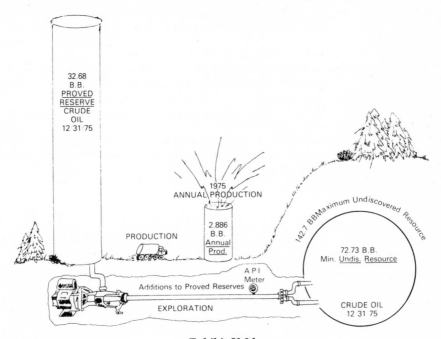

Exhibit X-21

The numbers most important to our forecast identify the rate of production, which is the actual annual withdrawal from the proved reserves. Our sample of the largest fields, accounting for 52 percent of the total reserve at the beginning of 1974, provides an excellent basis for starting the forecasting process. The tabulation on the next page summarizes these figures in six groups, beginning with the single Prudhoe Bay field, then groups of ten fields graduating to the last eleven fields in the sample. It is immediately apparent that these fields, grouped by size, are radically different from each other in their physical characteristics, and that the summation of all fields produces a misleading conclusion as to the pattern of withdrawal.

Between 1973 and 1984, the production from this 52-percent sample is projected to decline by only 3 percent. This conclusion cannot be accepted. It results from the increasing production from Prudhoe Bay combined with decreasing production from all other fields. The Alaskan pipeline had not been completed in 1973. Not until 1980 could the pipeline be operated at capacity and production at this level could be maintained through 1985 before the physical limits of the proved reserve would begin to reduce annual production.

Another pattern develops from this analysis of fields by size. The withdrawal rate (ratio of annual production to remaining proved reserve) is smaller for the large fields and the decline in the proved reserves for these large fields is much slower. As noted, the largest ten fields in the lower 48 states still will be producing 63 percent of their 1973 production in 1984. This compares with only 16 percent for the fourth group of ten fields and only 2 percent for the final grouping.

Summation of Petroleum Engineers Production Estimates of the 59 Oil and Gas Fields Which Represented 52% of U.S. Proved Reserves of Crude Oil on December 31, 1974

Reserves and Annual Production in $\overline{M}$ Barrels $^{-}$

Field	Proved Reserves 12/31/74	Production			Percentage of 1973 Production expected in 1984
		1973	1980	1984	
Alaska	8,759	– –	548	548	∝
Lower 48:					
1st 10 fields	7,093	477	372	302	63%
2nd 10 fields	1,975	219	140	68	31%
3rd 10 fields	957	155	62	31	20%
4th 10 fields	500	97	32	16	16%
5th 11 fields	134	52	10	1	2%
Total Sample	19,418	1,000	1,164	966	97%

Exhibit X-22

Also note the pattern of the field size. The Prudhoe Bay (Alaska) proved reserves are greater than the sum of the reserves in the ten next largest fields, and these first ten greatly exceed the reserves in the remaining 41 fields. The same pattern exists in the crude oil basins all over the world. We have depended on a few giant fields for over half of total world production. The significance of this distribution is the increasing difficulty in finding more giant fields.

The figures in Exhibit X-23 identify the probable petroleum that will be available to the United States from oil and gas fields within our national borders through the end of the century. In a 1979 forecast, Exxon anticipated 7.2 million barrels per day for 1990. The forecast prepared for President Ford in 1976* projected 7.1 million barrels per day for 1990 employing a methodology based on the undiscovered resource, assuming proved reserve flow-through. In 1980 Exxon reduced its estimate for 1990 to 6.3 million barrels per day. Today we no longer can find evidence to support the discovery rate required either for this author's earlier forecast or Exxon's 1979 forecast. In both 1979 and 1980 the difference between the two forecasts is small. It is now clear that it is physically impossible for America to produce much more liquid petroleum in the next two decades. After that, there will be even less.

**Forecast of Total Petroleum Liquids Million Barrels/Day	
1979	9.9
1980	9.9
1981	9.5
1982	9.2
1983	8.9
1984	8.6
1985	8.4
1986	8.0
1987	7.7
1988	7.3
1989	7.0
1990	6.7
1991	6.4
1992	6.1
1993	5.8
1994	5.6
1995	5.5
1996	5.3
1997	5.1
1998	4.8
1999	4.6
2000	4.4

Exhibit X-23

In mid-May 1980, the American Petroleum Institute released its annual year-end proved reserves report.*** For those concerned with this country's capacity to produce crude oil, natural gas, and natural gas liquids, this would be the most important information of the year. It summarized the petroleum engineers' analysis of every crude oil reservoir in the country, identifying all on-going activities to produce oil and gas and taking into consideration the economic influences on oil and gas producers. Changes in the wellhead price of crude oil and natural gas were reflected in the practicability of secondary and tertiary removal methods. The remaining reserves were evaluated on the basis of the current state of the art, current costs, and current price. Heavy oils, not economically producible in previous years, were now added to the nation's producible reserve. All the oil and gas known definitely to be available for production in future years were added field by field.

Total crude oil reserves were identified as 27,051,280,000 barrels. The obvious reason for the 3/4 billion barrel decline was the continued high rate of production, the oil removed from the reserve during 1979.

The good news was the addition to proved reserves, 2.205 billion barrels, the greatest addition in one year since 1971. 49,816 wells had been drilled, the

*Last Report to President Ford delivered in October 1976, by Samuel M. Dix, published as Energy—A Critical Decision for the United States Economy, 1977 by Energy Education Publishers.

**A graphic summary of U.S. petroleum resources and discussion of the controversy over their determination will be found in Derivation and Development section B. The 20-year forecast of U.S. crude oil production is detailed in Derivation and Development section C.

***This would be the last of these A.P.I. reports as the government's Energy Information Administration is now performing this service and no report was issued in 1981.

highest level of activity in twenty years, but these new wells accounted for less than half of the additions. 1.49 billion barrels of the increase was represented by revisions to the estimated production of existing reservoirs, the application of new techniques in reworking old fields to produce more oil and the correction of previous estimates. New reservoirs represented only .108 billion barrels, new fields added .239 billion barrels and extensions of existing fields represented .368 billion barrels. These were the critical statistics.

More oil was added to the proved reserve for this year than was anticipated by .7 billion barrels. This is not an insignificant addition. If the addition had occurred in finding new reservoirs or new fields, it would support a small, optimistic adjustment. Seven hundred million barrels represent a 2.7-percent increase in the projected reserve at the beginning of 1980, but 1979 had experienced another radical increase in oil prices as well as the relaxation of price controls. Petroleum engineers had been given more than the average expectancy of economic assistance to apply high cost removal methods to the remaining resource.

News of the new oil and gas reserve figures issued by the A.P.I. was not headlined in the *Wall Street Journal.* The confirmation of nine years of declining oil and gas reserves apparently was not news that the financial community wished to publicize.

Chapter 11
Natural Gas

Synopsis

Production is forecast through the year 2000 based on proved reserves and the probable additions to proved reserves from the identified undiscovered resource.

The year-to-year production of natural gas is much more difficult to forecast than the production of crude oil, but the total natural gas production anticipation to the end of the century is not subject to the same forecast difficulty. It is simply easier to draw down on the proved reserve of natural gas in any current year at the expense of future production.

Natural gas can be imported only from Canada and Mexico. Liquefying natural gas is an expensive process for ocean transport. The political forecast for natural gas importation from Canada and Mexico in the decade of the 90s must be viewed pessimistically.

N atural gas is second only to liquid petroleum as a source of energy for the United States. In terms of domestic production, natural gas exceeds the energy contribution of crude oil.

Natural gas production is more susceptible to economic and political persuasion than petroleum. Almost 70 percent of the U.S. natural gas reserves are not associated with crude oil and are independent of oil production scheduling. The flow of gas from these fields is much less restricted than the flow of oil. Thus, the quantity of gas that can be expected to be produced relates to the size of the field and the cost of constructing pipeline from the field to the point of use. Once the economics of this delivery have been determined, the size of the pipeline is not likely to be changed, but these physical and economic influences are not necessarily controlling on natural gas production and consumption.

During the 1980s, America can maintain or even increase its annual consumption of natural gas if its political leaders are able to keep hidden the costs to future generations. That cost is the unavailability of this critical resource in the quantities that will be required in the next century. America has been consuming 20 trillion cubic feet of dry natural gas per year. Our average findings have been less than half this amount each year since 1969, but proved reserves at the beginning of the year 1980 stood at 195 trillion cubic feet and the

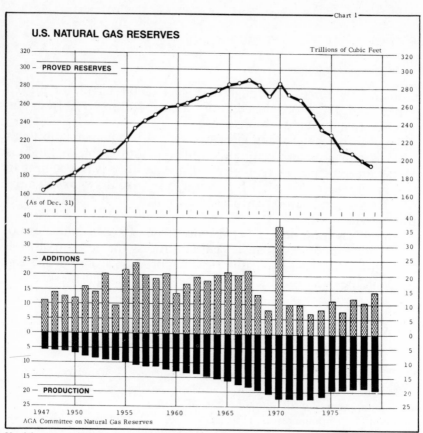

Chart 1

U.S. NATURAL GAS RESERVES

Trillions of Cubic Feet

PROVED RESERVES

(As of Dec. 31)

ADDITIONS

PRODUCTION

1947   1950   1955   1960   1965   1970   1975

AGA Committee on Natural Gas Reserves

Used by permission of the copyright holder, American Gas Association.

Exhibit XI-24

undiscovered resource was conservatively estimated at 258 trillion cubic feet at the beginning of 1975. Subtracting 55 trillion of discoveries, this leaves almost ten years' supply in the undiscovered resource in addition to approximately ten years of proved reserve. We can make it to the end of the century and we can have even more each year at the beginning. When we use our natural gas is a political-economic decision.

The sanguine voices for natural gas consumption assume the future availability of Mexican gas and a greater contribution from Canada despite the fact that the nations have given us contrary advice. The Canadian central government would like to maintain its gas and oil reserves for its own future, and after the Arab boycott, Canada advised our country to prepare for zero exports. Mexico has advised that their oil and gas production policy would be based on their own economic needs.

Despite the temporary economic and political advantage of the optimistic future gas production expectancy, neither the gas industry nor the government regulators is ignorant of the physical facts of our natural gas supply. As withdrawals exceed additions, each year less gas will be available and this trend can be interrupted only temporarily. As fields run out, production should be cut back although new fields will be developed and new lines will be laid to slow the decline in supply. Heroic efforts to increase the capacity of natural gas gathering lines and trunklines will prove an uneconomical capital investment in the long run.

The physical forecast of anticipated natural gas for the years through the end of the century is based on the implementation of a conservative gas production policy, maintaining the discovery and delivery capacities of the industry and following the established pattern of a retreating undiscovered resource. This forecast will be found in Derivation and Development section D. It follows the methodology employed for crude oil on a simplified form. Only one proved reserve category plus the category representing additions to reserves was used in the natural gas forecast.

The 31 trillion cubic feet of gas isolated on Alaska's North Slope has been subtracted from the year-end proved reserve before computing annual withdrawal expectancy and the annual level of remaining reserves.

Today the annual production from the lower 48 states represents the total quantity of the U.S. produced natural gas made available to the gas industry. A small amount of gas produced in southern Alaska is being liquefied and shipped to Japan. We have been importing natural gas from Canada. As Canadian exports decrease, we can anticipate future Mexican exports to replace this quantity, but the U.S. produced portion will control our use of natural gas. The forecast of natural gas production, natural gas liquids production, and the total of the two in terms of equivalent barrels of oil is summarized in Exhibit XI-25.

The reporting of natural gas liquids in terms of million barrels per day permits direct comparison with the summation of crude oil production in Chapter X. Annual production is 365 times this daily figure. Similarly, the combined natural gas and natural gas liquids can be identified in equivalent barrels of oil completing the comparison of oil and gas expectancy through the year 2000 as forecast in these two chapters.

This is not all the gas we will have, but it is all the low cost gas and all of the high quality gas. We so easily forget that the gas we are using is measured in trillions of cubic feet on an annual basis (and this converts directly to quadrillion Btu). A billion cubic feet or even a million sounds impressive if we do not take into account that it takes 19 million times a million cubic feet just to replace the natural gas we consumed in one year, 1979.

One promising addition to the future gas supply is the Prudhoe Bay, Alaska reserve, the 31 trillion cubic feet, which lacks only a pipeline for delivery, a pipeline that has been approved by both the Canadian and U.S. governments. The barrier is financing. It will cost between $30 and $40 billion, 40 percent of the money for the pipeline in Alaska, 40 percent for the Canadian section, and

GAS INDUSTRY FORECAST*

Year	Natural Gas Production Trillion Cu. Ft./Year	Natural Gas Liquids Production M̄ Bbls./Day	Total Gas & NGL Oil Equivalent M̄ Bbls./Day
1974	21.32	724	12.1
1975	19.72	701	11.3
1976	19.54	701	11.2
1977	19.45	699	11.1
1978	19.31	664	10.9
1979	18.96	649	10.7
1980	18.60	634	10.5
1981	18.31	618	10.3
1982	18.08	594	10.2
1983	18.06	579	10.1
1984	17.92	563	10.0
1985	17.91	547	9.9
1986	17.67	531	9.8
1987	17.39	516	9.6
1988	16.79	501	9.3
1989	16.68	485	9.2
1990	16.30	470	9.0
1991	15.88	456	8.8
1992	15.15	441	8.4
1993	14.48	427	8.0
1994	13.87	413	7.7
1995	13.30	446	7.5
1996	12.78	427	7.2
1997	12.29	409	6.9
1998	11.84	393	6.7
1999	11.41	377	6.4
2000	11.01	362	6.2

*The natural gas and natural gas liquids forecasts are fully explained in Derivation and Development section D.

Exhibit XI-25

20 percent for the connecting lines in the lower 48 states. The central figure for the United States' portion is only $20 billion, not a tremendous sum for a nation that measures Gross National Product in trillions, but $20 billion is more than twice the total investment equity generated by the United States stock markets in recent years. The 1980 price of natural gas did not produce the margins required to find the needed combination of equity and loan capital in the private sector. The pipeline as planned will carry .876 trillion cubic feet per year, generating $3.5 billion at $4 a cubic foot, not enough revenue to cover the costs required by the producers of the gas and the builders of the pipeline.

Potential Alaskan gas production is too small a proportion of our total consumption to influence public policy and trigger public financing. If the price of gas rises faster than the cost of the pipeline, the private economy will undertake the construction. Otherwise, public funds will continue to be required. In the meantime, the Alaskan gas is not being wasted. The gas which accumulates with the production of oil is being pumped back into the reservoir, employing giant gas-driven turbines. This process maintains the oil production of the reservoir as well as reserving the gas for future delivery.

The cost of the pipeline in terms of physical energy appears to center on one quadrillion Btu and the proved reserve is 31 times this amount. Thus, the physical energy profit that can be released by building the pipeline appears obvious unless the long-term future energy needs of the country are introduced. Then, speculation on the pipeline necessity produces interesting considerations. Presently identified producible American reserves of oil will be below one billion barrels by the end of the century and we may find no more than another 3 or 4 billion barrels on Alaska's North Slope during the next 20 years—a pessimistic but probable view. Some time after the year 2010 it might be desirable to give oil production on the North Slope a rest and refit the pipeline to bring the gas down to Valdez. A gas liquefaction plant or alcohol conversion plant could move the energy product to market without an additional pipeline. At 20 billion current dollars for the U.S. part of the pipeline, the investment represents the equivalent of the book value of the steel industry of the United States. The problem of finding this amount of capital in the equity market already has been indicated.

The importation of natural gas into the United States is limited to our neighbors, Canada and Mexico. Canadian imports have centered on one trillion cubic feet (one quadrillion Btu) a year. After the Arab oil boycott, the Canadians announced plans to reduce exports to near zero, but this has not yet been carried out. Canadian production is in the west and the gas is needed in eastern Canada, so a pipeline must be built if the Canadians are to conserve and use their own gas.

The Mexican contribution is in the future and they almost surely will exceed Canada's contribution at some time, but Mexico has made it clear that it has no intention of gearing gas production to U.S. market requirements. They would prefer to develop industries using oil and gas to build their own economy. The 5 percent represented by Canadian exports may not be exceeded by the combined Canadian and Mexican contribution in the future, but some increase is hoped for.

Two types of liquefied gas product are now being produced in the world market. Liquefied petroleum gas (LPG) is the common product distributed in this country in pressure cylinders for use as fuel for transportation vehicles and residential heating and cooking where pipeline gas is not available. The product provides a backup for utility systems and for industry purchasing interruptible natural gas. This gas represents the borderline hydrocarbons (primarily butane) that are found in crude oil and natural gas liquids. The product can be manufactured from liquid petroleum, selecting the light ends.

Liquefied natural gas (LNG) derives from primary natural gas, methane and ethane. It becomes a liquid at minus 450° Fahrenheit and must be held at this very low temperature during ocean transport. The cost of producing the low temperature and the insulation required for its maintenance, with container materials behaving peculiarly at this temperature, create problems. In early experiments, the containers fractured, releasing the frigid liquid and precipitating death and destruction. A harbor collision with a ship carrying liquefied natural gas could be devastating. The liquid floats on water and will quickly freeze anything in its path. As the liquid boils at 450° below zero and as the gas combines with air, an explosive cloud can move downwind and become ignited.

To import the abundant supplies of natural gas that are in the Persian Gulf and Africa would require a liquefaction industry in these supplying countries and ships for transport and ports for receiving the liquid product in this country. The economics of this supply are discouraging. The European economy is being geared to natural gas and the product can be delivered to that mass market by pipeline. Some of these are in process, some are in the planning stage. Obviously, a much shorter transport of the liquid version would be required.

Natural gas can be produced from coal more easily than liquid petroleum. Before the natural gas pipeline distribution systems were developed, coal gas, a low Btu product, was produced for distribution within major metropolitan areas of this country. Actually, gas distribution preceded the development of electricity in our eastern cities. In the beginning, gas lights were the most important contribution, followed by gas range cooking and gas hot water heaters. Coal gas has approximately one-third the Btu content of natural gas and this would require radical changes today to adapt pipelines for its distribution and use. Coal gas is uneconomical for transport over significant distances, but a high Btu coal gas product is available if we accept its cost. The production of this high Btu content substitute for natural gas is expensive in terms of time, money and materials required to build the process plants. Also, the environmental depredations now projected for their operation may be critical.

The difficulties with importing or synthesizing a substitute for natural gas have put pressure on futurists to seek exotic new natural sources. As previously noted, a large portion of the gas we are finding and using today is not associated with petroleum. How did this gas come into existence? The deep-earth-gas-hypothesis offers a tantalizing ultimate solution. It suggests that gas is being formed out of the primary substance of the earth, independently of the solar energy flow that created fossil fuels as they are generally understood. There could be a virtually unlimited supply if the hypothesis were proved. Methane (CH_4) could have been present in the earth's primitive atmosphere. Limestone ($CaCO_3$) is abundant in the earth's crust as is water (H_2O). The hypothesis suggests that natural gas is being formed deep in the earth and may associate with conventional solar-generated hydrocarbons. Unfortunately, there is a practical problem with the optimistic view. If non-fossil-fuel gas is contributing to our current supply, then this gas already is being counted by the petroleum and gas engineers in their evaluation of the existing fields and their annual determination of the proved reserve and this proved reserve has not been increasing.

A second natural gas hypothesis falls into the same trap. Large quantities of brine lie deep under the Gulf of Mexico and the borderline states. Below 30,000 feet, this brine is under very high pressure and contains small quantities of natural gas. However, the brine volume is so large that the potential gas contribution becomes significant if a way can be found to release the gas from the brine and then dispose of the unwanted liquid. The energy potential is increased by the fact that the brine is hot. Wells have been drilled and the high pressure has been confirmed, as well as the presence of gas. So far, the contribution to the proved reserve has not been significant.

When we get to the end of the line with the difficulties of importation or substitution or finding exotic new sources, we are faced with statistical evidence of a long-term, declining proved reserve of natural gas. Natural gas is too valuable to burn under electric utility and industrial boilers where alternative sources of heat are available. It should be conserved.

To substitute coal for residential heating means introducing atmospheric pollution at an unacceptable level. An economically feasible technology for control of pollutants in these small coal burners is improbable. Thus, natural gas is the primary candidate for maintaining the nation's investment in residential homes and commercial buildings that require seasonal heat.

But the gas industry depends on year-round sales to maintain its own economic balance. If the year-round customers for natural gas are required to seek more economical sources of heat, the industry could very well fall out of the private sector. Thus, it is the gas industry that faces politicians and economists with their most difficult decisions. It is no accident that the U.S. Congress spent a year debating the natural gas bill and then found a compromise that avoided recognition of the facts and their implications.

As the American economy entered the 1980s, spokesmen for the natural gas industry appeared to be approximately ten years behind their associates in liquid petroleum who have come to recognize the limits in the physical supply of oil. The American natural gas industry is isolated from world economics by the physical nature of the product and it is protected from immediate supply problems by the immense reserves that were accumulated when natural gas was a by-product of petroleum exploration, difficult to dispose of economically. Although the decrease in the volume of these reserves is obviously projectible as additions fail to match withdrawals year after year, industry spokesmen are very nearly unanimous in refusing to discuss a future production shortfall.

Chapter 12
Our World
Energy Dependence

Synopsis

The United States energy problem is revealed in the comparison of U.S. production with imports required to maintain our supply and the future stability of these sources in the international market. Between January 1980 and January 1981, the total net energy imports declined by the equivalent of 2.2 million barrels per day, but during 1980, oil imports had represented 7.47 million barrels per day and crude oil alone had ranged from 4.5 to 6.4 million barrels per day from month to month. These imports continue to represent the margin of energy required to maintain our free economy.

Future imports of oil and gas are threatened by political instability and the physical facts of a decreasing world proved reserve. There is significant evidence that future discoveries will not replace these reserves of oil and gas. America's future imports require a country-by-country analysis of the trend in the petroleum production capacity and the political as well as economic motivations of each of our suppliers.

During the 1970s, the United States became dependent on imports for a critical portion of its energy supply. In the last half of the decade, we imported over 50 percent of our total petroleum for several months. Years before, the major oil companies had shifted to exploring and producing oil outside our borders while, at the same time, promoting the sale of petroleum products to the world market.

In 1970, U.S. petroleum production turned down while world consumption continued to accelerate. Market forces shifted primary control of oil prices from the demand to the supply side of the economist's equation. The political and economic significance of this shift was highlighted by the concentration of oil in the Persian Gulf.

The world appetite for petroleum products had reached the point where all of the world's producers began to be needed to maintain a balance with demand. When higher prices generated revenues permitting production cutbacks without reducing the income of producing countries, a new element was introduced into the economist's supply-demand-price syllogism. It now developed that price increases cause production to drop when producing countries cannot effectively use increased income and when the annual rate of inflation exceeds the rate of return on investment.

The free market process handed control of the free world's economy to the Organization of Petroleum Exporting Countries (OPEC). Cartel rhetoric and anticipation of a decline in oil prices had little impact once the 1973-1974 boycott demonstrated world dependence on OPEC oil and oil price increases began to influence economic decisions in the producing countries. OPEC nations with large oil reserves and large current production capacities did not need and could not economically use the money generated from increased oil production.

There was no way to reduce the free world's demand for oil enough to avoid inflation. As world currencies began to lose value, oil in the ground began to be worth more than money in the bank. The inflation rate began to exceed the interest that could be earned. This became the controlling economic fact. The OPEC countries which continued to produce oil over and above the minimum requirements to maintain their economies did so for reasons other than simple economic motivation. This changed economic environment must now be recognized in projecting probable U.S. oil and gas imports, but economic practice is tied to current market responses and the world's limited capacity to store petroleum products.

Beginning in 1979, American politicians began to be impressed with the reality of their nation's energy problem, releasing oil price control. The average wellhead price in 1978 was $9 a barrel. By February of 1981 the indicated price was more than $34. The public responded with active conservation. Between January 1, 1980 and 1981, total net energy imports decreased by the equivalent of 2.19 million barrels per day with the help of economic recession and, in the first half of 1981, accelerating recession in Europe further reduced world consumption. In February of 1981, the landed price of crude oil in the United States ranged from $31.64 (Venezuela) to $42.05 (Libya). More oil was being produced than was needed and a price reduction was anticipated.

These economic facts and figures are important in marketplace transaction from month to month, but they will have little influence on the world energy balance for the remainder of the 1980s and into the next century. The quantities of energy available in world reserves and the quantities estimated in the undiscovered resources and the economic and political stability of the petroleum producing countries will control the availability of crude oil, and this is the energy resource that controls the free world economies. The United States consumption can have a substantial effect on the balance, but the spectacular reduction during 1980 and the first half of 1981 will be difficult to continue. America has been reducing its obvious excess consumption and recession has contributed. Further reductions and a real depression will be economically painful.

As the physical facts of petroleum availability will control energy economics in future years and decades, the sources and quantities of America's energy imports since 1973 provide important evidence of future supply expectancy. First, the non-OPEC suppliers tend to be our most reliable sources.

Petroleum

Petroleum Imports from Non-OPEC Sources

	Bahamas	Canada	Mexico	Netherlands Antilles	Puerto Rico	Trinidad and Tobago	Virgin Islands	Other[1]	Total
				Thousand barrels per day					
1973	174	1,325	16	585	99	255	329	480	3,263
1978	160	467	318	229	94	253	429	663	2,613
1980	78	R446	R530	226	85	176	383	R656	R2,580

[1] Includes Non-OPEC Arab, Western Europe, Angola, U.S.S.R., Rumania, other Western Hemisphere and other Eastern Hemisphere.

Exhibit XII-26

With the exception of Mexico, the contribution from these countries has been decreasing since 1973. Only Venezuela, our South American neighbor who is a member of OPEC, is not included among these more reliable sources of crude and Venezuela's contributions have been decreasing relatively rapidly.

The OPEC countries have the largest proved reserves and undiscovered resources.

Petroleum

Petroleum Imports from OPEC Sources

	Algeria	Indonesia	Iran	Libya	Nigeria	Saudi Arabia	United Arab Emirates	Venezuela	Total OPEC
					Thousand barrels per day				
1973	136	213	223	164	459	486	71	1,135	2,993
1978	649	573	555	654	919	1,144	385	645	5,751
1980	R483	R341	8	R552	R847	R1,257	179	R463	R4,251

[1] Includes Ecuador, Gabon, Iraq, Kuwait and Qatar.
[2] Includes Algeria, Libya, Saudi Arabia, United Arab Emirates, Iraq, Kuwait and Qatar.

Exhibit XII-27

Our dependence on the OPEC petroleum producers has increased substantially since 1973 and this dependence can be reduced only by successful future conservation over and above the requirement to cover the probable reduction in our domestic crude oil production. The ultimate question becomes the quantity of oil these exporting countries can be expected to produce in future years and the economic and political capacity of the United States to claim these resources in competition with world demand.

World production peaked at 62.4 million barrels per day in 1979 before falling back to an average of 59.5 in 1980. The figures for 1973, 1978, and 1980 indicate the capacities of the major petroleum producers. The listing begins with the Arab members of OPEC.

International

Crude Oil Production
for Major Petroleum Exporting Countries *
Thousand barrels per day

	Algeria	Iraq	Kuwait[1]	Libya	**Qatar	Saudi Arabia[1]	United Arab Emirates	Arab Members of OPEC[2]	Indo- nesia	Iran
1973	1,070	2,018	3,020	2,175	570	7,596	1,533	17,982	1,339	5,860
1978	1,160	2,560	2,135	1,985	485	8,300	1,830	18,455	1,635	5,240
1980	R1,012	2,514	R1,656	1,787	472	R9,900	1,709	R19,050	1,577	1,662

[1] Includes about one-half of the production in the former Kuwait-Saudi Arabia Neutral Zone. In January 1981 total production in this region amounted to approximately 528,000 barrels per day.
[2] Arab members of OPEC include Algeria, Iraq, Kuwait, Libya, Qatar, Saudi Arabia, and the United Arab Emirates.
R = Revised data.

Exhibit XII-28

Algerian production is peaking, an apparent physical restraint. Iraq has substantially greater capacity, more than another million barrels a day, but the production is economically optional. The smaller Arabian countries do not need more oil income and can be expected to decrease production. Saudi Arabia has current capacity in excess of 10.5 million barrels a day and there are no obvious physical restraints on substantially more production. Iran's production capacity remains politically restrained.

The world's remaining production capacity divides between the United States and its primary suppliers on the one hand and the Communist countries on the other.

Nigeria can produce more crude oil, but Venezuela and Canada cannot. Mexico and the United Kingdom are the new producers, but the level of their production is low. There is a substantial increase in production from Russia, but current news is a factor. In 1979, Russia began to fall behind in commitments to her eastern provinces. Russia cannot maintain the production increase required for the country's planned economic growth.

Since most of the world's recent increase in production can be accounted for by Russia, and since there are now political and economic restraints on increased production from the OPEC countries, a decline in world production during the 1980s is inevitable.

World crude oil reserves peaked at 712 billion barrels in 1975. At the beginning of 1978, they were estimated at 646 billion, a 66-billion barrel decline

International
Crude Oil Production
for Major Petroleum Exporting Countries

	Nigeria	Vene-zuela	Total OPEC[3]	Canada	Mexico	United Kingdom	United States	China	USSR	Other[4]*	World
				Thousand barrels per day							
1973	2,054	3,366	30,961	1,800	450	8	9,208	1,140	8,420	3,843	55,830
1978	1,895	2,165	29,800	1,315	1,215	1,080	8,707	2,080	11,215	4,698	60,190
1980	2,055	2,167	R26,890	R1,424	1,937	R1,622	R8,597	2,114	11,720	R5,151	R59,455

[3]OPEC total includes production in Algeria, Iraq, Kuwait, Libya, Qatar, Saudi Arabia, United Arab Emirates, Indonesia, Iran, Nigeria, Venezuela, Ecuador, and Gabon.

[4]Other is a calculated total derived from the difference between world production and the nations represented above.

R = Revised data.

Sources: *1973-1978 annual data (except U.S.): Central Intelligence Agency, *International Energy Statistical Review.*

*1979 annual data (except U.S. and OPEC nations): Central Intelligence Agency, *International Energy Statistical Review.*

*1979 annual data for OPEC nations: *OPEC Annual Statistical Bulletin 1979.*

*1979 monthly data (except U.S.) are EIA estimates based on CIA revisions to annual data.

*1973-1980 United States data: See sources on the last page of the Petroleum Section.

*1980 and 1981 monthly and 1980 annual data (except U.S. and World total): Central Intelligence Agency, *International Energy Statistical Review.*

Exhibit XII-28 (continued)

in three years (the total world production was estimated at 22.4 billion barrels for the year 1977). We know there is a great deal more oil to be found in the Middle East but the downward revisions and extractions substantially exceeded additions during these three years. Also, we know that more oil is being found and will be proved in Mexico, but we must maintain our perspective on the actual decline in the total world reserves and the evidence that these reserves have already peaked and the physical limits on annual extraction will follow within a few years.

Can America buy an increased share of the world's decreasing crude oil production? This we have been doing, employing our financial power in the world community. When our problem with the Euro-dollar is recognized, it appears improbable that we will be able to continue this process for long.

America's merchandise trade balance becomes a factor in this equation.

Merchandise Trade Value

	Exports		*Million dollars*		Imports		
Energy	Manu- factured Products	Agricultural, Chemical, and Other	Total	Energy	Manu- factured Products	Agricultural, Chemical, and Other	Total
1973 1,671	38,982	29,643	70,296	8,173	42,537	19,122	69,832
1978 3,881	81,850	55,310	141,041	42,096	93,887	35,996	171,979
1980 7,982	123,151	85,303	216,436	79,058	116,447	45,330	240,834

Source: U.S. Department of Commerce, Bureau of the Census (BOC) publication FT 900, *Summary of U.S. Export and Import Merchandise Trade.*

Exhibit XII-29

The cost for America's imports of energy very nearly doubled between 1978 and 1980. In the year of the Arab boycott, export dollars were 8.5 times the cost of energy imports. In 1980, the margin had been reduced to a 2.7 multiple and the cost of energy imports was close to the value of all agricultural and other raw material exports. Our energy exports included obligations related to the nation's defense. Our agricultural and chemical imports had also increased 2.4 times since the Arab boycott. America's trade deficit was being supported by the exported dollars that become claims on the nation's assets in expanding Euro-dollar bank deposits.

The world's economy appears as a balance of terror. The balance can be maintained only so long as there is free movement of basic physical resources of which oil is the most critical. The world must find ways to adjust to the quantities available, the physical supplies. This is the all-important linkage between future economics and the present economics of international finance. It is also the all-important linkage between energy economics and political reality in the United States.

Chapter 13

Coal, Shale, and The Synthetics

Synopsis

Coal was the principal energy resource of the last century and still contributes substantially to the production of electricity and industrial heat. A rapid increase in the use of coal is restricted by the time and cost of putting in place the capacity to convert coal to electricity or to liquid and gaseous hydrocarbons to substitute for natural gas and petroleum products. The coal supply would be exhausted before the middle of the next century if it were employed to replace all oil and gas. The shale supply is much larger but its economic use is more limited.

The production of usable energy forms from shale and coal is more visible and environmentally disruptive than the oil and gas industry. For practical purposes, we must supply the economy with oil and natural gas substitutes. The dimensions of the problem become evident when we analyze the size and number of the conversion plants that will be needed.

C oal was the energy resource in the transition from the solar energy society of colonial America to the oil and gas-powered twentieth century. Coal is relatively abundant but the supply has limits. Production of coal is costly in terms of human life and effort and in terms of air and water pollution. Also, more coal cannot be used for power until an expensive conversion industry is put in place: the electric generating plants and the synthetic oil and gas plants.

Coal and uranium are the principal future resources that can maintain electric power, the sine qua non of our industrial society. Our progression towards a post-industrial society is measurable in terms of the rate at which electricity ceases to be.

High grade shale has approximately half the Btu energy content of the middle grades of coal, and the lower grades of shale have much less energy. When shale is heated, keragin, which solidifies at 600° Fahrenheit, can be removed and employed to produce petroleum products, but the by-products of shale production are extremely disruptive to the environment and the shale resource is located in a sensitive geographic area in the headwaters of the Colorado River basin. Indiscriminate shale production could release these by-products and other natural contaminates into the aquifers threatening the water supply of the southwest.

The transportation economics of both coal and shale require that the mining facilities and conversion plants be located near the resource. Liquid petroleum and synthetic gas products are much easier to move. Thus, the line between the environmentally disruptive production of this energy resource and the economic benefits to the consumer becomes the critical problem. We can support the eastern population at its customary comfort level by using coal and shale, but only if the western states accept social and environmental disruption. The real problem becomes evident when the required quantities are identified.

The supply of coal is limited despite its relative abundance in comparison with oil and gas. As of January 1976, the United States Bureau of Mines reported that legally and economically accessible coal deposits totaled 438.3 billion short tons. This optimistic estimate is now disputed. Unlike the oil and gas industry, coal production in the United States never experienced a resource restriction. The Appalachian coal fields were convenient to the center of industrial America in the last century and they had not approached extraction limits when oil and gas began to take over the coal industry's markets. As the finding of coal was not critical economically, no industry accounting of producible reserves was needed to guide marketing and pricing policy. The coal producers were primarily concerned with production methods that would control costs. For years, the national coal reserve was estimated at 500 billion tons with the notation that this was a minimum expectancy. After 1973, when the reserve began to be important for the future, test borings were undertaken to verify the geological estimates. The coal seams proved to be much thinner than anticipated.

The task of proving the extent of our coal reserves has not been completed and there is concern as to the accuracy of current estimates. If we begin by accepting the Bureau of Mines' 438 billion ton estimate in the year 1976, and if we accept .7 billion tons as the production figure for that year, the actual limits of our coal reserve become apparent. We would need to be restricted to a 1.77 percent annual increase in coal consumption if any of this reserve is to be left after the next century (in 120 years). This compares with the Carter administration's 1978 National Energy Plan which called for a 5-percent annual increase in coal usage. At that rate, the reserve estimated by the Bureau of Mines would run out in the year 2038. Children in grammar school today would live to see the end of coal.

The shale resource is so large that its physical limits are less important than the political, social, environmental, and physical costs of the industry development and the net energy that can be delivered. This shale resource was identified and small quantities had been produced in the United States for a hundred years. Shale is being used to produce energy in Poland both by refining and by burning the raw product, an inefficient fuel, to produce electricity. Keragin has been produced from western Colorado shale both by mining and refining the product and by in situ blasting, heating, and removing the hot liquid.

Exxon Corporation is optimistic about the production of intermediate petroleum feed stocks from the Tosco Corporation plant in Colorado which they acquired. Shale is mined and the keragin is removed above ground, avoiding critical environmental problems that have developed with the in situ process. Exxon believes it can market its product in competition with $40 a barrel petroleum and with a substantial operating cost advantage over petroleum feed stocks produced from coal. They anticipate production in 1985 at the level of 47,000 barrels per day after expenditures of $3 billion. The plant appears to require 66,000 tons of shale a day for operation.

Four barriers must be overcome before shale can contribute energy to the U.S. economy. The first of these barriers is the water requirement for the process, approximately four barrels of water to produce one barrel of petroleum feed stock from shale. This is not very much, but all of the water in the Colorado River basin is now claimed for some other future use. The agricultural claim boils down to denying only a one-percent increase in the West's irrigated land potential if shale production replaced current petroleum imports and new agriculture were restricted to one acre foot (only the marginal land agricultural requirement, not the conversion of desert lands). Shale production should win this argument. The other principal competitor for the Colorado River basin water is population increase in the Southwest. On the same hypothesis of replacing our imports with shale production, they represent the needs of a one million person population increase. There may be political problems with this trade-off, but the interests of the nation clearly favor use of the water in the shale operation.

The second barrier is the disposal of physical waste. Mountains of a disagreeable, chalky, corrosive material will be produced. Some canyons will be filled and it will be difficult to keep the dust under control, but there is no reason to believe that this physical and environmental problem cannot be resolved.

The third barrier is more serious. Water pollution can develop from the mining operation and the waste disposal. At the present time, this problem virtually eliminates consideration of the in situ process of obtaining shale. The aquifers in the area are too vulnerable to the indiscriminate underground operation for the presently proposed in situ process. However, scientists should be able to resolve the surface run-off problem for controlled shale removal.

The fourth barrier is the cost of putting in place the mining and conversion industry and this cost must be stated in terms of time, material requirements, social disruption, and political reality. The dimensions of an industry capable of replacing our petroleum supplies staggers the imagination. When the Exxon investment figures are compared with projection of the cost for coal conversion, there is only a 15 percent advantage for the shale process. Obviously, all of these figures are too preliminary to be precise. They simply indicate that a single analysis of the conversion of either shale or coal to produce a liquid or gaseous fuel resource will identify the problem.

Oil and gas can be produced from coal, but to do so we must accept a 40 percent efficiency loss for the conversion industry plus the energy cost of building and maintaining this industry. A net 55 percent return seems optimistic. At this rate, 32 quads of coal will be required to replace presently imported oil and gas. The 18 quad decrease in U.S. oil and gas production by the year 2000 becomes another 33 quads, for a total of 65 quads.

ENERGY EQUIVALENTS

English System: Ft., Lb., Bbl., Btu[1]

Magnitude: M   MM   B   T   Q

Exponent: 3   6   9   12   15

Common Units of Energy Measure

THERM = 1 million Btu (appx. 1,000 cu. ft. natural gas)
Giga Watt = 1 million Kw/hr. electric output capacity
1 million bbls. of oil
1 million bbls. of oil per day, annual use equivalent
QUAD = 1 quadrillion Btu, annual measure of energy use
1 billion bbls. of oil, annual use measure

Basic Fuel Heat Equivalents

	Unit	Btu/Unit
GAS	Thousand cubic feet	1.0 million =
OIL	Barrel of 42 gallons	5.8 million =
COAL	Short ton of 2,000 lbs.	22.0 million =

United States Annual Use and Equivalents

Recent U.S. Use

	Units	Units/Year	Quads/Unit	Units/Quad
GAS	Trillion cu. ft.	21.0	1.000	1.00
OIL	Billion bbls/yr.	6.2	5.800	.17
	Million bbls/day equiv.	17.0	2.120	.47
COAL	Million tons	700.0	.022	45.45

Exhibit XIII-30

When we apply these parameters to shale, the process is totally different. The 40 percent efficiency loss becomes replaced with a 50 percent material handling multiple as the average ton of coal has twice the energy content of shale. If we accept the dollar cost comparison of the two types of plant construction—and they are very similar—the analysis can continue employing the coal conversion parameters.

The time required to build the process plants that would convert coal or shale to oil and gas becomes the critical factor. It will take all the rest of this century and more. During this time the adult population will be increasing at approximately 1.5 percent per year, with children already born and immigration assuring this minimum increase. The projected 65 quad deficiency gap in our oil and gas requirements now becomes 85.5 quads to the year 2000 (twenty years at 1.5 percent annual increase).

The economic and physical facts of synthetic oil and gas production help us to understand the nature of our dependence on oil and natural gas. The figure of a million barrels of oil a day has little significance to the average individual. Oil moves mysteriously out of the earth and through pipelines that crisscross the country. Only the retail delivery tanker trucks are in evidence and there have been fewer of these as natural gas replaced home heating oil. For most, the million-barrel-per-day average annual increase in U.S. oil consumption is only a statistic which occasionally makes the front page of the newspapers.

Actually, a million barrels of oil per day is a tremendous quantity. On an annual basis, it represents 2.12 quadrillion Btu. We move from thousands, to millions, to billions, to trillions, to quadrillions in accounting for our energy consumption.

Exhibit XIII-31 gives data for oil and gas conversion from coal. Plans for a conversion plant for the United States were first conceived in the late 1960's, based on the German Lurgi process which had been proved in World War II and now is considered the "first generation" of conversion plants. We have not yet built one of these plants. Second and third generation designs are still in the

OIL and GAS CONVERSION from COAL
The significance of a coal-based economy

	Standard plant (in planning stage) Estimated cost $1.5 billion	Million Tons Coal Per Year Input
Input	10,000 tons of coal per day 60% thermal efficiency 330 days/yr. effective operation, appx. 90% tons/yr. (330x10,000=3,300,000 tons) per plant	3.3
Output	Per Plant (60% of $72.6 \cdot 10^{12} = 43.56 \cdot 10^{12}$ Btu/yr.) QUADS per YEAR .04356 or $.044 \cdot 10^{15}$ Btu/yr. 23 plants required to produce 1 QUAD/yr. $$\frac{1 \cdot 10^{15} \text{ Btu}}{\text{Quad}} \times \frac{1 \text{ plant}}{.044 \cdot 10^{15} \text{ Btu}} = \frac{\text{plants}}{\text{Quad}}$$	76.
OIL	49 plants required for 1 million bbls./day 134 plants required for 1 billion bbls./year	162. 442.
GAS	23 plants required for 1 trillion cu.ft/year	76.

Exhibit XIII-31

experimental stage. The sought-for improvements over the original plant have been generally disappointing but we still are seeking greater efficiency or lower costs for the plant of the future. A 10 percent improvement in costs now is indicated in the indirect process wherein low Btu gas is first produced from coal followed by either enrichment of the gas to pipeline grade (equivalent to natural gas) or liquefaction for conversion to a refinery feed stock (source of gasoline, diesel oil, and jet fuel).

ELECTRIC POWER GENERATING PLANT

(Standard size for nuclear or coal)	Million Tons Coal
1 Gigawatt (1 million Kw or 1 billion watt) hrly. peak load	Per Year
32% avg. industry efficiency	Input
50% of capacity average effective operation	

Input   Per Plant
Coal in million tons per year   2.123

$$\left(\frac{1 \cdot 10^9 \, w}{1 \, h} \; x \; \frac{8760h}{1 \, Y} \; x \; \frac{3.413H}{1 \, w} \; x \; \frac{1 \, T}{22 \cdot 10^6 H} \; x \; \frac{.50}{.32}\right)$$

Output   Per Generating Plant
12 million Kwh per average day $(12 \cdot 10^9 \, wh)$
4380 million Kwh per average year $(4.38 \cdot 10^{12} \, wh)$
.01495 quad Btu/yr. $(4.38 \cdot 10^{12} \; x \; 3.413 = 15 \cdot 10^{12})$

67 standard plants to produce 1 Quad/yr.   142.2

142 standard plants to produce $1\overline{M}$ bbls. oil/day equiv.   301.5

Exhibit XIII-32

The original plant was designed around a basic production unit which would handle 10,000 tons of coal per day, and this is still our best point of reference. 10,000 tons of coal represents 100 gondola cars (each holding 100 tons), a trainload. Thermal efficiency was expected at 60 percent, and if the plant was down for maintenance and other reasons for only 22 days a year, its operational efficiency would represent 90 percent. This is the basis of the coal input and oil and gas output projected on the chart. The output is indicated in Btu energy units rather than specific combinations of oil and gas. Each plant would produce approximately .044 quadrillion Btu per year. This would represent .044 trillion cubic feet of natural gas (at the nominal 1,000 Btu per cubic foot). As a barrel of oil represents 5.8 million Btu, 7.6 million barrels of oil could be produced per year.

Returning to production output in terms of common units, 23 plants would be required to produce one quadrillion Btu per year, 49 plants would be required for one million barrels of oil equivalent per day, and 134 plants would be required to produce the equivalent of one billion barrels of oil per year. Thus, if the United States is to domestically produce oil and gas for the current rate of per capita consumption, the 85.5 quads of synthetic product required at the end of this century represents 1,966.5 synthetic oil and gas conversion plants, each dependent on a trainload of coal a day.

The country cannot begin to build these conversion plants until 1985. That is the earliest that present designs can be proved, when we would be able to begin turning out these plants on a production basis. In the 1960's the estimated cost of one plant unit was $1 billion. Today, that same unit would approach a cost of $2 billion, but there is hope that the cost can be reduced to somewhere near $1.5 billion with improvements in design and mass production efficiency. The 15 years between 1985 and the end of the century would give us 5,475 days or a little less than three days between plant openings. These figures bring into focus the significance of our nation's energy decision.

Chapter 14
The Nuclear Resource

Synopsis

Nuclear power is a necessity for the continuation of our industrial economy despite the dangers of plutonium in the hands of terrorists. The radiation fears for the domestic nuclear industry have been overstated and the time lost in developing the United States nuclear industry has contributed to our country's loss of world leadership. The practical employment of atomic fusion for energy production is improbable even in the next century.

Nuclear power is many things to the people of the Western world, but fear of its destructive power seems to overcome rational evaluation of its crucial importance for the future. Nuclear power plants are large. They are associated with big business, big government, and an expanding economy. Nuclear power has become a symbol of the destructive forces in the free economy. The protectors of the wilderness and primitive life processes have chosen nuclear power as their enemy.

Nuclear power can neither guarantee an expanding economy nor does its peaceful use threaten society and the natural world. It is a transition energy resource. Development of nuclear technology and the known world uranium resources will permit our society to maintain electrical power options if electric power use is combined with conservation. We must not continue to waste electricity in seasonal residential heating and non-essential industrial processing. We will not be able to afford to use nuclear electricity to produce hydrogen and extend indefinitely our individual transportation system. But we can use it to maintain the power required for communications and light and some of the luxuries electric power already has demonstrated. We can use it to electrify our railroads and extend electrified mass transit in our cities. With full development of the nuclear energy potential, we can promise our children a natural life expectancy in a world not too different from our world today.

Unless we accept a premature phasing out of our industrial economy, there is no viable alternative to the full employment of nuclear power. Although nuclear power accounted for only 13 percent of the United States' electrical supply in 1978, some regions of the country already were 40 percent dependent on it.

Energy will be required to develop an energy-efficient society and more energy is required to shift our source of energy from one resource to another. The physical energy component of capital investment is widely variable but substantial quantities of energy are required to build all types of plants and machinery. All of our energy resources will be required to alter our transportation systems, our industries, and our lifestyles. Nuclear electric energy either directly contributes or provides an alternative for some part of all production processes.

The United States has now lost most of its momentum in nuclear power development. This may cost us our world supremacy. Looking to the future, we must recover as much of this disadvantage as we can.

Mortality is the underlying issue in the nuclear argument. The probability of accidental death is mathematical and ultimate death is a certainty, but our society cannot deal objectively with morbidity statistics. Evidence shows that the greater dangers in the nuclear power industry actually are in the mining and processing of ore, that radiation is a lesser contributor to disabilities and loss of life than other mining accidents, and that the quantity of ore required by the nuclear industry is only one percent of the quantity of coal required for an equal amount of electric power generation. Actually, the nation can expect a higher rate of casualties with coal-fired electric generators than nuclear.

Similarly, the arguments surrounding nuclear waste contradict the definitions of what is waste and what is an energy resource. The nuclear industry is growing and developing and changing. Today the United States is producing electricity with light water reactors (LWR's), 66 of them with a generating capacity of 52 billion watts (52 gigawatts) in 1978. These are first generation plants which are able to use only 0.6 percent of the fission energy potentially available in their fuel. If this fuel is reprocessed and fed into a fast breeder with subsequent reprocessing, it is possible to recover 70 percent of the energy in the original uranium ore. Finally, "most experts are of the opinion that no technical obstacles stand in the way of safe management of any of these wastes."*

The significance of this waste discussion is the limited amount of uranium ore which is capable of producing net energy. Low grade ores require more energy for processing than the energy that can be produced from the ores. The 1977 study of the Uranium Resource Group of the National Research Council identified not more than 1.8 million tons in the United States. The Department of Energy expects a somewhat greater supply, motivating a 2.4 million compromise estimate by the Committee on Nuclear Energy Alternatives. This higher figure provides enough uranium for the lifetime expectancy of 400 gigawatts of capacity (400 average size nuclear power generators) if the United States does not proceed beyond development of the light water reactors designed for a one-time-through fuel cycle.

---

*"Report of the American Physical Society by the Study Group on Nuclear Fuel Cycles and Waste Management," *Reviews of Modern Physics* 50 (January 1978); and National Research Council, *Radioactive Waste at the Hanford Reservation: a Technical Review,* Commission on Natural Resources, Committee on Radioactive Waste Management (Washington, D.C.: National Academy of Sciences, 1978).

The importance of this 400 gigawatt limitation is its relationship to the size of the industry in the United States. In 1970, this country had nuclear and non-nuclear electric generating plants with an installed capacity of 360 gigawatts. In 1975 it had reached 527 and by the early 1980's was over 600. For practical purposes, our nation's supply of uranium will be exhausted early in the next century if we do not employ the breeder and if we treat the by-product of the present generation of nuclear power plants as disposable waste.

Plutonium is the public's problem with uranium recycling. The industry has been looking for alternatives to a recycling process that will avoid plutonium but this does not now appear to be possible. The breeder improves energy recovery by a factor of over 100 times the electric power generated from the same quantity of uranium restricted to its single use in a light water reactor, and this is not all.

As stated in the National Research Council's CONAES report,* "In addition to recovering a large fraction of the energy in uranium 238, it is possible to recover the energy in another element, thorium, that is probably four times more abundant in the earth's crust than uranium. The single isotope of thorium, thorium-232, can be converted to another fissile isotope of uranium, uranium-233, in nuclear reactors. Various combinations of thorium-uranium and uranium-plutonium fuel cycles can greatly multiply energy resources." Thus, the necessity for the breeder. Thus, the seriousness of the environmentalist's confrontation. Thus, the importance of energy-economics understanding.

*"The breeder design closest to commercial status in the United States and elsewhere is the liquid-metal fast breeder reactor (LMFBR). In the most resource-efficient version, this reactor would be fueled with plutonium separated from the spent fuel of light water reactors and with depleted uranium left behind in the enrichment process for today's light water reactor fuel. The energy available from uranium already mined and stored as depleted tails from domestic enrichment plants, if used in LMFBR's could provide one-third to one-half of the energy recoverable from domestic coal reserves and resources.

"The advanced converter most widely used in the world is the natural-uranium, heavy water CANDU, developed in Canada. The advanced converter closest to commercial status in the United States is the high-temperature gas-cooled reactor and the light water breeder reactor (LWBR). They both use the thorium-uranium cycle with enriched U-235 feed."

Evidence points to one conclusion: America cannot have nuclear energy in the next century without plutonium. England, France, and the Soviet Union have been taking full advantage of the United States' moratorium on breeder development, taking over the lead position abandoned by the United States. France has little problem with public objections. Russia has no problem.

*Discussion of nuclear power in *Energy in Transition 1985-2010,* The National Research Council, National Academy of Sciences, final report of the Committee on Nuclear & Alternative Energy Systems, to be published by W. H. Freeman and Company, San Francisco, 1980.

England is moving ahead in developing public acceptance. The United States appears to have succumbed to economic bloodletting as a consequence of the anti-nuclear movement.

The dangers of plutonium are real. It must be guarded to prevent radiation damage to persons and property. If properly prepared, it can be made into bombs. The manufacture of atomic bombs is no longer a secret matter and world terrorists could find physicists capable of producing bombs. However, will the availability of plutonium be more attractive to terrorists than the accessibility of thousands of nuclear bombs and warheads in the world's military arsenals? "A graver possibility than illicit diversion is that countries installing reprocessing plants would thereby have the means to build up arsenals of nuclear weapons in short order."*

In abandoning our lead position in the development of the breeder reactor and in refusing to reprocess nuclear waste for the countries that installed our first generation reactors, we have stimulated the industry's development among foreign competitors. Yet, the fact is that we are going to live in a nuclear world whether or not we are leaders of the nuclear industrial society.

The nuclear concept that avoids plutonium and the breeder is fusion, the energy release demonstrated by the hydrogen bomb. This is the ultimate power resource, the consequence of two molecules of heavy hydrogen coming together to produce helium-3 plus a neutron of tritium plus elemental hydrogen. Nuclear fusion is a darling of the futurists who have faith in the scientific rescue.

Edward Teller, the scientist who is credited with the success of the hydrogen bomb, is a primary authority on the nuclear fusion potential. The first sentence of the fusion chapter in his 1979 book, *Energy From Heaven and Earth,*** reads: "Too often those who know least about a subject are the ones who talk the most about it. This seems to be the case with controlled fusion." Dr. Teller's book is optimistic in presenting his view of this country's energy future, but his analysis of the problems we must overcome before we can achieve controlled fusion is precise in its identification of the obstacles. The theoretical physicist may score a laboratory success in this decade, but that will be only the beginning. The engineering tasks of designing the process equipment to provide a continuous flow of energy from the fusion reaction are formidable. Dr. Teller's final caution is economic: "the process may be too expensive to be affordable except for space travel."

Nuclear fusion has almost nothing in common with the atomic fission process which is able to control the release of heat in the radiant breakdown of uranium isotopes. Nuclear fusion requires the miniaturization of H-bomb explosions in rapid succession. The physicist's task is to find a way to actuate the first miniature explosion, producing a greater energy output than the energy input required. So far, this has not happened. The H-bomb itself was detonated with a full scale fission bomb and there is no thought of miniaturizing this process.

* Ibid.
**W. H. Freeman and Company, San Francisco 1979

There are now two approaches for achieving a controlled nuclear fusion reaction, and they are proceeding independently. The first uses nuclear fuel in great dilution in a high-pressure vacuum which is described as a few particles with enormous energies. Density in this vacuum is reduced to one 100 millionth of the normal density to avoid the uncontrolled bomb syndrome. The container is called a magnetic bottle, created by electrical magnetic fields. The nuclear fuel is called the plasma and the most efficient selection consists of deuterium (hydrogen-2) or deuterium plus tritium (hydrogen-3). The shape of the bottle is critical to the success of the process and here the Russians have contributed the Tokamak configuration, now believed to represent the most probable solution.

The second approach seeks to achieve very high density (a thousand times the normal density of the liquids) by use of laser energy input concentration. Control is achieved by confinement of the reaction in a very small space. The great compression reduces the expansion potential of the explosion. So far, the laser approach has only achieved a compression of ten times liquid density. Thus, the energy input appears to require a one hundred times increase beyond present achievement to realize a net energy output. Then, the engineers will have to find a method to produce this reaction several times a second.

The physicist's problem of achieving the single successful reaction appears difficult enough. However, physicists believe that one or the other of these approaches will succeed. Probably both will succeed before much progress is made with the engineering problem. This may take us all the way through the twenty-first century. No responsible scientist promises fusion energy in economically significant quantities except in terms of the indefinite future.

Chapter 15

The Solar Society

Synopsis

The solar complex of energy resources includes all energy capture emanating from the solar flow with its wind and rain consequences. Secondary effects include ocean waves and tides (with the assistance of the moon's circumnavigation). Wood burned for heat and charcoal smelting, wind-driven sailing ships, and horses were the principal energy resources of colonial America and through the first half of the nineteenth century. Hydroelectric energy is much the largest contributor today but expansion of this energy resource is limited. The solar society of the future will closely resemble the solar society of the past despite the claims for solar voltaic cells, new forms of biomass, passive and direct solar collection, and new designs for wind generators.

S olar energy will become a significant exogenous energy resource in the twenty-first century, but that significance will be very different from the expectations of the great majority of voters in 1980. Ecologists, environmentalists, and virtually all anti-establishment groups have pushed solar society enthusiasm beyond reality. We will require greater quantities of solar energy, but we will be clearer about the future if we study the past.

Solar energy exemplified by wood for fuel and wind for ocean transport and water power and grass fueled horse power was the primary source of power throughout the nineteenth century. In 1800, total fossil fuel in the United States was represented by 108,000 tons of coal, the equivalent of forty pounds or one-half million Btu per person. There were 1,400,000 horses delivering another 70 million Btu per person at the equivalent efficiency of alternative sources of power. The nation was more than 99 percent solar energy dependent.

In 1850, we were still 97 percent dependent on solar energy. In 1900, 18,730,000 horses represented one horse for every four persons, very little different from the 3.9 person per horse in 1850 and 3.8 in 1800. In 1900, our dependence on wood for heat had dropped to 27 million Btu per person from 92 in 1850. Coal represented 2.8 tons per person or 96 million Btu and we had begun to use gas and oil, reducing our solar energy dependence below 40 percent.

The year 1900 is important to our energy perspective. The country supported a population of 76 million and the oil and gas economy was just beginning. There had been no significant increase in the consumption of these two fuels since 1890 (the economic depression was a principal contributor). But in the next ten years, oil consumption increased five times and then settled down to doubling every ten or fifteen years until the present restraints on physical supply. There was a balanced energy economy in 1900, with coal fueling our factories and railroads. 1900 saw the beginning of the electric power industry and the automobile. America had 5,737,000 farms.

We will not go back to a nineteenth century economy in the twenty-first century, but our only solid solar society facts lie in past history.

The new, primary solar energy resources will be disappointing. We will improve on passive solar collection with modern building materials, glass and insulation and computer-controlled radiation shields, but reduced levels of comfort and luxury will account for much of our energy savings. Experience with direct terrestrial solar heat collectors has been discouraging. Fifteen percent total system efficiency in mile-high Colorado cities is about the best we have experienced so far with affordable collector designs. Perhaps the radiant losses can be reduced. Collectors which track the sun can approximately double inputs. But when the days are short and there is haze or intermittent cloud cover, very little energy is available for collection. These conditions are the rule in many areas of the country during the five-month heating season. Direct solar collectors are a luxury, primarily conversation pieces today. They will continue to be a luxury despite the success of hot water heater collectors in the southern states. Running hot water itself was a luxury in the last century.

Solar collectors in space, transmitting electrical energy to the earth, are theoretically possible but practically improbable. The cost of resolving technical problems will be unaffordable until we have a world order guaranteeing that our space station electric power source will not become the target of unfriendly nations or individuals.

Hydroelectric power can be expanded, but most of the available dam sites are in the northwest, and this form of solar power is not cheap or permanent. Dams silt up and must be abandoned and dams develop leaks. When one lets go, the damage to life and property is frightening.

In 1860, the water power resources of this country were only four percent efficient. Around 1800, before electricity, the water wheels and primitive steam engines could not have been more than two percent efficient. This efficiency is less than that of the horse which was capable of delivering 15 percent of the thermal energy in his feed as measurable pulling power in controlled observations. By the 1970s, the average efficiency of the U.S.-operated power plants was 32 percent, a remarkable progression of technical improvements.

The comparison of past and future uses of wind energy puts the solar economy in perspective. The clipper ships of the nineteenth century were the most efficient wind machines man had conceived. The sailing ship itself had been developed by man's earliest civilizations and it was responsible for human progress in exploration and commerce on the waterways of the world until the middle of the nineteenth century. The swiftest and most celebrated British clipper was completed in 1869 (the Cuttysark) to compete with steam vessels. Until then, sailing ships were the fastest and most economical ocean transport available.

What was the nature of these ships? Wind power was teamed with man power. The crews climbed the rigging to furl and unfurl and set the sails. The last of the clippers were steel hulled with metal masts and wire rope stays. They were large (up to one-quarter the size of the World War II steam "victory" cargo ships) and they were almost as fast. They could compete economically, carrying commodities such as grain and coal from either England or the U.S. east coast ports around the Horn of South America to San Francisco. But there were no creature comforts on these ships, no cabin heat. The galley was on the open deck. The crews were paid five pounds a month into the last half of the nineteenth century.

The social implications of a return to wind-powered ocean transport are obvious. To provide comfort heat would require fossil fuel. Auxiliary propulsion power would be needed to reduce the risk of loss on rocky shoals. Powered winches would require more fossil fuel. Reduced hazard in working aloft would reduce sail efficiency. A 40-hour week would increase the crew by one-third with all the costs of berthing and feeding. The sailing ship of the twenty-first century surely will be less efficient than the sailing ships of the nineteenth century. Only nylon sails and lines can be identified as a principal improvement and these require another assist from the fossil fuels.

Wind generators can produce electricity. They did on prairie state farms before rural electricity was financed by the federal government. They can again, but not in great quantities, nor with continuous reliability, nor in all parts of the country. Very little energy is available from winds below 18 miles per hour, and the generator must be protected from too high velocities. There are locations on the Hawaiian Islands that have the necessary conditions for steady wind generation, justifying a major contribution to an electric power grid. Battery storage is the weak link in a system serving most areas of the United States without alternative generation.

Ocean wave motion energy is a wind-related solar power source for some parts of the world. It has potential for the western British islands and our west coast. Surely something will be developed from the on-going experimentation. The ideal condition for wave power generation is an uninterrupted sweep of open sea—no continental obstruction. Latitudes 55° to 60° south around Antarctica below the tip of South America meet this requirement.

Energy captured from ocean thermodifferentials are only theoretically possible. The temperature differences are not great enough to produce enough energy to overcome the physical problems and costs of the required massive structures. The problem of delivering the produced energy can be solved by collecting hydrogen as the energy product, but this thought is quite useless without resolving the primary production problem.

Geothermal energy is not solar energy and it is not renewable energy and its contribution is very small, but geothermal energy is spectacular. It is demonstrated by the geysers in Yellowstone National Park, an electric generating plant in northern California and a project in the Mojave Desert that is bogged down with the problem of handing the corrosive hot effluent. Even on the world scene, the total electric power generation from geothermal resources is less than the equivalent of one large, coal fired plant.

The technology for reaching miles down to the hot rock above the center of the earth has not been developed. Rather, the geothermal resource consists of pockets in the upper part of the earth's crust where hot water and steam have been trapped in much the same way that oil and gas have been preserved under geological formations. These pockets tend to be located along the dividing lines of tectonic plates where earthquakes and volcanos are common. Few of these locations are in the United States.

Biomass represents the greatest potential solar energy resource after hydro-electric power. It was the principal source of energy in the nineteenth century. It depends on the chlorophyll in plants which converts the energy of the sun to vegetation, grasses, grains, and timber. Historically, biomass has supplied wood burned for fuel, grasses and grains fed to draft animals, and sugars fermented and distilled to produce ethyl alcohol.

Perspective can be gained on wood-burning potential from an *American Forests** editorial in March 1980:

"In northern New England, 20 percent of all homeowners use wood as their primary heat source compared with 1 percent in 1973. In Vermont, two-thirds of all households now use wood to some degree with heavier reliance growing. Burlington Electric is seeking state approval to construct a 50 megawatt, wood-fired electric plant that will require 80,000 green tons of wood chips yearly; this, according to a United States Department of Commerce study would preempt most of the present surplus of low-quality wood in northern Vermont and will limit the use of this wood for small scale power generation, domestic or commercial heating, or material fabrication. In Massachusetts, where homeowners burned nearly a million cords in 1978, state officials have estimated that there is only about one and one-half million cords of annual growth suitable for burning. And that assumes harvesting is being done properly.

"The bottom line is clear. New England is on the brink of a new era of forest exploitation. Not only is the region approaching the limits of its firewood resource, but there is every indication that the present fuel wood cutting is threatening the future of forest productivity of higher quality wood. The same trends are evident elsewhere."

To put these facts in perspective: the proposed Burlington Electric wood-fired generator represents just 5 percent of the size of the average nuclear-powered or coal-fired electric generating plant (50 compared to 1,000 megawatt capacity), and the new plants are becoming larger. In 1970, New

England consumed 65.6 billion kilowatt hours of electricity, equivalent to 14,260 megawatts of capacity (at the national average reported production ratio that year). The proposed Vermont wood-fired plant would thus represent less than four-tenths of one percent of the region's electric power requirement. Wood burning plants in southern Vermont and Maine and New Hampshire might make a larger contribution, but little could be expected from the southern New England states beyond their own wood stove requirements. Then consider the cutting and transporting of all this firewood. How much motor fuel would be required? The last century used manpower and horsepower.

The biomass enthusiasts expect to produce motor fuel in the form of ethanol and butanol/lignin distilled from wood and food crops. Internal combustion engines can be developed to employ these fuels. Rapidly growing seaweed and tropical vegetation could produce fuels wherever there is abundant sun and water. The growing and the conversion techniques are feasible. The only problem is the total quantity of net energy that can be produced and delivered to the market.

The efficiency of solar fuel production must be judged by the energy cost of the total process compared with the energy value of the finished product, eliminating all fossil fuels by replacing them with the solar-generated product. The process does not begin with an excess of corn or wheat which has no alternative use. The physicist's measure of energy in heat units (Btu or calories) can be employed in this balance analysis, but all steps must be included. The land must be prepared and cultivated and the machines employed must be first built and then replaced as they serve their time. The crop must be fertilized and harvested and delivered to the process plant. Then heat energy must be supplied to convert the crop to liquid fuel which must be stored and delivered to the ultimate user. The energy cost of all the process and transportation machinery, both for operating and for replacement, must be added. All along the way gaseous and liquid fossil fuels will be required and all must be subtracted. In the end, there may be no surplus liquid fuel available to the economy beyond maintaining the process. No auditable figures have been produced for the production of a net quantity of liquid fuel from food crops.

Biomass energy will not be ignored in the twenty-first century. Brazil already is producing significant quantities of alcohol from sugar cane with the country's ample sun, water, and inexpensive labor. It is not a new combination. In the eighteenth and nineteenth centuries the alcohol was rum and New Englanders traded it for slaves employed to produce the sugar cane. The linkage between cheap manpower and liquid fuels produced from vegetation is apt to remain substantially intact.

For the middle latitudes in the United States, hybrid poplars hold promise of producing ethanol as a gasoline extender and butanol/lignin as a heating fuel. Less energy input is required to raise trees. Production would be possible on marginal land, avoiding direct competition with food crops. Is a 1,500 gallon per acre yield possible? How can one balance the energy inputs? Horsepower and manpower may be a factor in this process too.

The lure of a solar society is irresistible to environmental and ecology buffs. Actually, a future solar society may be inevitable. We do not have to hasten its arrival, but we must face up to the necessary alterations to our economic and political systems before this solar society becomes a reality.

Part Three

Solutions

The physical restraints on the political economy of our free society are now clearly discernible. The crisis time will occur in this decade. How will it be met? What path will we take when decisions are no longer avoidable? The evidence as to the limits of our physical world, interpreted by physical scientists, is pitted against custom, tradition, the political-economic structure of our society, and our religious beliefs. These are not apt to change under any evolutionary process that can be projected. There is no precedence in human history for the alteration of a society's ideology, employing the power within that society to accomplish the change that now is indicated.

The betting man will concentrate his attention on projecting probable social-political-economic responses to the strangulation of the free world's national economies by energy attrition and the curtailment of trade as the international credit system breaks down. The betting man will calculate the power of competing social forces. Money is power. The law, nationalism, liberalism, conservative religion, youth, the contract, property rights, union loyalty, traditional economics: these and many others will exert influence and in turn will be influenced by the rising tide of money-credit and the ebbing flow of the real wealth of nations. Starvation will stem population increase in the developing nations. Inflation and depression will occupy the politicians in the advanced nations. The reality of petroleum dependence will invite war in the Middle East and the probability of its avoidance will diminish with each advance in the arms race.

The betting man will be concerned with the balance of political forces that will decide the economic question. Will it be runaway inflation or depression or will we hold a middle course as the economy runs down, the prisons overflow, and riots are routinely put down while we slowly alter our moral concepts? In which direction will alteration move? Not all potential life on a finite planet can be preserved. This is the bottom line in the moral and physical accounting. The realization and acceptance of this simple fact will mark the beginning for solutions, but the process of finding solutions must start much earlier.

Solutions will be found on the social side of the conflict between irrestible political-economic forces and immovable physical reality. The earth will not provide more. Man must adjust. The solution finding can begin now for those who seek solutions. There are few real obstacles. It is possible for a few seekers to find the way and show the way and lead our free world out of its wilderness with only a few casualties. We can begin with the present and the recent past.

Since 1973, American politicians and economic leaders have vigorously denied or studiously avoided the physical evidence of energy limits. Little has changed during this time except that the physical limits have become more obvious and the time lost has increased the cost of an ultimate solution.

Looking back, we can think of the condition of our physical, social, and economic world 30 years ago when M. King Hubbert demonstrated the limits of U.S. and world petroleum, 50 years ago when world depression exploded primary economic myths, 55 years ago when Frederick Soddy identified the limits of credit and the necessity of physical energy; and then there were Malthus, Marx, and the social philosophers who identified the weaknesses in our laissez-faire economy during its first century.

We can view our history optimistically and recognize that much has been good. America and the world have enjoyed the fossil fuel age but now we must get on with the realities of our future.

Solution-finding begins with solution elimination. Our economic community has become the world community and this world community depends on world-wide political integration. International interdependence requires international law and order and unified credit control, but these three ingredients are perilously tentative in the world today.

There have been times when the world has been close to order in the international community, but there has never been a time when the tribes and nations of men have accepted willingly the rule of a foreign culture and there seems to be a limit on the size of the community that can develop the respect required to rule the people who are counted as its subjects. Freedom is the force that upsets order and produces nationalism. A nationalistic, fragmented world can be welded into an international community only with great difficulty. There is no evidence today that this solution can be relied upon, desirable as it may be.

The international solution becomes more remote when the parts of our political-economic problem are analyzed. Solutions to the primary problems faced by our world culture cannot be applied to the world community until those solutions are accepted by the smallest of the community's subdivisions. The necessity for and the method of credit control, energy supply maintenance, and population control may be recognized in physical science circles, but there is neither understanding nor acceptance of solutions in any major political subdivisions of America. This is where we must begin.

Political reality points in a direction of a retreat from the international community, a devastating conclusion for Americans who have won two world wars and have achieved near universal acceptance of much of their political-economic ideology. We will find solutions to our economic problems only when we are able to read the signs of the future and abandon the myths that have developed from our past successes, the origin of which we never understood and so gratuitously misinterpreted.

We do not lack for information. We have the mathematical and analytical tools to interpret our future. We also have the knowledge required to alter our ideologies and balance the sacrifices that must be made with the good that can be achieved. We can have a new economic game that can be rewarding and challenging. Most of the problems will be found in the transition, most of the resistance from the institutions and individuals who understand only the economics of the immediate past. But before any progress can be made towards solutions, the gravity of our situation must be broadly recognized. Solution acceptance will require more problem recognition than has been achieved. Society's capacity for looking into the future is limited. A democracy tends to wait for events to develop to the point where change can no longer be avoided, but we can escape chaos only if the solutions are available when the nation is ready to consider them. This is the meaning of solution-finding today.

In part three, we must go beyond theory and face real conflict. Polite hypocrisy has been a cornerstone of our civilization and many will be offended when we consider the consequences. Aldous Huxley pictured our new world 50 years ago. Now we must recognize the necessity for its acceptance.

Chapter 16
Recognize The Limits of Pecuniary Economics

Synopsis

Solutions begin with the assumption that we cannot go on with our dreaming, that as a society we must look for new economic solutions and accept drastic change.

Time is the most critical concept dividing the physical and social sciences. Market theory deals with the economic forces of supply and demand acting in the present, and political practice is similarly dependent on constantly current opinion and immediate responses. Our banking system dominates economic theory imposing interest costs that preclude long-term conservation. Physical economics requires time to build process plants and the conservation of critical material supplies. Planning must be introduced into economics.

Market, competition, and price will always contribute to the economic process in a free society; however, there is no mystery or magic in their functioning. Economic decisions are man-made. The critical function for a future economics is timely material supply, and energy is the ultimate material.

N o progress can be made in resolving our economic problems so long as political leaders believe that credit can be expanded without limits and that energy is infinitely available. Once this bridge is crossed, it is a matter of taking one problem at a time and finding solutions. The economic sacred cows of competition, the free market, and price solutions for material substitutions will continue to contribute in the economic process, but all have their limits and these limits must be recognized. First, we must deal with an apparent abstraction that is the controlling influence on politics and economics and which identifies the difference between physical economic reality and pecuniary economic practice.

Time—The Critical Element

The free political economy is highly focused on the present. Political efficiency is measured by the capacity of the system to transmit public opinion and satisfy the demands of the nation's people. In its practical application, every advance in communications technology has been brought to bear on this political process with remarkable success. We can know each evening what transpired in any part of the globe that day for longitudes east of our position, and instant transmission can be arranged for any scheduled event. We know what happened and we see what happeded any place our news organizations anticipate action they wish to report and our television crews are permitted to set up.

Time has been all but eliminated in information distribution. Politicians can obtain nearly instant polls of the opinion of their constituents. The pure democracy of every man affecting government decision is more nearly realized in our country today than in the Greek city state where the democratic ideals were promulgated before the Christian era, but the democratic ideal then and now has serious liabilities. Instant political decision proved to be undesirable when it became attainable. Instant political decision avoids both the past and the future and we cannot live in the present. There is no time in the present. It is an instant that divides the past from the future.

Our political system is suffering from the consequences of communications overload and communications capture by minority interests in every part of the country. The Congress of the United States is so highly focused on its representation responsibility and the representation process that it has lost the capacity to consider the national interest. There is no isolation from the momentary ignorance of the electorate as its desire is perceived by its representatives. Legislation that restricts consumption potential for the current year is considered politically impossible. The obviously necessary restraints on energy consumption from 1973 to 1980 failed in the legislative process.

Economic theory has its answer for the representation of future time in the decision process. Every man with economic power (money to buy product or money to invest in producing future product) has an opportunity to contribute in the economy's forecasting process. The national market pulls this forecast together. The price system distributes product in proportion to demand. The market clears each day, satisfying the buyers with purchasing power and rewarding those who anticipated the demand of the day. No more democratic forecasting system could be devised. Economic theory extends the present to include the future. Every man can determine his own time horizons limited only by his capacity to see the future, and in this process he serves his fellow man.

The emptiness of economic theory becomes apparent when we view energy's contribution to the sequence of economic events. The economist's dream of a perfect answer was first defeated by the reality of political domination. Uncontrollable political demand for instant satisfaction defeated the economist's plan for control of time. The economist has not been able to see beyond this defeat.

The second *time* problem in economic theory is more serious. The time scale of value is determined by the banker's interest charge for borrowed money. The current value of a resource (oil) to be mined (produced) at a future time is diminished in proportion to the time that its use (marketing) is delayed. The economist assumes that the money to pay for the resource must be borrowed and thus the interest cost for not using that resource must be paid each year. The higher the rate of interest, the greater the interest cost, and this affects a reduction in the present value of the resource. Thus, the present value of benefits to be received many years in the future become smaller and smaller as the time is extended. No person or organization can afford the cost of conservation for very long.

A conservation ethic cannot be imposed on our political-economic system without recognizing this fundamental problem with economic value. The money lenders' value prescription has been with us since the dawn of history. It was the prescription that built the economy of our country moving from land purchases at five cents an acre to land purchases representing hundreds of dollars a square foot, harvesting the forests and the minerals and the indigenous animal populations, and building our farms and factories and cities.

The money-lender's market economics responds to conservation that relates to cost reduction and the economic system is sensitive to all forms of tax advantage, but these two have limited application in an economics that requires conserving known energy supplies for future generations. And this is not all. The political system also is geared to the primacy of the present.

The politician who proposes denying any significant good to the nation will fail in election or, if elected, will fail in reelection. The director of a public corporation who fails to take advantage of opportunities to produce profits today faces unattractive alternatives; undistributed rewards to his stockholders lower the market value of the company's stock, inviting take-over by a more sanguine corporation, or the stockholders will organize to directly replace their directors. By either course, the conserving director's life would be short. Neither the politician nor the corporate director can become concerned with the mathematical impossibility of energy conservation. Each has prior concerns that stand in the way of conservation. Today, the political-economic system functions independently of realistic time and mathematical considerations or concern for the generations to come, even the life expectancy of today's children.

In the economics of the future, the physical science time perspective must prevail. The future of our society cannot be left hanging on the uncertainty of the economist's ever-advancing present when the future is predictable in terms of solid mathematical probability. We know the physical limits of our energy supplies. We know the political limits of credit expansion. We can extrapolate the quantities in both series and see the inevitability of economic collapse and the necessity for picking up the physical pieces.

The question then focuses on the employment of the time that remains. How can it best be used. The present cannot be ignored. Politicians and economists must deal with this present: the revolutions must be put down; the wheel of credit must be kept turning; the public must be kept informed and amused by the news of the day. Reality can be slowly introduced in this process. A few hundred thousand readers have been fed factual information in serious publications and foundations have come to the rescue of the publishers who could not find economic support for this information flow in the marketplace.

The facts have been presented and discussed widely. Those who wish to know can know the parameters and can compute the time limits.

The academically approved literature was discussed in Chapter VII, and its inadequacy is obvious. A primary contributor to our problem is the limitation of the academic community, their prejudices, the physical science fixation of the social disciplines, and the privileges that this community has won for its members by employing laissez-faire economic power to subvert a unifying, purposeful university structure. The serious periodical press, with all of its market limitations, has been outproducing our universities in meaningful discussion.

How can the evidence be organized and presented to achieve acceptance in a democratic society? This is an educational problem in its broadest definition and again time becomes a critical factor. What is the rate of change that the public will accept in altering comfortable ideologies that are reinforced by established institutional leaders and charismatic personalities whose economic fortunes depend on maintaining the myths and denying the evidence? The balance of these forces moves slowly in the direction of change as the factual information develops: anticipated oil fields that prove to be dry when billions of dollars are expended as well after well is drilled; a revolution here, a war there; stagflation in contradiction of economic theory; an election that throws out one group of dreamers and replaces them with another.

The public is not yet ready for cold, factual information on the limits of sacred economic myths but the time for revelation is not too far away. Time continues to represent the critical element in the process.

In its specific application, a conservation economy will require insulation of the segment of the economy which must be subjected to the conservation ethic, and that insulation must be permanent. There is no evidence that the free world will resolve its energy supply problem in the twenty-first century or any future century. It is not a matter of one or two decades, the cover that has been employed to reduce future shock in almost every political-economic prescription.

The time spectrum must be recognized in future economics replacing in some part the timeless or constant present hypothesized in the market theory of supply, demand, and price control. At the same time, the planning concept that is the consequence of time spectrum recognition will not replace the timeless, unplanned market concept that supports the economic and political process. Both must be recognized. Both must be employed in theory and practice.

The Free Market's Limits

The concept of economic freedom and its market dependence is the abused cliche in our culture's ideology. Actually the market is indestructible in the affairs of men. It needs no defense. It will survive and exert its influence in the dark alleys of the most organized monolithic political-economic structure. Men will trade for pleasure and for the necessities of life and to multiply their productive efficiency. The development of the market instinct identifies our higher form of life. Price and competition are indispensable in the market function. The market identifies the human process in elementary economics.

The market is also primitive, inefficient, and destructive in an advanced culture. The market is more useful in its political function than its economic function. The timeless nature of the market limits its effectiveness in major economic decisions. The market does not plan. Market economists are thus restricted from effective planning and faith in the free, unrestricted market becomes a burden to constructive rational processes.

The market cannot solve the major problems that face the free economy today, the supply of energy, transportation, and money with a stable value. The market did not play a significant role in the decision processes of the past that kept these major segments of the economy under control or that led to our present problems. These decisions were made by men who understood the market's limitations. The audit path of this decision process is discoverable, much of it in the public record. The pretension of the market dependence of our free society is a cover for political and economic power manipulation and for the failure of the social sciences. Little progress can be expected either in resolving the major political-economic problems that impact our society or in developing a rational social science until this cover is removed and we recognize the nature of the market function, its necessity as well as its limits.

The market's economic contribution is limited to secondary decisions in measuring buyer preference after a product or a service has been conceived and in supplying secondary products and services in support of major items produced in volume and accounting for the nation's primary economy. The free market keeps open the avenues for product and service improvement. The market is the scavenger that liquidates obsolete inventories and facilities, and the market is the final judge of economic decision. The private economy is able to effect elimination of inefficient persons and functions. These are the tasks that democratic government finds difficult or impossible to perform.

Competition

Competition and price are the handmaidens of the market economy. Where competition and price can function freely, the market is effective in performing its supply function. The availability of time, primary materials, and economic freedom are the critical elements in the functioning of the free market. When any one of these three is unavailable, the market ceases to function as a controlling influence.

When competition is free and unrestricted it is amazingly effective in squeezing the cost of a product or service to the economic breaking point. Karl Marx did not dispute the efficiency record of Adam Smith's system. He was concerned for the entrepreneur as well as the laborer. Both suffered in the cyclical process that lassaiz-faire economics generated. But competition does not reduce costs controlled by physical limits or a more powerful organization than the individual entrepreneur, and government policy which focuses on controlling business activities that restrict competition has been a conspicuous failure.

Competition between the employer and the individual for his labor is the critical element in economic theory and practice. Personal services are the ultimate costs of production. The materials of the earth are free goods and title to these goods is limited by our political and social conventions as is the cost of credit. The capital that constitutes real wealth is a combination of these three. The unionization of labor is a natural consequence of laissez-faire economics, so is the warfare that unionization produces. Government protection of unions was motivated by the objective of boosting purchasing power as much as by social and humanitarian consideration; but, when competition is limited by political protection of the union organization and unions are successful in organizing an industry, then the balance of economic forces moves into the political arena and the efficiency of the political structure becomes the measure of progress. Today, the American political economy is in an unstable equilibrium as a consequence of the incomplete process of political and economic accommodation. Our cities, states, and critical industries are held hostage by organized labor exercising political-economic power for the benefit of its members. Economic competition is no longer effective. The evidence of this process is in the international community. The economies that have found an accommodation for competitive labor strife have overtaken the free market economies despite natural resource limitations.

International competition has been the American politicians' surrogate policeman of labor costs. He has been able to escape the decision process in dispute between labor's quest for higher wages and the consumer's desire for lower costs by citing economic principles of free trade and broadening the argument to include constituent exporters. Legislation that increases labor costs only defers the economic consequence in a free world market. The obsolescence of our political and economic theory is buried from one Congressional term to the next with no limitation on the extension of this process.

The failure of economics in the United States must be recognized as its political connection. Economic theory independent of political support has never been viable, even rational. Economic man independent of the influence of social humanity and unaware of political power is a fiction. Economic and political power are inseparable and it is the power of this connection that describes the economic process.

Competition is the primary force that must be dealt with in the human community. Economic organization seeks to control or eliminate competition. Competition threatens every economic activity: the mobster rubs out or drugs his competition; unrestrained business buys out its competition; restrained business markets its product under special labeling and advertising to set it aside from competing commodities and to provide a basis for customer loyalty, the secure market that every business seeks. National competition is controlled by war or threat of war. Ideological, artistic, and physical sport competition feeds the nation's culture and advances civilization, but it destroys individuals.

Competition and the method of controlling competition defines a nation's culture. Economic competition must take its place in this spectrum. The ideological competition of pecuniary economics must face these realities if economics is to develop a scientific basis.

The theory of our dependence on market, price, and competition is the principal barrier to a rational approach to the economics of the future. This future economics could be called supply economics if that word had not been claimed in the last hurrah of Adam Smith's apologists, swept into influence by the election of President Reagan. The drama of this ascendancy will have to be played out and it will clear away some of the illusions of political omnipotence in the credit economics of the Keynesian school that has confused America's economic theory for the last forty years.

Material Supply, Productivity, and Price

The economic system comes into focus in its supply function. The purpose of every system is to supply human needs and desires. Laissez-faire goes one step beyond need in emphasizing consumption as a good in itself and by measuring success in terms of a nation's consumption of natural resources, and the employment of labor and credit. The measure is called gross national product. GNP measures the total consumption activity. Separating out the portion of this activity that contributed to the putting in place of capital structures proved too difficult for the economic statistician who sought consistency.

Productivity, the second measure of economic success, has more interesting implications with respect to the energy attrition that will pierce economic theory. Individual productivity is a sacred symbol of success in our advanced culture. It measures human worth as well as individual and national progress, but a major component of this productivity has been mechanization and most mechanization introduces quantities of exogenous energy into the economic process. There are virtually no measures of the exchange of energy for human labor in economic history despite the evidence that the rewards to labor which have increased in every decade are energy-dependent. During the 200 years of our history we shifted the burden of process work from man to energy-supplied machines. We thought we had an unlimited supply of no-cost energy: we produced wealth and leisure; we paid off displaced farm laborers and factory laborers and dock laborers with welfare checks and housed them in cities while we moved the new, automated factories to the suburbs, serviced by highways and trucks and private cars. Now, we face the necessity of reversing this process. It will prove far easier for the private sector than for the public sector. The manufacturer will be able to decide whether or not it will pay him to reduce his transportation costs and begin supplying local markets with local production. The problem in the public sector will remain and this problem will motivate alterations in our political and economic theory.

Under our current economic theory, demand anticipates consumption and pushes prices up. At the increased price, men are encouraged to increase production by every means at their disposal. Enlarged manufacturing facilities can be built and the cost of invested capital can be paid. Miners can dig deeper and carry ores farther and refine lower grades to supply the market at the higher price. But the economic process is limited by the ultimate material supply and no multiplication of price will produce energy after the threshold of net energy has been passed for each energy resource. The final balance is in physical terms and price economics will become totally inoperative.

Chapter 17

Learn From the Failures
Of Market Ideology

Synopsis

Four political-economic problems will concern America in the 1980's. Each are the consequence of past and current market decisions. Each tests our economic theory.

Transportation will be the most critical problem for America in the future. This nation has developed economic and political dependence on a liquid petroleum powered individual transportation system. Our first concern is the inefficiency of the American private car. Solutions for this problem will strain economic theory, but this is only the beginning.

The origin of America's spiraling health care costs involves moral problems that exceed the limits of economics. Similarly, this nation's concern with defense and its economic implications involves solutions to political and moral problems.

Inflation is the most specific test of economic theory identifying past failures and accelerating difficulties for our political-economic system in the future.

The four problems demonstrate the pretension at the heart of market economic theory. Economics is guided by the decisions of men and these decisions involve political and moral consideration.

A nation's destiny is determined by the consequences of major political-economic decisions and the theory that guides these decisions. We have been talking and acting as though the market had magic power to deliver critically-needed resources and find answers for political problems. Danger lies in this decision.

The market reacts to economic decisions made by political and economic leaders. The market may be consulted in opinion surveys, but the surveys only reflect the decision capacity of the respondents to the survey at the time of the survey. The respondent's opinion on a conceptual product is tentative at the most. Years are involved in the design, tooling, and marketing process that is finally tested in an actual market reaction. The over-simplification of this process in the rhetoric of economic and political decision dependence on the market must be recognized if solutions are to be found for an economics that will be useful in the future.

America's Critical Automotive Industry
Decision Was Not Made by the Market

The automotive industry is ruggedly competitive and dependent on the whim of its buyers, the American public. One-sixth of the American economy generally is recognized as having dependence on the automotive supply and maintenance market. This market is associated with the success of America and its current dilemma affects the confidence of Americans in their political-economic machinery. But the marketplace cannot be held responsible for the decision process that has led to the American automotive industry's loss of position in the world markets, the potential bankruptcy of the corporations serving this market, and the capacity of America to resolve its transportation problem.

The decisions that have laid low the American automotive industry are identifiable. Public and private sector decisions were involved with a minimum of debate or discussion. America's competitive ideology, private sector independence, and the forebearance of government from interference was played out in its traditional form. All aspects of the market contributed to the process, but the market had very little influence on the controlling decisions.

Leadership in the decision process can be credited to General Motors Corporation. The date can be identified as April 11, 1974. In the previous five months, America had discovered its dependence on foreign oil imports and had time to take stock of the domestic oil reserves and resources that could be expected to be discovered in the future. America had had twenty years to analyze the facts and figures relating to its petroleum supply and no informed industrial leader needed to doubt the spectrum of probable future oil available to the American economy.

General Motors Corporation had employed a former undersecretary of the Department of the Interior to become the head of its new energy resource department. The Corporation had a decision to make. Over the years, their industry had been committed to the production and marketing of automobiles designed for speed, comfort, and every form of luxury. The U.S. industry had totally ignored the potentially dominant consideration of fuel efficiency. Billions of dollars had been committed to each corporation's capital stocks, irretrievably focused on the production of these vehicles. Tooling commitments extended five years into the future. Redesign of a corporation's product line would have meant operating losses beginning immediately and probably extending for most of those five years. A redesigned new line of fuel efficient automobiles could be marketed only through a cooperative effort with the government of the United States wherein increased taxes on automotive fuel would be scheduled, permitting the automotive industry to phase out the production of low mileage cars while building a foundation in the market for the demand for the fuel-efficient automobiles of the future.

Thus, two decisions were involved: first, the acceptance of operating losses in the immediate future, and second, a departure from the isolation in the government and industry decision processes. President Gerald Ford's administration was ready for this decision, but the industry was not.

On April 11, 1974 the President of General Motors Corporation, E. N. Cole, went public with his corporation's decision, announcing to a businessman's luncheon club that the boycott was over and that America would not again face a petroleum supply problem. America had 485* years' supply of petroleum resources within its borders and need not fear for a repetition of the recently experienced petroleum shortage. The automotive industry appeared to be ready to throw its weight behind lobbying efforts to forestall any increase in taxes or any restriction on petroleum imports. General Motors mustered its political influence in the considerable number of local communities where its plants and suppliers are located. The critical number, the unsupportable 485 years of petroleum resource supply was not openly questioned in the press and General Motors' leadership on the question was accepted by the automotive industry and its petroleum suppliers.

The source of the General Motors' figure on U.S. oil resources is traceable to the director of the United States Geological Survey and the committee process through which this organization and other organizations of the United States Interior Department are administered.** Market economics are not involved. The spectrum of petroleum resources estimates and a summary of the General Motors interpretation of these figures is reproduced in Derivation and Development section B.

America's Health Care Problem Cannot Be Resolved through Competition Alone

Free market principles are limited in their application to the health care industry. The market for medical care is sick and dying people, a peculiarly inappropriate market for promotional stimulation.

In America's first century, health care services were supplied by self-educated, entrepreneur medical men and women who competed for the loyalty of their patients, propelled by horsepower in making housecalls. Michigan did not have a hospital code before 1968,*** but the profit hospitals of that decade competed for government-supported patients and the transition to a de facto state control of medicine was well along. Today, little is left of the wholly independent medical service industry. No medical school can function without heavy endowment and government support. No doctor begins practice free of the financial obligation to past generations and the state. Only the theory and privilege of private medical practice remains.

The insurance industry has taken over health services in a misapplication of economic principles that avoids both marketplace influence and responsible

---

*Cole also anticipated 4,300 years of oil shale petroleum supply to the U.S. economy.

**U.S. Geological Survey Circular 650, 1972, U.S.G.S., Washington, D.C. 20242; The Energy Cartel, 1974, Uttenberg, Friedman, Gilgallon, Gutchess & Associates, Inc., 1211 Connecticut Avenue, N.W., Washington, D.C. 20036.

***Michigan Public Act 17 of 1968, Licensing of Hospitals.

administration. By calling our prepaid health plans an insurance program and setting up competition between programs, the health delivery service organizations are free to increase their costs without effective limits. The medical costs of the elderly and the indigent are covered by state and federal programs placing a floor under medical costs. The practice of medicine has become a state financed privilege and the medical men dedicated to patient care become fewer each year.

In medicine, science has displaced God and the law prohibits death from being an option to be chosen by man. Not even the poor can escape the tortures of intensive care with its television monitors, oxygen supply, tube feeding, and catheter. No hospital can resist the latest diagnostic machine and the banks compete to finance a cost that surely will be paid. "Thank goodness his heart gave out" has become the epitaph for our society. Spiraling medical costs are a secondary consideration, but the economic connection cannot be ignored. It encapsulates our political-economic dilemma.

Politicians are intimidated by the life issues. A tiny minority now holds most state and federal legislators hostage to its desire to eliminate legal abortion and restrict birth control information. A one-woman filibuster defeated legislation in Connecticut to support the living will that would preserve the dignity of dying. The living will will not be legal and binding without such legislation. Our culture cannot define life and cannot deal with mortality.

When Joseph Califano, President Carter's Secretary of Health, Education and Welfare, saw a correlation between the nation's hospital costs and the number of licensed physicians, he announced a cutback in the federal support for medical schools and requested the states and private sector to follow his lead. Predictably, the shortage of physicians to staff the nation's medical facilities affected further increases in salary demands. Fifty thousand dollars a year was no longer adequate to attract a graduate from an American medical school. With excess incomes, mature physicians work less, further increasing service needs and salary demands.

In economics, the expanding health care industry has become the leading contributor to the nation's economic growth. While seeking tax advantages from the government, the Independent Petroleum Association of America which claims credit for the great majority of oil and gas exploration and the discovery of new reservoirs identified their typical financier as a doctor or dentist. Thus, the economic circle is closed: government support of health care expansion stimulates the economy and increases Gross National Product; the excess income of practitioners in the industry provides venture capital; the banking industry profitably supports the construction of medical facilities and advanced life support systems; employee unions force members' wages upward to correspond with upper level salary increases. Competition has been eliminated from the system and the health care investment adds little to the nation's productive capacity. The great wheel of credit cranks out inflation.

The problem with the health industry involves all aspects of our culture. Its purpose is not defined and lacking an agreement on definition, all life must be preserved at all cost. All risk must be avoided, imagined or real. Practically speaking, it is illegal to practice medicine in the United States under principles of economy and human charity. The doctor must charge his patients for the insurance cost of avoiding personal responsibility for this service. The first patient to imagine a discourtesy or an impropriety or to suffer from the laws of probability in the development of his disease can find a lawyer able to take from the uninsured medical man all of his earthly possessions.

Medical costs can be radically reduced if the objectives of health care are defined and removed from the influence of political and legal profiteering. Competition in the delivery of health services could realize spectacular gains. Many surgical procedures can be performed by training the average orderly who would be happy to earn $10 an hour under medical supervision in an economy-conscious society. Instead, the cost approaches $1,000 an hour in the hands of overtrained professionals who compete only for the practice privilege.

Health care costs will continue to escalate until our society comes to terms with the mortality of man. Economics is subservient to social ideology.

War and Defense

The largest single cost in the federal budget concerns past and future wars. War and economics are intimately related and here economics comes first. War can be waged only by the nations that can afford war and a war is won or lost by the nation whose economic support holds or crumbles; but few marketplace economic principles apply in the administration and organization of war. The attempt by the United States to apply marketplace economic principles to its defense planning is doomed to failure.

A social, political, and economic metamorphosis is required for the peace to war transition of a democratic society. The oratory, flags, and music responsible for a war decision disguise the reality of military organization. Repression and fear are principal motivations in military life. Individual rights, privileges, and even human concern are subordinated to the military objective. The interdependence of the men in a military unit takes precedence over concern for the mortality of the individual. Arrogance becomes a virtue. Charity is a liability.*

Militarism rejects the open, democratic society in all its forms. Individual freedom in expression and action is a centrifugal force intolerable to military organization. Mortal fear and charity must be repressed. The profit motive that defines our laissez-faire economy cannot be eliminated in the conversion for war but it must be controlled overtly or covertly. Government for the people and by the people must become government of the people if the military organization is to succeed.

A military organization exists to destroy persons and property and these persons and property are a part of our world community. The enemy must be

---

*The philosophy that governs organization for war is discussed in Derivation and Development section F.

identified in military preparation and defense is a totally inadequate term to describe the purpose of this preparation. More than semantics is involved in the choice of a name for a peacetime military organization.

The military organization can be organized to promote either war or peace, diametrically opposed objectives, and the means and methods of organization are totally different. Peace can be achieved in a world community of independent nations only within the physical boundaries of a nation. Military preparations which extend beyond the nation's own boundaries can only promote war.

Internal or external military organization may more accurately define the purpose of military preparations. Defense of the world community was the recognized objective of the United States military establishment. It is an external defense posture assuming a responsibility that is becoming incompatible with physical reality. The more limited purpose of maintaining a balance of military power in the world may represent a compromise definition to describe the physical and ideological transition currently in progress, but this definition only emphasizes the decision avoidance in our political process. We cannot have a rational military structure if the purpose of that structure becomes subordinate to its momentary physical strengths and weaknesses.

America's voluntary military force cannot compete with Russia's universal conscription and cannot provide the basis for an immediately expandable American conscription as the army recruited from the unemployed does not represent the social structure of the nation. A military organization that must compete with peacetime civilian employment and peacetime civilian ideologies becomes both excessively expensive and militarily inefficient. The Russian soldier may not be happy with his five cents per hour compensation but his nation can afford a large army and a military organization does not depend on economic incentives. America's $5 an hour soldier may be happier but he is militarily less efficient. The dollars America spends do not buy military capacity comparable to Russia's conscripted army. Russia expects men to be expendable in war and does not waste irreplaceable resources in building safe military hardware.

The war we are preparing for is total war. It will be won by the adversary who knows when his defenses are adequate to his purpose and has the wisdom to reserve his strength to serve that purpose. Our nation's defense problem is not in our arsenals or our budget or in the field. Our defense problem is education and communication and political organization. Our democracy must know its limits and define its purpose and select leaders who represent the interest of the nation.

Inflation

Inflation is the harbinger of economic trouble, the measure of the public's confidence in their government, and the product of the banking industry. Gradual inflation stimulates economic activity, enhances the value of real property investment and relieves the debtor of part of his burden. Precipitous inflation risks panic, deflation, and the collapse of the economy.

Controlled inflation is politically and economically irresistable. The inflationary tendency is built into our political-economic system and the resistance to inflationary influences has been weakening for the last fifty years, encouraged by both liberal and conservative persuasion. The long-term inflationary trend begins with the earliest recorded history.

The problem with inflation in the free world of the 1980's is its indeterminate state. The value of money results from the relationship between the quantity of money in circulation and the real, physical wealth which supports that money. No measure of wealth is available. The measures of the money supply are difficult to interpret and they are not available to the millions of deciders in the free market. Panic inflation can be precipitated when ultimate wealth is either adequate or inadequate. The solid evidence of declining, ultimate wealth faces this free economy with the necessity of controlling the inflationary influences on the money supply or accepting greatly accelerated rates of inflation, rates so high that panic and economic collapse are constantly at risk.

We have no precedent for the developing world problem with resource limits. In the past, the limits have applied to relatively small regions and no world community existed. We have no precedent for holding growth at the near zero level required to avoid accelerating inflation in a contracting real-wealth world. The problem cannot be confined within the parameters of the banking industry which controls the engines of monetary increase. Zero growth is a cultural as well as an economic problem.

We have not run the inflationary course and as a consequence, the lessons are too few to be persuasive in influencing market activity. The ultimate problem is the cost of the adequate lesson. Are we so wedded to our economic theory of market response that the physical evidence of decreasing wealth and expanding credit cannot be interpreted until the economy of one or more modern, industrial nations goes into the panic stage? Is this the meaning of our competitive market ideology?

Chapter 18

Employ Cooperation and Human Judgment

Synopsis

Both economic theory and practice require a balance of competition and cooperation for primary motivation. Laissez-faire economics is heavily weighted towards unrestricted competition but our politically dominant humanitarian interests restrict effective competition. We have sought compromise in the political arena destroying our economic system without providing for its replacement.

The economics of the future must recognize the effectiveness of cooperation in resolving economic problems, the necessity for human judgment, and the inclusion of relevant physical science fact and mathematical methodologies.

In approaching a new economics, we must recognize that our political integrity has been dependent upon market economic illusion. When these illusions are swept away, political panic can result unless prior consideration is given to providing primary material supports for economic planning. A feasible balance of energy supply and demand must be projected. Cooperative economic theory and practice must be demonstrated. Credit controls must be in place. Finally, we must find a method for reaching national consensus and executing political decision.

Man's capacity to reason and to cooperate with his kind in common purpose has contributed most to his supremacy over the creatures of the earth. Man's competitive savagery and will to live is shared with other creatures at the top of the food chain. Our economic theory has been tied to man's primitive competitive instincts in an effort to avoid political dictation and the subordination of individual economic initiative. It was a beautiful theory and the accomplishments were magnificent until the limits of the world's resources became apparent.

Human judgment is indispensable to economic planning and economic planning is now indispensable to the survival of our free society. Our problem is political. How do we find judges? How do we say goodbye to the theories that avoided the judges?

In searching history for answers, the long span must take precedence. America's 200 year experience with political organization is totally dominated by Adam Smith's laissez-faire economic theory and is totally dependent on the natural resources of this virtually uninhabited continent. Our theory of government and our form of government require the frontier that is no longer available.

Where does America look for patterns that will be useful in the design of a future society? We cannot abandon the old without an alternative that gives promise of improvement. No matter how dismal the present may appear, we will not abandon the ideologies that guide our decision process until our future becomes brighter with altered political structure and social objectives.

Fortunately a wealth of information is available from the political-economic experimentations of the countries influenced by our Western culture. While America was enjoying its resource binge, less favorably situated nations were finding ways to satisfy human wants with lesser supplies of energy and basic materials, limiting competitive consumption and controlling political decision-makers. Sweden's middle-way, cooperative economy was well advanced and available to economic theorists in the 1930's. The Japanese cooperative political economic system has demonstrated its efficiency with the most limited natural material resources. New Zealand has experimented with a restrictive distribution system that has maintained personal freedom. The developing countries of the world have been trying out political structures related to their cultural inheritance with varied degrees of success. None has employed the U.S. form of divided political authority.

The design of a new economic structure must begin with identifying the primary function and the general form of that structure. There also appears to be a necessary sequence to political-economic change. The nation must have political decision capacity before alteration of either the economic or political system can be entertained. Because energy is absolutely essential to the functioning of our economy, the assurance of a minimum energy supply must precede the introduction of cooperative economic principles. These must be identified and generally accepted before altering the nation's control over the generation of credit, the heart of the economic system.

Political Decision Capacity

Political efficiency in the United States requires drastic change both at the national level and in the relationship of the states. Our federal government is a luxury we will not always be able to afford. The separation of power between the legislature and the administrative branch of the government effectively stymies political decision. The organization of the legislature gives veto power to special interests of every kind whether organized by economic, ideological, or regional interests. The nation is represented only in the person of the President, a single individual who brings to office his own economic inheritance and prejudices and has no politically responsible structure to guide his decisions. The United States government is organized to restrict political decision. It cannot serve a political economy that recognizes the necessity for decisive human judgment.

The states and regions of our country compete for economic advantage. States offer deferred tax privileges and financing to the industry that will locate within its borders, boosting employment, future tax revenues, and future population increase for that state. Welfare benefits vary widely from state to state encouraging migration of the economically disadvantaged. Barriers to migration set up by state law have been overridden by the federal courts. Natural resource rich southern and western states restrict the development of the resources needed by the nation. State legislatures and state courts hamper the development of industry and multiply the costs to business, rewarding only an army of lawyers and state bureaucrats.

Our federal government is an archaic inheritance from our colonial past. The independence of the states has been eroded by the federal courts and the federal legislature, and the original independence cannot be reestablished. What is left of state authority restricts efficient national government.

Energy Supply Assurance

Economic fiction will not give way to physical reality until energy supply can be provided for the life expectancy of current generations. The unpredictability of the future under market economic theory is essential for the maintenance of social sanity when our energy dependence is recognized. Early on, our Western society accepted the exchange of a predictable, slowly developing or unchanging solar society for the dynamics of exploration and we invested the energy surplus of each generation in conquest. As we have seen, our physical capacity multiplied with each energy resource discovery. Our predecessor civilizations only halfheartedly attempted to wall out marauding barbarians and revolutionary ideas. The barriers to change never lasted very long and unpredictability has become our preferred state, buttressed by romantic notions of another world where eternal bliss can be tolerated.

Actually, energy supply planning today is not difficult. Science has given us enough information to predict both the geological limits of the fossil fuels and the technical barriers to nuclear alternatives. There is no secret to the required political and economic organization needed to achieve and maintain equilibrium. The numbers can be projected and the plan can be put in place. But how can it be implemented?

Our society will not give up its romance with unpredictability and this is the real appeal of our economic theory. Perhaps this is the meaning of market economics—man's faith in his own capacity to resolve tomorrow's problems tomorrow until the last hope is eliminated and political action takes over. For the last 150 years, America has offered the principal avenue of escape for Europeans caught up in national disaster or failed economic foresight. It is difficult to believe that energy supply remains the key to the continued functioning of our economic system, but acceptance of controls to assure the continuance of energy supply will persist as a prerequisite to progress in the resolution of the political-economic problems. The energy segment of the American economy must be brought under rational control before alterations to our political structure can be carried beyond the conceptional stage and before change in economic ideology can be accepted.

Cooperative Economics

Cooperative economics can bring management, labor, and credit authority together to realize production and marketing objectives that are compatible with physical reality. The antithesis of cooperative economics is the economic law produced in the United States by the logrolling of senators from northern and southern states and the game played by the elected representatives to state and federal legislatures in running interference for their constituents with the bureaucrats who interpret and try to enforce the laws that the legislators write. Cooperative economics will involve wage controls and acceptance of long term employment responsibility by industrial management. We will need to limit our dependence on adversary litigation and this will be difficult for a society that is dominated by legal professionals. Cooperative economics will require an underpinning of ideological support including acceptance of man's mortality, population control, and limits on personal freedom. Cooperative economics may require regional reorganization of the government of the United States to reduce the problem of government to manageable levels.

Private economic warfare is natural enough and it has been fun for the generals and their tacticians during most of recorded history, but it is already an anachronism. The individual can no longer command the resources required to retreat from the battlefield and wait for the opportunity to carve out a significant piece of the common domain. The early laissez-faire economists belonged to a solar society that was independent of utility and credit and transportation systems in protecting individual turf. A private army could guard a man's castle when Jefferson disputed Hamilton's theories of a national credit system supporting trade and manufacturing in the United States.

The generation of independent achievers was largely eliminated in the war that reduced the capital stocks of Japan to rubble, and the British and European victors were not too far behind. In Japan, the new achievers sought cooperation between the government and industry in developing primary units of production. Their tradition included tolerance for governmental dictation and restrictions on individual privilege. Cooperation between labor and manufacturing management and banking and government developed naturally.

The Swedes and Swiss had observed the collapse of the world around them through two world wars, subordinating individual ideologies to national survival. They developed cooperative economics between the two wars and reinforced their concepts of national defense through neutrality. The pattern for cooperative economics and the replacement of laissez-faire economic competition with national decision is well established. The success of these national patterns is available for the American observer and the literature need not be reviewed in this discussion.

But the economic game does not end here. These countries have their own problems in adjusting to a future of restricted energy resources. Their political economic decision capacity will be tested as this future unfolds. Their problems with natural resources are more severe than the problems facing America today but these countries may continue to show the way in problem solving.

Credit Control

Credit control is our country's first and last economic problem. As discussed in Chapter VI, Euro-dollar deposits are expanding out of control and they threaten to engulf the U.S. economy. This cannot be allowed to happen but the obvious cures have drastic consequences and this fact delays decision. Restrictions on credit transfer have been employed many times and in many forms by the nations of the world to protect currency value or balance of trade or natural resource depletion or native control of land and production facilities. Credit transfer restrictions have always limited international trade and reduced the efficiency of the international economic community. Almost always, credit restrictions have affected most severely the interests of the citizens of the nation employing the restrictions. Trade and credit transfer restrictions interpose the interest of the nation in opposition to the interest of its citizens as individuals, but this fact does not mitigate the necessity or desirability of the restriction when a nation's total economy is threatened.

The introduction of control over credit transfer between the United States credit system and the international credit system today is not that simple. The U.S. economy provides the principal support for international trade and that support cannot be withdrawn without drastic consequences. The world has become dependent on international trade, specifically the international trade in oil. This trade cannot be returned to barter without collapsing the economy of Japan and throwing the economies of most European countries into chaos. The oil exporting countries do not need any of America's food when we recognize the availability of surpluses in other agricultural countries who have greater need for oil and thus a greater desire to barter food. The barter of military hardware for oil is already well advanced, and barter has moved into the realm of the intangibles, the contribution to peace and defense of the oil producing countries.

America can survive on its own energy resources and America can write off a trillion dollars in foreign investment if the international market collapses, but we would be living in a very different kind of America and in a very different world community. American politicians cannot close the window on the inflow of Euro-dollars without consideration of these consequences.

The relationship of the international banking community to the Euro-dollar credit problem is one of the consequences that must be dealt with in finding a solution. The Euro-dollar deposits are liabilities owed by the banks to their depositors and payable in dollars. These dollars have been lent to the bank's borrowers, returnable in the same kind of dollars plus interest, and the original dollars have been lent and deposited repeatedly with no reserve requirements. This credit process has gone on multiplying Euro-dollars and can continue to go on multiplying Euro-dollars without limit under the present international banking structure and the control of these banks. The customer borrowers and depositors have had no reason for complaining. The dollars are backed by the full faith and credit of the United States' government and its total economy.

The international banking system does not have any geographic limits and it is not politically restrained. Bank lend money to customers who, they anticipate, will be able to repay the loan with interest when it comes due. If the loan is not repaid, the banker will be the loser and the stock of Euro-dollars will be reduced. The Euro-dollars involved in these transactions are not expected to be returned to the United States for conversion into any other kind of credit or currency, although they could be employed to buy American goods or services or property if by chance these were desired.

So what is the problem with the restrictions on the privilege of transferring Euro-dollar credits into the United States? Maybe there isn't a problem. The University of Chicago School of Economics has advanced the theory that these external dollar deposits do not flow into this country because the national economy is so large relative to the world economy and because the world economy needs the dollars to handle the international credit demand. They call the process the sterilization of external credits. But will this credit system work if the United States closes the credit window? Even if no one had come to the window for years—and this is not quite the way it has been happening—it seems improbable that Euro-dollars could retain their value in the absence of any realistic support. It is the full faith and credit of the United States economy and the obligation to accept dollars in the payment of U.S. debt that makes the dollars valuable and acceptable.

The Euro-dollar credits could be supported by substituting an international guarantee, payment in a basket of currencies for instance, but could this basket exclude dollars that account for more than half the credits in international trade? And what nation would be willing to step into the shoes left vacant by the United States in allowing its credit to become the primary support for world trade? The bankers and the principal depositors of Euro-dollars are not apt to be pleased with any credit transfer restrictions or substitution for the full backing of the United States economy in the support of the dollar. The Euro-dollar separation from the reserve restricted deposits of American banks will unquestionably create different values for the former dollars and, understandable as a separation may be, it will not win friends for America in the international community; as a consequence, it will affect our influence on this community and our ability to import the oil that now requires the largest quantity of export dollars. Thus, any alteration in this country's relationship with the Euro-dollar market and the tacit approval of Euro-dollar credit multiplication immune from reserve requirements or other controls by the government or Federal Reserve System must be preceded by consideration of the nation's energy supply problem. The maintenance of energy supplies remains the controlling economic fact limiting political decision.

Chapter 19
Integrate
Social Science

Synopsis

The ultimate problem with economics is its claim to represent a scientific discipline independent of the humanities and physical science. Economics must take its place in an integrated social science. Its methodologies must be radically altered. But prior to the change in economic theory, solutions must be found for our society's major moral questions. The church and our concepts of freedom and education are involved.

Mortality is the first of the prerequisite building blocks for a social science. The employment of control over mortality and the power of immortal promise now stand in the way of any social science development.

Education is the key to a future integrated social science. The power of education must be released in any formula or system for the salvation of our free society. Personal freedom, religious freedom, and political freedom must be defined.

The most obvious necessity for the survival of a scientific society is population control. Solutions to this problem will identify political progress and test the free society's survival potential.

Our economic problems extend beyond the recognized limits of the economic discipline. This becomes the revolutionary conclusion in the energy-economics analysis. In the total perspective, our primary economic problem is the isolation of present economics from physical science, the humanities, and the other social sciences. We must find a way to integrate economics with physical, social, and political reality.

We have known the limits of impersonal justice for at least 5,000 years. Men can be led and they will sacrifice their lives for what they believe to be their interest; but what they believe may have little relationship to justice or truth by any name. The accumulation of isolated fact and the weight of uninformed opinion does not reduce the distance between the present state of our knowledge and relative truth in social relationships.

The physical science methodology of division, separation, and specialized research ignores the connectedness that is critical to solution finding for social problems. A problem may be divisible into many parts and the parts may be independently analyzed, but the solution to the parts of a problem cannot contribute to the solution of the whole problem by an impersonal, decision-avoiding process.

Economic theory is motivated by the desire to avoid directed human judgment because of the inevitable involvement of political decision that is implied by any form of organized economic direction. Economic theorists sacrifice rational conclusion in the protection of their position.

In the political process, laws are written without regard for their enforceability, anticipating that clerks and computers will run the circus. Then we attempt to protect the interest of all individuals in the name of practical politics. Civil law which is the final arbiter of both economic and social behavior depends on the same human judgment. With no restrictions on legal procedure, the self-interest of adversary attorneys takes precedence over the interest of society. The law has a life of its own and its practice can absorb the economic resources of the nation.

Order in our society depends on human judgment, leadership, and material resources. The maintenance of society's physical supports requires integration of all relevant information. The privilege to ignore or be ignorant of physical fact and the mathematics of their relationships is no longer tolerable. Scientific objectivity and social justice are only relatively realizable.

We can have a free society with its free press and democratic government if we can accept limited objectives. All life cannot be preserved. Ultimate truth can only be approached. The social structure and its physical support must be protected from destructive forces, ideologies, and individuals. We must identify the measure of ultimate value, the balance between the self-interests of individuals and the protection of the social-political-economic community.

The academic communities of the Western world are involved in the failed social science research method. The separation of the social disciplines has been sanctioned by our universities as has been curriculum that develops ignorance and encourages dependence on incomplete knowledge. If the word science is to be employed in describing the methodology of the natural sciences, then meaningful knowledge in the social disciplines must find a new word for objective research and conclusion. The physical science methodology applied in social research has failed.

A prescription for an integrated social science is possible. The social sciences grew out of integrated physical and social philosophies. All of the social science discoveries are available for testing in an integrated science approach. The laws of the physical sciences, constantly changing and constantly supported by the physical science community can be employed in testing social principles and eliminating the impractical. A new generation of physical scientists can be grown to integrate physical knowledge and present this physical knowledge to a new generation of integrated social scientists. The only barriers to the future are the barriers that have been constructed in our academic communities by the social scientists of past generations. These social scientists cannot be expected to radically alter their persuasions, but true scientists of one generation have not prevented true scientists from growing up in a new generation. Although the scientific principle of specialization has failed in the social disciplines, the scientific principles of objectivity and rational analysis are available to an integrated social science of the future.

The necessity for decision on the current state of relative truth is a primary ingredient in defining the development of an integrated social science. The employment of tentative decision must be accepted before a community of social scientists can develop. Truth must be sought and separated from fiction. The impossible dream with all its romantic implications must be identified and the dreamers must have another place in our society. The need to judge returns. It is the hurdle our society must negotiate. It is this capacity that now separates the physical sciences from the social disciplines. The denial of relatively known fact separates the economic opportunist from the physically oriented engineer and scientist. Relative truth is the currency of the physical scientist. This currency is fragile and constantly manipulated to a limited degree, but its fragile nature is not a barrier to human progress when the necessity for that progress is recognized.

The integrated social science will be tested by its capacity to answer the critical questions that plague the integration of social and physical science. Our society must have answers to the question of man's mortality, the proper functioning of the educational process and effective political decision.

The Mortality Problem in Developing an Integrated Social Science

The broad implications of human mortality have forestalled the development of a society of rational beings. Man, the individual, can have everlasting life only through his community, only through that which he leaves behind him, only through those who remember. To expect more degrades the individual. To promise more is tyranny.

Manipulation of mortal expectancy has been a principal lever for the control of society through the ages. The power to destroy life is ultimate power. The temptation to promise life and deny mortality has been irresistible to men who would control their communities and the community became the known world as modern transportation, communications, and social organization developed.

Mortality is more rationally represented in the mythology of the ancient Greeks than in our modern age. Rationality wars with the power of immortal promise. Rationality can overcome the organization that rests its power on promises of immortality, but rationality gives way to power when rationality is restricted by established social, political, and religious doctrine.

Our society fears discussion of mortality. The power of immortality stands against the power of mortality, the power to deliver death and rule by force of arms. The power inherent in promising immortality rests on the good that has been achieved and that good is indispensable in the balance of political forces.

Rationality has not dared to unbalance the power of mortality and immortality, but rationality is the only hope for an effective social science.

The difficulty of achieving a new balance between the power of religion and science must be recognized. Science has been stopped at the gate of social understanding by fear of the powers of mortality and immortality. Science knew enough to challenge religious doctrine long ago but social science did not dare grasp the levers of power. Social science has tried to avoid the levers of power, seeking to find science without power, to find a way to overcome the necessity of power, to avoid the pretension of possessing the truth while searching for knowledge and the knowledge it has sought has been buried under its own outpourings.

The answers are so awfully obvious. Man is subject to the laws of nature and limited by the power and resources of the physical world. Rationality can be taught in a democracy but rationality cannot be subordinated to fear of death or promise of everlasting life. War, the unlimited employment of death, can no longer be relied upon to clear a living space for the strong within the developed community or tame the infidel to serve that developed community. The world has become too small, the concentration of power too great.

Crime in all its forms employs the power of death as its enforcer. It is outside the law but not outside society. Its influence penetrates the political and legal defenses of an open society creating satellite protectors. There is no escape from the power of the fear of death and a society that dares not face the most obvious dimension of its physical limits will sacrifice survival in a world where ultimate destruction is available.

The power to represent immortality, although less sinister, is no less powerful and may introduce the chaos that releases the final deluge. The representatives of immortality are privileged to seek power both at the heart and on the fringes of our society, to contest the democratic majority, to sow seeds of doubt and counter the power of the state. Energy attrition will enhance the social position of the claimants to the power of immortality. The test of a new economic theory will be found at its margin, the frontier between the economically organized society and the primitive world. Primitive societies measure progress in terms of the mortal balance. Economics is housekeeping. Economic success is food and shelter for the living. Economic failure is hunger and cold. Mortality controls economics in primitive societies. Economics that is incapable of dealing with mortality can only fail these societies.

The mortal fixation of our Western culture has built a hospital and prison society. In America, these have been the growth industries in the 1960s and 1970s and these growth industries now collide with the reality of energy attrition. Without surplus energy, our society will not be able to afford this growth industry. Again, look to the margin for proof. Early on we exported our hospital and prison mortality to the primitive cultures of arctic and desert people. We destroyed their culture in saving the remaining inhabitants while claiming their land area. They have become our wards. How does this civilizing process come to conclusion if we cannot recognize the source of the problem? How many prisons and hospitals would be needed north of the Arctic Circle, in the deserts, and the rain forests; or shall we devise an independent morality for these people? Energy attrition will bring the problem from the geographic margin to the center of our society as population pressures build.

An integrated social science must include the humanities and must face the problem of the influence of historic conceptions of reality. Staying with the power of the concepts of mortality in influencing human behavior, consider one of the most powerful influences the world has known, the influence that contributed to conquering half of Western civilization in the seventh century, an influence that is very much alive and effective today, the influence of Mohammed's promise of reward to the warrior who died in battle, the seventh heaven of the hereafter:

> "Good believers will go there, and those who die for Allah's cause in war; and the poor will enter 500 years before the rich. Paradise is in or above the seventh astronomic heaven; it is one vast garden, watered with pleasant rivers and shaded with spreading trees; the blessed there will be dressed in silk brocades, and be adorned with gems; they will recline on couches, be served by handsome youths, and eat fruit from trees bowing down to fill their hands. There will be rivers of milk, honey, and wine. The saved will drink wine from silver goblets, and will suffer no aftereffects. By the mercy of Allah there will be no speeches at these heavenly banquets; instead there will be virgins never yet touched by man or jinn, . . . in beauty like the jacinth and coral stone, . . . with swelling bosoms but modest gaze, with eyes as fair and pure as sheltered eggs, and bodies made of musk, and free from the imperfections and indignities of mortal flesh. Each blessed male will have seventy-two of these houris for his reward, and neither age nor weariness nor death shall mar the loveliness of these maidens, or their comrades' bliss."*

Will science under any name be able to put this appealing poetry into perspective? This is the reality of the decision process in separating today's accepted truth from the impossible dream that still motivates.

Education Defined

An acceptable definition of the place of education in our democratic society will be as difficult as the mortality question. Education is the totality of man's communication with his society. It begins in the womb. It has no end: diminishing as the influence of a life on the living community fades or multiplies.

---

*Selections from the Koran, XLIV, 53; XXXV, 33; XLVII, 15; LXXVI, 14-15; LV, 56-87; LXXVIII, 33 & 35; XXXVII, 48; XLIV, 56, by Will Durant, *The Age of Faith,* Simon & Schuster, 1950. Page 179.

Education shapes the community and the community shapes its members. Control of education is the jealously fought-over engine of social change.

In a totalitarian state the place of education is well defined, as is its purpose and its methods. There is no interference with the planned educational process. No mechanisms escape the plan. No individual interferes with the purpose.

The free society is faced with an educational dilemma. Definitions fail. Freedom, the most powerful political force the world has known, must be controlled if society is to survive. The principal means of control is education. We avoid the confrontation by dividing and limiting both freedom and effective education. The church and the state shall be separate. The press will be free. Formal education will be guaranteed to all but its purpose will be defined in indefinite terms. We will rely heavily on platitudes and impossible goals, and we will weave faith and hope and charity into our prescription.

In our free society, education threatens science and science threatens education. Who knows the truth and who shall be its keeper? The physical science community has avoided this problem by segregation. Within the community, science consensus establishes what is presently known and avoids calling it the truth. We have institutionalized this delicate compromise and we are so proud of our achievement that we dare not lift the lid on its true nature. The system works. Science is free to pursue truth by its own methods within its own sphere of influence, delivering up to the world gifts to improve man's material housekeeping. Outside the scientist's community we will test truth with political economic power and a system of legal controversy. Education will be divided against itself. The church and press will be given special privilege to roam the jungle for economic sustenance, each relying on the goodness of man to raise its standards.

The system has worked because there has been enough goodness in man and because the resources of the world have not been exhausted by man's multiplication. The system has broken down when these two have failed. Cycles of rising and falling civilizations have passed over the developed world, but never before now has the world been so nearly integrated or so nearly controlled its supporting environment. Man has eliminated the scourges that kept his population in check, protecting the survival of the human community. Science has given society the power to elevate the individual, reduce his sorrow and burdens, extend his life, and eliminate fear of the natural world; but that same power now threatens the total human community and the community is divided against itself.

Man has become dependent on exogenous energy. He is no longer a creature of the solar-powered annual cycle, taking his place in the natural world at the top of the food chain. He has altered the food chain with the energy inputs he discovered in his capture of the fossil fuels. He has employed science to build molecules not found in nature which threaten individual and community life. Now, future life is threatened by a combination of the failure of the natural energy supplies and the failure of man to control his community.

Today, we know enough about the limits of the energy resource to project the level of future life supports. We can solve our problem with self-annihilation and we have the means at hand. There would be suffering only on the fringes. Society marches towards this eventual conclusion with all the joy of the thirteenth-century Inquisition and with few more detractors now than then.

Today, we have a problem with the nuclear bomb. Our economic theory fails to explain and guide future economic activity and our political systems cannot keep order in the world. But solutions to all of these problems are possible if we unleash education. This is the system that must look into itself, must be taken apart and put back together. We will be dealing with surgery on the heart of the free society. It is fearsome to contemplate. There is no question about the necessity. Why is there no big beginning, not even a general recognition of the need for a beginning? Can a free society recognize its own problem and find the means for its solution?

Population Control

Now let us consider another decision that future society must make, another question for the integrated social science capable of guiding this society. Future population must be controlled, but population control produces an automatic political response of horror.

Population pressure creates real estate value and fuels product demand. Population increases bring young, strong workers into the labor market, clearing the market of obsolete skills and demands for job protection. Population growth is almost a necessity for economic growth. No free market economist wants to consider alternatives to population increase and few have considered the possibility seriously. Population age distribution is dynamic and decreasing growth would overload the upper age bracket. There would be too few young workers able to support the growing number of retirees. Without the margin of growth provided by population increases, economic planners and risk-takers would no longer be protected from the majority of their expansion errors.

It is almost impossible to separate economic and moral influences on political decision. Conservative religion adamantly opposes population growth restraints. The moral or economic source of these strong opinions, although critical to their potential alteration, are incidental to the conclusion in the practicalities of rational discussion today. The combination of economic interest and conservative religious interest has shaped American politics in a defense of motherhood and the privilege of the individual to reproduce without limit.

The children that are the consequence of this political persuasion become an independent barrier to population control. No political organization can oppose public support for the nation's children and survive. That support now includes the rights of the unborn in direct opposition to the rights of the nation's living, recognizable citizens, the true members of our society. As we enter the 1980s, the nation's moral development is still directed towards unlimited humanity to an ever-expanding world population.

The populations of the underdeveloped countries seeking escape from political oppression must be admitted to the United States under current law. Restricting the interpretation of this privilege is politically dangerous. Restraints are sabotaged by subtle political processes and there are positive political gains to be achieved by supporting ever more liberal immigration rules. The entry privilege for political oppression can be interpreted to include economic oppression generated by the population control failure in the country of origin.

We continue to associate the welcoming to America of the world's population excess with a moral good. The more thoughtful moral arguments gravitate to the opposite side of the question. America is not immune from responsibility for the developed world population problem. America inherited the culture, the science, the religions, and the economics of western Europe. We contributed in its export to the underdeveloped world. In the name of humanity, we reduced the death rate and doubled the life expectancy of primitive populations. We created economic dependence and cultural dependence and expected political development that was improbable if not impossible. Six hundred million persons are living on the threshold of starvation in these countries. Are we prepared to welcome them to an America that must now resolve the problem of an unprecedented transition to reduced energy availability, reversing economic growth? At four times our present population and with restricted liquid petroleum for our agricultural industry, America would not only be short of meat, there would be a sharing of the world's starvation.

The population problem must be recognized. We have already passed the time for easy solutions based on simple, rational decision. Now we must wait for the economic problems to grow and develop to a crisis stage in the political process, the point of revolution. Then we will be able to face the population problem and after that, the acceptance of energy economics and the survival of what is left of our free society will be practicable.

We will approach a rational political solution to the Western world's energy problem when environmentalists and ecologists begin to recognize and accept the primary relationship between environmental deterioration and the limits of the human population that the earth can support. We have a choice of denying life supports to the living community or controlling the size of that community. Arguments which suggest that the physical quality of life can be reduced to accommodate arbitrary levels of starvation and air and water pollution are politically naive.

Population control does not threaten the free economy or the free political society. Positive population control has been demonstrated in democratic Singapore and the moral principles have been accepted by liberal churches in America. The problem is tradition, the conservative mind set, the fear of offense to political elements assumed to be required to maintain the practical balances of influence that all add to the assumed "political necessity" which is pitted against physical reality.

If a positive social-political counterforce does not develop, this mind set will continue. We will continue to avoid approaching energy economics by a direct, rational route. We will move from crisis to crisis with wage control and price control and the creation of a government-supported energy industry, holding off solutions to the international problems with threat of war and impossible promises to shape the world in the image of our conquering ideology.

If we desire more lasting solutions, we must break down the barriers that have divided society and we must consider the basic motivators: our impossible dreams, our prejudices, our traditional irrationality. The religions of America are economic and political as well as ecclesiastical. All are involved and must be recognized. The poetry of the Koran can better be understood in terms of its relationship to our problems with education and population control. The humanities are responsible for the social sciences and must be included in the integration. A free society can be preserved only by free men seeking understanding of their total world, without prejudice. The physical sciences have shown the way to identify relative truth, the truth that is kept alive with doubt, the truth that reflects its early discoveries without the dead hand of deification, the truth that allows its society to move on to meet the survival priorities of each generation. America still has the physical resources and we have the knowledge. We lack only understanding of the necessity for putting it all together. Then we can recognize present priorities. The test will come in our capacity to develop a political organization that respects freedom, understands physical limits, and is capable of decision.

Part Four

Derivation and Development

In the beginning there were numbers and the words required for their understanding. These numbers are still the primary support for the discussion and conclusions that have been reached in this writing. However, numeric resources and their development become difficult when the emphasis is shifted to philological conclusion.

In the first three parts of this book, numeric tables and references have been held to the minimum requirement of the discussion. Reference is made to primary resources and their development in this final section. Part Four is intended to be readable. The discussion is carried to greater depth and the numeric proofs are fully developed.

Derivation and Development

Section A

Euro-dollar

Record and Projection

Bank for International Settlements
Basle, Switzerland

T he three key tables for the fourth quarter of 1980 reported by The Bank for International Settlements on May 14, 1981 are reproduced for immediate reference. Figures from these tables were employed in Exhibit VI-4 which was discussed in Chapter VI in computing the indicated quantity of Euro-dollars that were in circulation at the end of the years 1977 through 1980.

The Bank for International Settlements identifies the external position of the reporting banks, country by country. The external position represents both deposits and loans made to banks and individuals located outside of the country of the reporting bank and thus outside the jurisdiction of the central bank responsible for the control of the domestic currency.

Both domestic currency and foreign currencies are employed in a bank's external position. The sum of the foreign and domestic currencies are counted the total Euro-currency of the reporting bank.

The Bank for International Settlements has identified the foreign currency liabilities (deposits) and assets by currency denomination only for the European banks. These banks constituted the original contributors to the reporting structure serviced by the Bank for International Settlements.

The quarterly reports now include the European countries, plus the United States, Canada, Japan, and offshore branches of U.S. banks. The grand total of reported deposits at the end of the year 1980 was indicated at $1,334.6 billion U.S. dollar equivalents in the external position of all currencies. This grand total was corrected to eliminate double counting due to the redepositing among the reporting banks for a net International Bank credit position for the external accounts of $810 billion.

The gross, grand total ($1,334.6 billion) is the primary reference in identifying deposits by country each quarter (Table 7) and by major geographic sections of the world (Table 6). The estimated source and use of Euro-currency funds (Table 5) accounted for $575 billion at the end of 1980 for the major economic groupings, United States, OPEC, developing countries, etc.

Most of the activity in the Euro-currency market is between banks. Page 2 of Table 2 identifies the non-bank deposits and loans made to individuals in the reporting European countries by currency. The dollar denominated deposits of residents in the European countries total $83.9 billion compared with $27.5 of all other foreign currencies. The other foreign currencies are identified as the Deutsche mark, the Swiss franc, the British pound sterling, the Dutch guilder, the French franc, the Japanese yen, and the Belgian franc.

BANK FOR INTERNATIONAL SETTLEMENTS
Monetary and Economic Department
BASLE

TABLE 1 (page 1)

External positions of banks of fourteen reporting countries
and the United States and of certain offshore branches of US banks

Reporting country / End of month	European reporting countries — Foreign currency (Euro-currency market)										Switzerland	United Kingdom	Total
	Austria	Belgium	Luxembourg	Denmark	France	Germany	Ireland	Italy	Netherlands	Sweden			

Assets

Amounts outstanding in billions of US dollars

Reporting country / End of month	Austria	Belgium	Luxembourg	Denmark	France	Germany	Ireland	Italy	Netherlands	Sweden	Switzerland	United Kingdom	Total
1977 Dec.	7.4	22.9	44.0	2.1	62.2	17.3	1.5	14.8	27.2	3.2	23.0	159.2	386.8
1978 Dec.	9.6	31.8	58.3	2.8	80.8	20.8	1.5	22.2	36.6	3.4	31.4	202.8	502.0
1979 March	9.5	33.3	61.1	2.8	74.3	19.5	1.0	15.0	34.9	3.7	30.5	203.9	489.5
June	11.8	34.4	66.5	3.0	80.5	20.1	1.1	17.4	38.6	3.9	30.0	221.5	528.8
Sept.	12.7	38.5	72.1	3.3	87.2	21.3	1.2	17.9	40.5	4.1	32.0	252.5	583.3
Dec.	13.7	39.7	79.4	3.8	100.4	21.7	1.5	28.3	44.5	4.8	31.9	270.0	639.7
1980 March	13.7	41.9	77.5	3.6	95.7	19.8	1.4	21.0	45.8	5.0	31.4	286.4	643.2
June	14.5	48.9	87.7	3.5	101.0	22.0	2.0	21.5	49.5	6.0	30.8	304.1	691.5
Sept.	15.0	50.2	89.0	3.5	103.7	21.6	2.0	19.2	49.7	6.2	30.9	309.3	700.3
Dec.	15.0	52.4	87.3	3.6	118.8	21.5	2.0	29.7	50.8	6.4	30.1	333.6	751.2

Liabilities

Reporting country / End of month	Austria	Belgium	Luxembourg	Denmark	France	Germany	Ireland	Italy	Netherlands	Sweden	Switzerland	United Kingdom	Total
1977 Dec.	9.7	23.5	41.9	1.4	63.0	15.2	1.7	21.5	25.5	3.4	18.0	171.4	396.2
1978 Dec.	12.8	33.5	54.5	2.3	78.8	18.9	1.8	27.8	35.6	4.5	26.9	213.4	510.8
1979 March	12.3	35.5	57.0	2.4	72.8	17.5	1.4	21.9	34.1	5.7	25.1	216.7	502.4
June	14.5	37.5	62.5	2.4	78.7	18.1	1.3	25.3	38.0	6.3	26.4	234.4	545.4
Sept.	15.6	42.0	68.1	2.5	86.6	21.6	1.7	24.4	40.6	6.9	28.1	266.3	604.4
Dec.	17.9	43.6	75.6	3.3	99.6	23.4	2.0	35.2	44.6	7.8	30.8	282.0	665.8
1980 March	17.6	45.9	75.1	3.0	94.8	21.8	2.0	30.1	45.9	8.7	31.4	299.7	676.0
June	19.9	53.1	85.0	3.1	102.2	23.5	3.1	30.9	49.3	9.9	30.4	318.1	728.5
Sept.	21.4	55.7	85.9	3.1	105.8	24.8	3.1	30.0	49.7	10.1	29.9	322.4	741.9
Dec.	22.1	57.9	83.5	3.3	121.7	23.5	3.2	43.6	52.4	10.8	31.8	346.7	800.5

(A)

Note: The totals for the European reporting countries and the grand totals contain a large amount of double-counting arising out of interbank transactions within the respective areas. For example, the assets of US bank branches in certain offshore centres are largely funded by banks in the United States and the reporting European area.

May 1981

Exhibit A-33

BANK FOR INTERNATIONAL SETTLEMENTS
Monetary and Economic Department
BASLE

TABLE 1 (page 2)

Amounts outstanding in billions of US dollars

(A & B)

Reporting country or area	European reporting countries (contd.) Domestic currencies Total	of which: France	Germany	Switzerland	United Kingdom	Total foreign and domestic currency	United States	Canada	Japan	Offshore branches of US banks[1]	Grand Total	Net international bank credit[2]	Memo item: Non-reporting banks in offshore centres[3]
End of month													
Assets													
1977 Dec.	81.4	11.5	31.5	14.5	12.2	466.2	92.6	18.1	21.7	91.1	689.7	430	77
1978 Dec. I	109.4	18.2	40.3	19.3	14.7	611.4	130.8	22.3	33.7	106.5	904.7	540	107
Dec. II	109.4	18.2	40.3	19.3	14.7	611.4	119.2[5]	22.3	33.7	106.5	893.1	535	107
1979 March	112.6	18.1	40.2	21.4	14.9	602.1	111.0[5]	22.7	36.6	111.1	883.5	550	110
June	120.5	19.3	42.6	24.4	15.1	649.3	117.7[5]	23.8	37.1	118.6	946.5	580	117
Sept.	129.3	21.4	43.5	27.7	15.5	712.6	129.9[5]	25.4	45.0	128.6	1,041.5	630	128
Dec.	136.3	23.2	47.6	27.2	15.5	776.0	136.0[5]	25.6	45.5	127.6	1,110.7	665	135
1980 March	132.0	21.5	45.6	27.8	15.9	775.2	133.6[5]	28.9	49.8	129.9	1,117.4	680	142
June	148.7[4]	25.1	51.5	29.9	18.5	840.2	152.5[5]	30.5	51.3	131.5	1,206.0	745	154
Sept.	149.6	25.3	49.8	30.5	20.5	849.9	164.6[5]	32.9	60.1	140.4	1,247.9	775	165
Dec.	151.7	24.4	51.8	29.5	22.7	902.9	176.9[5]	35.5	65.7	142.1	1,323.1	810	175
(B) **Liabilities**													
1977 Dec.	57.7	4.2	24.3	5.7	11.1	453.9	78.8[6]	18.9	28.6	91.7	671.9	430	75
1978 Dec. I	82.0	5.7	40.2	6.8	11.9	592.8	101.6	25.0	39.0	107.5	865.9	540	101
Dec. II	82.0	5.7	40.2	6.8	11.9	592.8	92.0[7]	25.0	39.0	107.5	856.3	535	101
1979 March	81.9	5.8	37.3	6.4	13.3	584.3	98.6[7]	26.8	39.8	112.3	861.8	550	107
June	87.8	5.8	41.3	6.8	14.7	633.2	112.6[7]	29.7	39.7	118.3	933.5	580	111
Sept.	95.9	6.1	45.8	7.3	16.0	700.3	125.5[7]	30.8	50.4	129.0	1,036.0	630	119
Dec.	111.4	6.6	54.3	7.4	19.2	777.2	130.0[7]	32.8	50.5	128.8	1,119.3	665	125
1980 March	103.6	7.3	46.5	7.4	19.8	779.6	132.7[7]	35.4	57.8	131.5	1,136.5	680	133
June	125.6[4]	8.7	53.5	9.7	24.2	854.1	130.8[7]	37.2	67.7	133.5	1,223.3	745	143
Sept.	129.1	9.4	52.2	11.6	26.4	871.0	132.0[7]	39.4	75.1	142.3	1,259.8	775	153
Dec.	127.9	8.6	50.7	12.0	27.6	928.4	138.2[7]	43.6	80.2	144.2	1,334.6	810	164

1 In the Bahamas, the Cayman Islands, Panama, Lebanon (December 1977 and from September 1979 onwards), Hong Kong and Singapore.
2 "Grand total" adjusted on a partly estimated basis to exclude double-counting due to the redepositing among the reporting banks.
3 Estimates for non-reporting banks in offshore centres mentioned under footnote 1 and all banks located in Bahrain and the Netherlands Antilles.
4 Including for the first time positions of banks in Ireland. At the end of June 1980, these amounted to $0.1 billion on the assets side and to $1.8 billion on the liabilities side.
5 Excluding all custody items.
6 Excluding US Treasury bills and certificates held in custody on behalf of non-residents.
7 Excluding all custody items except negotiable US bank certificates of deposit held on behalf of non-residents.

May 1981

BANK FOR INTERNATIONAL SETTLEMENTS
Monetary and Economic Department
BASLE

TABLE 2 (page 1)

Currency breakdown of the external positions of banks
in the reporting European countries

a) Total

Amounts outstanding in billions of US dollars

End of month	Domestic currency	Foreign currencies		of which								Memorandum items — Positions in foreign currencies vis-à-vis residents	
		Dollars	Other foreign currencies	Deutsche Mark	Swiss francs	Sterling	Guilders	French francs	Yen	Belgian francs	Dollars	Other foreign currencies
Assets												
1977 Dec.	81.4	268.4	116.4	70.4	23.6	5.3	4.3	3.3	1.7	2.4	93.5	35.7
1978 Dec.	109.4	339.5	162.5	97.4	27.9	7.3	6.9	5.7	5.4	3.2	106.5	49.6
1979 March	112.6	327.2	162.3	94.9	26.0	8.3	7.7	6.4	6.1	4.0	107.3	50.8
June	120.5	351.1	177.7	104.8	31.5	8.3	7.4	6.8	5.7	3.5	110.5	59.3
Sept.	129.3	384.2	199.1	116.9	37.3	9.4	8.1	6.8	5.7	4.4	116.1	66.0
Dec.	136.3	428.0	211.7	124.4	38.7	11.1	8.5	7.8	6.3	4.9	126.6	69.6
1980 March	132.0	439.0	204.2	115.7	38.0	11.6	7.8	8.5	8.0	4.5	137.3	73.1
June	148.7[1]	456.7	234.8	129.8	46.2	13.6	8.7	9.1	9.6	6.1	148.7	82.0
Sept.	149.6	465.6	234.7	127.4	47.2	13.4	8.0	10.4	10.3	6.1	156.0	81.8
Dec.	151.7	518.7	232.5	122.9	49.6	13.0	7.4	11.6	10.5	5.9	169.6	85.4
Liabilities (1.)												
1977 Dec.	57.7	278.8	117.4	68.7	22.7	6.9	5.1	4.4	2.7	1.9	75.3	30.4
1978 Dec.	82.0	348.6	162.2	93.1	27.9	10.3	7.4	7.4	6.2	2.1	87.7	45.1
1979 March	81.9	336.6	165.8	93.2	26.8	12.0	8.1	8.2	7.2	1.9	85.4	45.1
June	87.8	359.9	185.5	104.6	32.3	13.1	7.7	8.9	7.8	2.0	90.7	50.0
Sept.	95.9	392.4	212.0	117.8	38.3	14.5	8.4	9.6	8.8	2.5	96.4	57.6
Dec.	111.4	436.6	229.2	127.9	40.7	15.2	6.8	11.4	10.3	2.9	108.9	63.9
1980 March	103.6	450.1	225.9	118.2	41.7	19.4	8.2	11.4	10.9	3.3	117.9	61.6
June	125.6[1]	474.0	254.5	133.0	49.2	22.9	9.4	12.6	10.0	3.7	124.7	68.7
Sept.	129.1	486.1	255.8	130.5	51.7	23.1	8.9	13.4	10.1	3.5	132.7	66.1
Dec.	127.9	548.4	252.1	125.3	51.6	23.8	8.3	14.5	11.2	3.7	148.1	66.6

1 Including for the first time positions of banks in Ireland. At the end of June 1980, these amounted to $0.1 billion on the assets side and to $1.8 billion on the liabilities side.

May 1981

Section B

The Relative Truth
of the Remaining
Undiscovered
Liquid Petroleum Resource
in the United States

A merica's economic future will depend on the quantity in the undiscovered petroleum resource within its borders. This factual information controls all physical forecasts of the energy that will be available to the United States economy at the end of this century, and the last years of this century will determine the political economy of the next. Alternative forms of energy have only theoretical significance for our liquid petroleum dependent society.

These physical and economic facts are most important for their moral and political implications. How is the quantity in the remaining resource to be determined? Who is privileged to interpret the available facts and guide critical economic decision? The nation must accept the consequences when anticipations are in significant variance with the actual outcome.

The time for decision was the beginning of the second quarter of 1974 when the illusion of a safe dependency on foreign oil imports was broken and the nation had had time to consider the geological evidence. For the previous fourteen years a battle for the relative truth as to the extent of U.S. petroleum resources had been in process in scientific, governmental, and business circles; but it was an unequal battle. Too much was at stake to trust a physical science conclusion. The weight of evidence was given to economically and politically oriented spokesmen during most of this period, but when the political answers had to stand up to analysis, conclusions began to change.

Energy—A Critical Decision for the United States Economy was totally concerned with this central question. The reports that became that book were first directed to Vice President Gerald Ford in the last two months of 1973. The evidence of the remaining crude oil resource is depicted graphically in Figure 1 on page 64 of that book, reproduced on the following page.

In the spring of 1974, the most recent information on the nation's petroleum resource was the March 26 news release by the United States Geological Survey. Knowledgeable geologists were aware of the 1956 estimate by Dr. M. King Hubbert and the contrasting conclusion published in 1972 as U.S. Geological Survey Circular 650. The 1974 news release was an obvious compromise of the Survey's earlier position and was easily interpretable as a transitional estimate to figures closely approximating Dr. Hubbert's fully documented prediction of the ultimate quantity of liquid petroleum that would be found.

Before the end of 1974, the Geological Survey undertook a massive study of the nation's undiscovered oil resources employing the exploratory records accumulated by the oil industry, interpreted by a broad segment of the nation's geologists. This became U.S.G.S. Circular 725, the most completely documented record up to that time. But even this study bears the imprint of politically-induced bias. The maximum estimate is identified as carrying a 5 percent probability of being realized or exceeded. Obviously, this maximum estimate

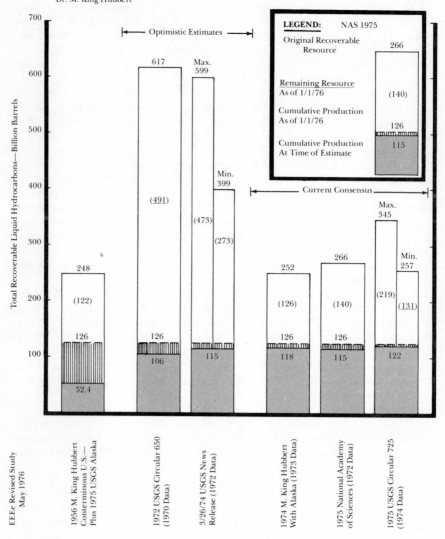

Figure 1

ESTIMATES OF ORIGINAL RECOVERABLE OIL IN PLACE

Including Crude Oil, Lease Condensate, & Natural Gas Liquids
By: United States Geological Survey
National Academy of Science
Dr. M. King Hubbert

Exhibit B-36

must be discounted almost totally. Five percent probability is translatable as close to impossible.

Paralleling the U.S.G.S. detail survey, the National Academy of Sciences undertook a study of the available data in 1974 and completed their report in 1975. Early in 1974, Dr. Hubbert updated his earlier study, confirming his original predictions for all practical purposes. The results of these three independent conclusions are graphically presented in the reference exhibit. However, this is not the total amount of information made available by these organizations. U.S. Geological Survey Circular 650 included much larger numbers for interpretation or misinterpretation by political economists.

The Survey's scaled diagram attempts to identify all the hydrocarbons in the geologic rock formations of our country. The small square in the upper left hand corner is the identified petroleum reserve of 52 billion barrels. The large square represents 2100 billion barrels in the submarginal undiscovered category. This

TOTAL CRUDE OIL AND NATURAL GAS LIQUIDS
U.S. Geological Survey Circular 650
**Proved Reserves, Undiscovered Resource,
and Submarginal, non-producible Hydro Carbons**
Billions of Barrels

	Identified resources	Undiscovered resources
Recoverable	52	450
Submarginal	290	2100

Figure 5.—Scaled diagram of crude oil and natural-gas liquids in the United States (including the continental margin to 2,500-m water depth) as of Dec. 31, 1970 (billions of barrels). Reliability of estimates decreases downward and to the right. Compiled by S. P. Schweinfurth.

Exhibit B-37

classification is defined as, "those quantities estimated to be present but that cannot be produced if found or that might never be found because of small size or remote location." Only the 450 billion barrels in the undiscovered, recoverable classification purports to identify the potential liquid product and only a portion of this liquid product (an unidentified portion) is recognized as economically producible. U.S.G.S. 650 does discuss the contradictory conclusions of independent analysts including M. King Hubbert who was a member of the U.S. Geological Survey when this report was published.

U.S.G.S. Circular 650 exemplifies a pattern in the relationship between physical scientists and political economists that is the heart of the moral problem. Science has been willing to produce evidence to a politicians' specification, covering its shame with careful labeling. The politician then delivers the information to his constituents, knowing that the label will not be read or if read will be ignored. The authority of the scientific organization will be used in selling the public. Everyone knows that ultimate truth is not realizable so the doubt which the scientist recognizes as a mathematically computable tolerance becomes a cover for any exaggeration of factual information that an economically motivated individual wishes to employ.

In 1974, the United States consumed a little over six billion barrels of petroleum products, and consumption had been increasing at the exponential rate of 4.2 percent per year for the previous 27 years, the post-World War II economy. The annual increase had been much greater over the hundred year span, back to 1874. Future annual consumption was very much in doubt. The reliable physical evidence indicated that the liquid product would not be available and thus consumption would have to begin decreasing each year, but the optimistic forecasts denied this evidence. At a 4.2 percent annual increase, we would consume 17.7 billion barrels (48.5 million barrels per day) in the year 2000. The potential computation from six or fewer to 18 billion barrels per year at the end of the century is sufficient to support a wide variety of political-economic forecasts. The potential consumption figures could be combined with a similarly wide variation in undiscovered resources.

The manipulation of these numbers by General Motors Corporation, appears to have been responsible for the keynote utterance for the automotive and petroleum industries. Grand Rapids Rotary, which includes the manufacturing executives of the second largest city in Michigan, was selected for the test of public acceptance. If President Cole's facts and figures were challenged, little harm would have been done. If accepted by this community and the press and the corporations that look to General Motors for leadership, industry policy would be established. In fact, no challenge was allowed to develop and the industry position is now history. Mr. Cole's talk is reported by Charles Fuller, co-editor of the Grand Rapids Rotary weekly publication. Cole is identified in the announcement in the bulletin of the previous week. Mr. Cole's 485-year supply of petroleum (exhibit B-38) indicates his corporate conclusion that U.S. consumption would back off very slightly from the 1974 record, an average 5.96 billion barrels per year for the next 500 years based on the most blatant misinterpretation of the government's figures and definitions. Seventy-three percent of the resource he claimed for future generations is labeled "cannot be produced if found."

SPOKES O' THE WHEEL

A Weekly News Bulletin Published in the Interest of the
GRAND RAPIDS ROTARY CLUB
Organized 1913, Club No. 77, District 629

ROTARY PROGRAM - APRIL 11, 1974

SPEAKER:	TOPIC:
EDWARD N. COLE	"SOME PEOPLE WONDER"

EDWARD N. COLE was elected president and chief operating officer of General Motors and appointed chairman of the Corporation's Administration Committee on October 30, 1967. He became chairman of the Executive Committee on January 1, 1972.

Mr. Cole is also a member of GM's third top policy-making body, the Finance Committee, and is on six of the Corporation's policy groups—Engineering, Industrial Relations and Public Relations, Marketing, Personnel Administration and Development, Research, and Overseas.

EDWARD N. COLE
PRESIDENT OF GENERAL MOTORS

PRESIDENT COLE grew up on a farm, near Coopersville, so there's hope for Farmer Blake* yet. From the Marne-Berlin High School (Class of 1927); he graduated from Grand Rapids Junior College; and then on to the General Motors Institute in Flint. Mr. Cole began his talk with several reminiscences and flash-backs to his earlier days in this area where he learned the free enterprise system the hard way during the depression.

President Cole was able to present the inside experts' view of both the energy problem and the fast changing market situation. The U.S. has the world's greatest supply of fossil fuel: enough coal to last 5,300 years; petroleum for 485 years; oil shale for 4,300 years; and natural gas for 290 years. So there is no energy shortage, only an energy management problem. Incentives are needed to explore and to invest. Only 20% of the earth's crust has been explored for petroleum and after the fossil fuels run out, we can always turn to synthetic fuels.

Detroit automobile executives are not dispirited or gloomy about the present market. They are busy adjusting to the desires of the people. They see no need for more bureaucratic decisions and rulings. The market is improving, even for large size cars. March was 6% above February and 23% above January. By 1975, GM will be building 2 million small cars a year. Fuel efficiency will be increased on all sizes of cars. The manufacture and sales of cars is still a growing industry and by 1980, sales will reach 17 million cars and trucks per year in the U.S. and 48 million in the world.

In Grand Rapids, GM has 7,500 employees and contributes $115 million/yr to our economy. "What's Good for General Motors is Good for Grand Rapids"!

CF

President of G.R. Rotary '73-'74.

Exhibit B-38

Derivation and Development

Section C

Forecast of United States Crude Oil and Total Petroleum Liquids Production 1980-2000

T he crude oil production forecast is based on a physical model that projects the first decade with a reasonably high degree of certainty. The primary inputs are hard data, proved petroleum reserves and engineering projections of U.S. oil field production capacities. Economic inputs are implied from market responses from 1974 to 1980. The source information, computation, and year-by-year conclusions are identified in the following discussion.

1. HARD DATA INPUTS
    (1) *U.S. proved reserves*
    The American Petroleum Institute's 33-year record of discoveries and revisions representing added potential production from the existing reserves is the primary forecast reference. Exhibit C-41 follows.
    (2) *Ten-year production forecast for sample representing 52% of U.S. proved reserve*
    The final report, Volume II, Oil & Gas Resources, Reserve and Productive Capacities, submitted in compliance with Public Law 93-275, Section 15b, published by the Federal Energy Administration in October 1975 provides a means for interpreting future production from the crude reserve. (exhibits X-16 through X-22 in Chapter X)
    (3) *U.S. Geological Survey Circular 725, geological estimates of undiscovered recoverable oil and gas resources in the United States*
    The quantity of the undiscovered oil and gas resource is the subject of this major geological study completed in 1975. The maximum and minimum expectancy stated in statistical probability terms brackets all responsible estimates of the United States resource base. (exhibit B-33)
    (4) *Energy—A Critical Decision for the United States Economy by Samuel M. Dix*
    This three-year study undertaken for President Ford interprets the petroleum resource base in terms of probable year-to-year (discovery) additions to the proved reserve. (Primary reference No. 1 of bibliography) Future annual production assumes a proved reserve flow-through.

2. IMPLIED ECONOMETRIC INPUTS
    (1) *Price influence on U.S. supply based on 100-year study including 1975 to 1980 experience*
    The effects of price on the level of petroleum production activity were studied in *Energy—A Critical Decision for the United States Economy.* Current price influence is interpreted from its effect on the rate of proved reserve revisions. The application of higher cost recovery methods to the

actual remaining reserves is indicated in the American Petroleum Institute annual survey of proved reserves (now taken over by the Energy Information Administration).

(2) *Other demand influences on supply*

Political and organizational influences other than price are affected through the same channels, interpreted in the annual proved reserve changes.

3. PHYSICAL ASSUMPTIONS

The hard data forecast is limited to a 20-year time span. Scientific discoveries which require a longer time to produce energy products are excluded from this forecast. However, most of the considered physical assumptions will influence the future a long time after the 20-year forecast. Accuracy in extrapolation beyond the 20 years will be reduced to the degree that the following physical assumptions are expected to give way:

(1) *No significant quantity of petroleum resource will enter the economic system without passing through and being accounted for in the proved reserve.*

The methodology for the proved reserve accounting and the establishment of procedures including the training of persons and the development of the petroleum engineering science supports the probability of continued, accurate reporting. This probability is reinforced by the federal government's present interest in these procedures which includes the failure of political investigation to find error or intentional misinterpretation of the data despite the legal privileges of private property under U.S. law.

(2) *The liquid petroleum dependence of Western civilization will hold for the 20 years of the forecast.*

The U.S. transportation system's dependence alone will maintain sufficient pressure on petroleum demand to support maximum domestic production. This demand is reinforced in depth by the economic and political realities of our democracy.

(3) *No new petroleum region comparable with the Persian Gulf will be discovered and developed within the time span.*

The probability of upsetting this assumption has become increasingly remote during the last seven years of maximum exploratory effort.

(4) *The laws of thermodynamics will hold.*

The probability of upsetting these physical laws has been considered more remote than in any other branch of physics.

(5) *Atomic fusion will not succeed in replacing liquid petroleum with a hydrogen economy during the time span.*

A physical breakthrough in 1981 could be expected to provide no significant atomic fusion energy supply in the next 20 years.

(6) *At least half the population of the developed world would survive atomic warfare during the time span.*

Obviously, a major disruption of civilization would reduce petroleum demand temporarily, but this demand can be expected to be returned in proportion to the reestablishment of industrial processes supporting a surviving population.

(7) *No other vital resource or combination of resources will preempt the role of energy as the primary support for our industrial civilization.*

All current information indicates that substitutes for all resources except energy will be available into the next century. Obviously, air and water are comparable to energy in their necessity but the deterioration in their quality will not immediately affect the economics of energy demand.

4.   POLITICAL-ECONOMIC ASSUMPTIONS

Liquid petroleum demand is sustained by every form of government and every variation of economic system known to the developed world today. Within the 55-year time span projected by "The Global 2000 Report" population pressures are expected to upset international relations in the world community, but the U.S. community that develops out of this international chaos will still require energy resources and the demand for fossil fuel production will continue. The forecast assumes that:

(1) *A conservation ethic will* not *take over the U.S. free economy and drastically restrict the employment of petroleum products for private transportation within the time span*

The necessity of this eventuality is already apparent, but the implementation of such a political alteration must be interpreted in relative terms. Encouragement to reduce petroleum consumption within the framework of the present U.S. political system can be expected to be constantly behind the projected decline in domestic petroleum production. Thus, continued excess demand for petroleum products is anticipated. Maximum development of the fossil fuel reserves will be required including the conversion of coal and shale as substitutes for petroleum.

(2) *Anarchy does not destroy the orderly processes of the economy under a civilized form of government*

Petroleum production can be anticipated to survive a relatively total disruption of our governmental processes, but it is possible for this eventuality to develop to the point of actually reducing liquid petroleum demand.

5.   MODEL CONSTRUCTION

The model was designed to accommodate the available physical data. The following decisions describe the model construction and indicate the characteristics of the forecast:

(1) *Acceptance of the petroleum engineers' ten-year forecast.*

This 52-percent sample of the remaining U.S. petroleum reserves and the proof of its accuracy through 1978 were described in Chapter X. The model construction begins with these data inputs.

(2) *Division of the petroleum engineers' sample into three segments for extrapolation*

In Chapter X the differences in field characteristics are described. A realistic forecast is possible only by separating these fields to represent common future production characteristics. In this forecast, Alaska, the first ten fields, and the next 41 are separately identified for extrapolation of production expectancy.

(3) *Total U.S. proved reserve universe employed to determine remaining fields in projecting production expectancy.*

The final segment of the forecast represents the 48 percent of the total universe for which a specific field-by-field production forecast is not available. The rate of withdrawal from this segment is based on the computed remainder production for the years 1975 through 1978 and extrapolation at maximum expectancy assumed to be 14 percent of the quantity remaining in this reserve each year.

(4) *Treatment of each segment of the identified proved reserve as a closed system*

The total reserve identified by petroleum engineers at the end of 1975 is isolated from all additions to this proved reserve for the remainder of the forecast. The sum of production from each identified reserve is considered actual for the four years under observation. Production from the remaining fields becomes the difference between the universe and the sample. Production expectancy for the remaining six years of the forecast continues this process for the sample. The universe differential segment is extrapolated as stated above. The total quantity in these reserves approaches zero as the forecast procedure is carried out with each year's production representing a percentage of the remainder, either a fixed percentage, or an extrapolation of the trend established in the engineers' sample.

(5) *Treatment of all additions to the proved reserve after 1974 as a separate segment of the forecast*

The reserve in this segment begins at zero in 1974 and represents the actual accumulation differential through 1978. The accumulation represents the difference between total reserve additions and (production) subtractions from the reserve projected at 13 percent annual rate. This reserve will build as all other reserves are depleted. (If more oil is found on the Alaskan North Slope and the pipeline is double looped to increase daily flow, the production will appear in this segment of the forecast.)

(6) *Projection of additions to the proved reserve based on the 1974 through 1978 additions experience applied to U.S.G.S. 725 resource estimate interpreted by "Energy–A Critical Decision for the United States Economy" forecast*

Experience since 1974 projects 50 percent actual finding of the anticipated annual rate of discovery computed from the 1975 resource statistics.

(7) *Maximum projection of proved reserve additions based on double the current finding rate* (Exhibit C-40)

A maximum petroleum resource projection was undertaken on the basis of an assumed doubling of the finding rate, bringing this finding rate back to the anticipation in the original resource study. The resulting year-by-year total U.S. production expectancy is summarized with the projection stated in millions of barrels per year for both the probable rate of additions to the reserve and the doubling of this rate, but only the probable forecast was carried into the text discussion.

(8) *Addition of a 4 percent correction factor to the summation of crude oil production expectancies by identified forecast segments in the probable forecast*

Lease condensate* was not projected in the petroleum engineers' crude oil production forecasts but lease condensate is included in the annual summation of the proved reserves. The employed computation methodology throws these lease condensates into the universe remainder segment. However, the history of proved reserve computation indicates an element of conservatism and lease condensate was not included in new discoveries (6). The 4 percent correction overcomes the conservatism in the engineering estimates of present reserves and provides for the lease condensate contribution to reserve additions.

(9) *Rate of future production employed for each forecast segment beyond 1985*

The following computed rates were applied to the three segments of the petroleum engineers' forecast:

Prudhoe Bay, Alaska	11.4%	
First 10 fields curvelinear extrapol-		
ation beginning with	7.4%	
developing to	14.4%	in the year 2000
Next 41 fields	12.0%	
Remaining fields (universe minus sample)	14.0%	
Additions to the proved reserve	13.0%	

---

*Lease condensate derives from small amounts of hydrocarbons that exist in the gaseous phase in natural underground reservoirs but are liquid at atmospheric pressure after being recovered from oil well gas and lease separators. Their contribution to total liquid petroleum recovery centers on 4 percent.

6.   MAXIMUM U.S. CRUDE PRODUCTION EXPECTANCY

Although economic and political influences on petroleum production are definitely limited in today's demand-dominated world economy, they cannot be ignored. As long as oil finding and production costs stated in physical terms are less than the value of the energy that is finally produced, political and economic influences can be effective. More new oil can be found and more intensive production methods can be employed to produce a higher percentage of the oil in the ground. The energy content of oil and gas is so great and the initial flow from new wells requires so little energy input that net energy production from discovered reserves has always been taken for granted. But this situation is already beginning to change. Despite the constant improvements in the techniques for discovering oil resources under the ground and beneath oceans, the ratio of oil finding per foot of exploratory drilling has continued to deteriorate, and this ratio is only part of the story. A foot of drilling on the North Slope of Alaska and the deep water off this coast and in the stormy Atlantic requires tremendous energy inputs that are not comparable with the first three million wells drilled on the flat land of the 48 states. A 20,000' to 30,000' well must produce many times the quantity of gas that the average 4,000' to 6,000' well requires to break even on energy input costs. The dollar cost at current gas prices are already too great to market the product from these deep wells and no oil is expected at these depths. The break-even point for oil and gas exploration and production, stated in ultimate physical terms, is now projectible. Economic and political pressure on finding and producing a maximum quantity of crude oil in this century will speed the end of the petroleum era and guarantee a crisis of unprecedented dimensions surely in the next century.

Interestingly, today's political encouragement of oil production is identical in its economic consequences with the political-economic policy of earlier periods: breaking up of Standard Oil, the approval of the Texas Railway Commission's control of production, the depletion allowance tax privilege, the restriction on foreign oil imports, and the deduction of foreign taxes from U.S. oil company income tax liability. In each era the United States' controlled oil companies were protected and encouraged to provide the U.S. economy with as much petroleum product as the economy could absorb at the minimum price consistent with political reality. The only variation was a slight shift between the influence of the domestic and international producers. Now, the physical reality must be recognized, the high cost of producing the last of this resource. Maximum supply requires maximum price and, for the first time in one hundred years, the free market can be allowed to set that price while maintaining the policy of supplying the U.S. economy with maximum product at the least cost.

More objectively, these physical data identify the desirability of employing political influence to curtail oil and gas discovery and reserve the high cost petroleum recovery method for the time when our economy will need this resource in phasing out liquid petroleum dependence. We know the oil is there and we know how much it will be needed in future decades. Accelerated discovery and production wastes energy. The free economic system's incredible focus on satisfying today's demands is capable of exceeding the projected discovery rate during the 1980s at the expense of the 1990s and the next century.

Unfortunately, accelerated oil and gas exploration is the cheapest and fastest way to increase energy availability to the U.S. economy today and the Reagan administration is moving political influence behind the release of these economic incentives. These political realities must be taken into consideration in any forecast of crude oil production expectancy from the United States resource.

Annual increases to U.S. crude oil reserves can be doubled if the United States Geological Survey estimates of the undiscovered resource prove to be accurate and if an all-out effort is made by the industry to find and produce the oil within our territorial limits. The forecast question then becomes how quickly and in what quantity these additions to the reserve will affect annual production. This exercise has been undertaken by applying the previously described analysis of the crude oil flow-through from 1979 through the year 2000 at double the annual addition to the reserves. As previously noted, the additions in 1979 were greater than the original forecast although they were far short of the quantity required for doubling.

Exhibit C-44 concludes with the additional annual production that will result from a doubling of annual additions. This quantity is added to the probable annual production in Exhibit C-40.

7. PETROLEUM LIQUIDS FORECAST CONCLUSION

Exhibit C-40 summarizes the conclusion for the total petroleum liquids production expectancy year-by-year to the end of the century for both the probable rate of discovery and the maximum rate. The production expectancies are indicated in the last two columns stated in the familiar million barrels per day. A doubling of crude oil discoveries beginning in 1980 will increase petroleum products availability from U.S. resources by two million barrels a day during 1984. The differential will build to 2.5 million barrels a day of increase by the end of the century if crude oil additions are maintained at this level, double probable expectancy.

No correction was made to the estimates of probable natural gas liquids production despite the anticipation that an increase in exploratory drilling will result in a higher level of natural gas production and a consequent increase in the by-product of this production which becomes petroleum liquids. The reason for this omission is the desire to reduce potential confusion. A doubling of crude oil resource finding represents an extreme expectancy. A higher level of petroleum liquids production will increase the probability of this maximum production potential. Derivation of these quantities appears in the first three columns of Exhibit C-44, stated in terms of million barrels per year. The natural gas liquids forecast is developed in Derivation and Development section D.

The supporting figures for the Exhibit C-40 forecast appear in the exhibits immediately following. The employment of these figures was previously discussed. The numbers will permit the reader to visualize the continuation of the American Petroleum Institute's 33-year record of crude oil reserves and production. The primary addition is the probable annual additions which appear on this page without the allowance employed in the forecast calculation.

Only the probable total petroleum liquids production, the extrapolation of the current rate, is considered realistic and discussed in the first three sections of Chapter XI. This probable forecast should not be interpreted as minimum. Between now and the end of the century, we will experience a reversal of the political influence on maximum crude oil production. A more rational energy policy for the United States would result in less than the probable forecast. Realistically, 1984 could be the earliest beginning for this political-economic reversal.

	Probable Annual additions to proved reserves '75 to '78 experience = 50% of U.S.G.S. 725 annual production interpretation
1974	1,994
1975	1,318
1976	1,085
1977	1,404
1978	1,348
1979	1,448
1980	1,435
1981	1,437
1982	1,418
1983	1,382
1984	1,348
1985	1,314
1986	1,283
1987	1,241
1988	1,199
1989	1,159
1990	1,120
1991	1,082
1992	1,046
1993	1,010
1994	976
1995	943
1996	911
1997	881
1998	851
1999	822
2000	795

Exhibit C-39

PRODUCTION FORECAST

	Billion Barrels/Year		Probable Total Petroleum Liquids Production	Additional Production @ Double Annual Crude Oil Additions	Million Barrels/Day Total Petroleum Liquids	
Year	Probable Crude Oil Production (1)	Natural Gas Liquids Probable Production (2)	(3)	(4)	@ Probable Discovery Rate (5)	@ Maximum Discovery Rate (6)
1975	2.89	701	3.58			
1976	2.83	701	3.53			
1977	2.86	699	3.56			
1978	3.03	664	3.69			
1979	2.96	649	3.61	--	9.88	9.88
1980	2.93	634	3.56	.19	9.87	10.27
1981	2.83	618	3.45	.35	9.45	10.41
1982	2.75	594	3.35	.49	9.17	10.52
1983	2.67	579	3.25	.61	8.90	10.58
1984	2.59	563	3.15	.71	8.64	10.59
1985	2.52	547	3.07	.79	8.41	10.58
1986	2.39	531	2.92	.86	8.01	10.37
1987	2.28	516	2.79	.92	7.65	10.16
1988	2.17	501	2.67	.96	7.31	9.93
1989	2.05	485	2.54	1.00	6.95	9.69
1990	1.96	470	2.43	1.01	6.67	9.44
1991	1.87	456	2.33	1.02	6.38	9.19
1992	1.79	441	2.23	1.03	6.10	8.93
1993	1.70	427	2.13	1.04	5.83	8.67
1994	1.63	413	2.04	1.03	5.59	8.42
1995	1.55	446	2.00	1.02	5.48	8.28
1996	1.48	427	1.91	1.02	5.24	8.02
1997	1.42	409	1.83	1.00	5.01	7.75
1998	1.36	393	1.75	.98	4.79	7.49
1999	1.29	377	1.67	.97	4.56	7.22
2000	1.22	362	1.59	.94	4.34	6.94

Exhibit C-40

ANNUAL ESTIMATES OF PROVED CRUDE OIL RESERVES
IN THE UNITED STATES 1946 THROUGH 1979
by American Petroleum Institute
(Thousands of Barrels of 42 U.S. Gallons)

Year (1)	Revisions (2)	Extensions (3)	New Field Discoveries (4)	New Reservoir Discoveries in Old Fields (5)
1946	1,254,075	1,158,923	(b)	244,434
1947	749,278	1,269,862	(b)	445,430
1948	1,958,853	1,439,873	269,438	127,043
1949	603,566	1,693,862	544,319	346,098
1950	663,378	1,334,391	407,739	157,177
1951	1,776,110	2,248,588	205,959	183,297
1952	743,729	1,509,131	280,066	216,362
1953	1,264,832	1,439,618	344,053	247,627
1954	537,788	1,749,443	307,625	278,181
1955	696,114	1,697,653	219,824	257,133
1956	804,803	1,702,311	234,727	232,495
1957	465,421	1,543,182	207,437	208,760
1958	954,605	1,338,908	151,210	163,519
1959	1,518,678	1,778,705	165,695	203,667
1960	787,934	1,323,538	141,296	112,560
1961	1,087,092	1,209,101	107,423	253,951
1962	759,053	1,041,257	92,488	288,098
1963	966,051	858,168	96,732	253,159
1964	899,292	1,419,182	126,682	219,611
1965	1,783,231	792,901	237,335	234,612
1966	1,839,307	814,249	160,384	150,038
1967	1,900,969	716,467	125,105	219,581
1968	1,320,109	776,780	166,291	191,455
1969	1,258,142	614,710	96,435	150,749
1970	2,088,927	631,354	9,852,512	116,125
1971	1,600,426	560,596	91,469	65,241
1972	820,107	459,311	123,210	155,220
1973	1,551,777	390,141	116,097	87,816
1974	1,310,929	368,918	226,163	87,563
1975	677,271	340,128	173,177	127,887
1976	488,659	466,279	67,842	62,511
1977	769,678	365,007	159,950	109,145
1978	707,190	366,589	199,994	73,483
1979	1,490,618	368,082	239,406	107,567

Exhibit C-41

ANNUAL ESTIMATES OF PROVED CRUDE OIL RESERVES
IN THE UNITED STATES 1946 THROUGH 1979
by American Petroleum Institute

(Thousands of Barrels of 42 U.S. Gallons)

Year (1)	Total of Discoveries, Revisions, and Extensions (6)	Production a (7)	Proved Reserves at End of Year (8)	Net Change From Previous Year (9)
1946	2,658,062	1,726,348	20,873,560	931,714
1947	2,464,570	1,850,445	21,487,685	614,125
1948	3,795,207	2,002,448	23,280,444	1,792,759
1949	3,187,845	1,818,800	24,649,489	1,369,045
1950	2,562,685	1,943,776	25,268,398	618,909
1951	4,413,954	2,214,321	27,468,031	2,199,633
1952	2,749,288	2,256,765	27,960,554	492,523
1953	3,296,130	2,311,856	28,944,828	984,274
1954	2,873,037	2,257,119	29,560,746	615,918
1955	2,870,724	2,419,300	30,012,170	451,424
1956	2,974,336	2,551,857	30,434,649	422,479
1957	2,424,800	2,559,044	30,300,405	(134,244)
1958	2,608,242	2,372,730	30,535,917	235,512
1959	3,666,745	2,483,315	31,719,347	1,183,430
1960	2,365,328	2,471,464	31,613,211	(106,136)
1961	2,657,567	2,512,273	31,758,505	145,294
1962	2,180,896	2,550,178	31,389,233	(369,282)
1963	2,174,110	2,593,343	30,969,990	(419,233)
1964	2,664,767	2,644,247	30,990,510	20,520
1965	3,048,079	2,686,198	31,352,391	361,881
1966	2,963,978	2,864,242	31,452,127	99,736
1967	2,962,122	3,037,579	31,376,670	(75,457)
1968	2,454,635	3,124,188	30,707,117	(669,553)
1969	2,120,036	3,195,291	29,631,862	(1,075,255)
1970	12,688,918	3,319,445	39,001,335	9,369,473
1971	2,317,732	3,256,110	38,062,957	(938,378)
1972	1,557,848	3,281,397	36,339,408	(1,723,549)
1973	2,145,831	3,185,400	35,299,839	(1,039,569)
1974	1,993,573	3,043,456	34,249,956	(1,049,883)
1975	1,318,463	2,886,292	32,682,127	(1,567;829)
1976	1,085,291	2,825,252	30,942,166	(1,739,961)
1977	1,403,780	2,859,544	29,486,402	(1,455,764)
1978	1,347,256	3,029,898	27,803,760	(1,682,642)
1979	2,205,673	2,958,144	27,051,289	(752,471)

Exhibit C-41, continued

PROJECTION OF
U.S. CRUDE OIL PRODUCTION
BY IDENTIFIED RESERVES

M̄ Barrels per Year
1975 to 2000

After	(1) Alaska Prudhoe Bay	(2) 1st 10 Fields	(3) Next 41 Fields	(4) Re-maining Fields	(5) Additions to Proved Reserve Annual Accumulation	(6) Total U.S. Production
1984*	11.4%	7.4% to 14.4%	12%	14%	13%	
1975	--	486	452	1,818	130	2,886
1976	--	479	389	1,794	154	2,825
1977	146	449	355	1,761	295	2,860
1978	515	419	317	1,333	440	3,030
1979	548	395	280	1,136	558	2,917
1980	548	372	244	977	673	2,814
1981	548	351	211	840	772	2,722
1982	548	333	184	723	859	2,647
1983	548	314	154	621	931	2,568
1984	548	302	116	534	990	2,490
1985	548	278	103	460	1,037	2,426
1986	485	258	90	395	1,073	2,301
1987	430	240	79	340	1,100	2,189
1988	381	222	70	292	1,118	2,083
1989	338	202	62	251	1,119	1,972
1990	299	186	54	216	1,133	1,888
1991	265	170	48	186	1,131	1,800
1992	235	155	42	160	1,125	1,717
1993	208	140	37	138	1,114	1,637
1994	185	128	32	118	1,101	1,564
1995	163	115	29	102	1,085	1,494
1996	145	103	25	88	1,066	1,427
1997	128	92	22	75	1,046	1,363
1998	113	82	19	65	1,025	1,304
1999	101	73	17	46	1,002	1,239
2000	78	64	15	40	979	1,176

Source: Oil and gas resources, reserves, and production capacity P.L. 93-275 Sec. 15(b) A.P.I. Reserves of Crude Oil etc., Volume 33 June 1979. *Energy—A Critical Decision for the United States Economy*—S. M. Dix 1977.

*Projection beyond petroleum engineer's production estimate based on identified percent of remaining proved reserve.

Exhibit C-42

RECONCILIATION OF REMAINING PROVED RESERVES
U.S. Crude Oil in Billion Barrels at Yearend

Year	Prudhoe Bay Alaska (1)	1st 10 Fields Lower 48 (2)	Next 41 Fields Lower 48 (3)	Remaining Fields (4)	Cumulative Net Addition to Pr. Res. After 1974 (5)	Year End Total A.P.I. Data to 1978, Comp. to 2000 (6)
1974	8.76	7.09	3.57	14.83	–	34.25
1975	8.76	6.61	3.11	13.02	1.19	32.68
1976	8.76	6.13	2.72	11.09	2.27	30.94
1977	8.61	5.68	2.36	9.45	3.82	29.49
1978	9.10	5.26	2.04	8.11	4.30	27.80
1979	7.55	4.866	1.76	6.98	4.18	26.34
1980	7.00	4.49	1.52	6.00	5.94	24.96
1981	6.45	4.14	1.31	5.16	6.61	23.67
1982	5.90	3.81	1.13	4.44	7.17	22.44
1983	3.36	3.50	.97	3.82	7.62	21.56
1984	4.81	3.19	.86	3.28	7.97	20.11
1985	4.26	2.89	.75	2.82	8.23	18.98
1986	3.78	2.61	.66	2.43	8.46	17.94
1987	3.35	2.35	.58	2,09	8.06	16.97
1988	2.96	2.11	.51	1.80	8.68	16.07
1989	2.63	1.89	.45	1.55	8.71	15.23
1990	2.33	1.69	.40	1.33	8.70	14.44
1991	2.06	1.50	.30	1.14	8.65	13.71
1992	1.83	1.33	.31	.98	8.57	13.02
1993	1.62	1.18	.27	.85	8.47	12.38
1994	1.43	1.04	.24	.73	8.34	11.78
1995	1.27	.91	.21	.63	8.20	11.28
1996	1.13	.80	.18	.54	8.05	10.70
1997	1.00	.69	.16	.46	7.88	10.20
1998	.88	.60	.14	.40	7.71	9.73
1999	.78	.52	.13	.33	7.53	9.49
2000	.68	.45	.11	.29	7.34	8.87

Exhibit C-43

MAXIMUM CRUDE OIL PRODUCTION FORECAST
Derivation of Addition to Proved Reserve
and Production at 2x Discovery Rate Used in Primary Forecast

Year	Addition at 2x Probable Discovery (1)	Cumulative Reserve Additions Yearend (2)	Annual Production at 2x Discovery (3)	New Reserves Annual Production & Probable Discovery (4)	Addition to Annual Production (5)
1978		4.30		.44	
1979	2.90	6.63	.56	.56	
1980	2.87	8.37	.86	.67	.19
1981	2.87	10.38	1.12	.77	.35
1982	2.84	11.87	1.35	.86	.49
1983	1.76	13.09	1.54	.93	.61
1984	2.70	14.09	1.70	.99	.71
1985	2.63	14.88	1.83	1.04	.79
1986	2.57	15.51	1.94	1.07	.86
1987	2.48	15.98	2.02	1.10	.92
1988	2.40	16.30	1.08	1.12	.96
1989	2.32	16.50	1.12	1.12	1.00
1990	2.24	16.60	2.15	1.13	1.01
1991	2.16	16.60	2.16	1.13	1.03
1992	2.09	16.53	2.16	1.14	1.03
1993	2.02	16.41	2.15	1.11	1.04
1994	1.95	16.23	2.13	1.10	1.03
1995	1.89	16.00	2.11	1.09	1.02
1996	1.82	15.75	2.08	1.07	1.02
1997	1.76	15.46	2.05	1.05	1.00
1998	1.70	15.15	1.01	1.03	.99
1999	1.64	14.83	1.97	1.00	.97
2000	1.59	14.49	1.93	.98	.95

Computation: 1. Begin with column (2) cumulative reserve addition in 1978 (see column (5) of Exhibit C-43)
2. Compute annual production for follwing year column (3) at 13% of 1.
3. Add probable discovery for that year column (1) to previous year's cumulative reserve column (2) and subtract annual production column (3) to obtain new yearend cumulative reserve column (2)
4. From computed annual production at 2x discovery rate column (3), subtract production at probable discovery rate column (4) [see Exhibit C-42, column (5)] = addition to annual production expectancy at double the probable annual additions to the proved reserve.

Exhibit C-44

Derivation and Development

Section D

Forecast of United States Natural Gas and Natural Gas Liquids Production 1980-2000

A lthough the energy content of natural gas products exceeds U.S. produced crude oil, natural gas is less critical to the U.S. economy and less information is available for a precise forecast. Gas is found in small quantities over wide sections of the country and it is economical to produce these small quantities when they can be found and piped to a user.

1. NATURAL GAS FORECAST

The natural gas forecast and the natural gas liquids forecast both follow the procedures defined in Derivation and Development section C for crude oil except that the reserve was not divided into segments. Thus, the forecast is greatly simplified.

The hard data inputs, the implied econometric inputs, the physical assumptions, and the political-economic assumption all follow the order and implication of the crude oil forecast with obvious variations. Natural gas is not the primary support for transportation in this country and consequently the demand for natural gas is not projectible with the same degree of certainty. A conservation ethic could very well enforce radical changes on the natural gas industry as discussed in Chapter XI. The exclusion in the forecast of the 31 trillion cubic feet of Prudhoe Bay natural gas is also discussed in Chapter XI.

The development of the natural gas forecast is evidenced in the following exhibits and in Chapter XI. For the years 1974-1978, total discoveries and additions to the proved reserve are taken from the American Gas Association's Reserves Committee record as of December 31, 1978, published in mid-1979 in conjunction with the similar report of the American Petroleum Institute. These figures deal with the proved reserve, annual production, and the total of all revisions, extensions, new field discoveries, and new reservoir discoveries in old fields. Total production is more than the reported quantity of marketed product and it is also greater than the reported consumption of dry gas, but the relationships between these three remained relatively constant. Obviously, gas is used and lost in the process of transport and conversion.

Annual production from the lower 48 states represents the total quantity of U.S. produced natural gas made available to the gas industry. A small amount of gas produced in southern Alaska is being liquefied and shipped to Japan. We have been importing natural gas from Canada and small quantities are exported, mostly for convenience in the border areas of the two countries. As Canadian gas exports decrease, we can anticipate future Mexican exports to this country.

The rate at which proved reserves are produced is indicated to begin at 9.74 percent of the previous year's proved reserve in 1974, ending at 10.86 percent in 1978. This rate was extrapolated on a straight-line basis to 15 percent per year in 1991. This is an optimistic anticipation as the industry has always considered production above 10 percent of proved reserve to be less than reliable. However, both the petroleum and gas industries have demonstrated their capacities to produce above this level. It is just a question of how far they can go from year to year. A more sophisticated projection would expect the topping off of the rate closer to 1985 instead of 1991.

The second most sensitive variable in the natural gas production projection is the quantity of total revisions, extensions, and additions to the proved reserve. These quantities are the source of future production even though only 10 or 15 percent can be made available in the year of discovery. Anticipated additions have been projected on the basis of two sources of information. First, the trend between 1974 and 1978 was extended by a straight-line extrapolation through 1983. This time span represents the post-Arab boycott economics of increased price and exploration activity. After 1983, anticipated additions to the proved reserve will become constrained by the quantity in the undiscovered resource. From 1984 through the year 2000, the analysis anticipates conversion of the undiscovered resource to proved reserve at the rate determined in *Energy—A Critical Decision for the United States Economy* published in 1977. This study anticipates that from a maximum addition of 13.6 trillion cubic feet in 1983, additions will fall off to 8.5 in the year 2000.

The remainder of the natural gas production forecast is purely mechanical. The computed rate of production for the year is applied to the quantity in the proved reserve at the end of the previous year identifying production. This quantity is subtracted from the proved reserve, the anticipated annual additions are added, and a new year-end reserve is determined. This is the way the industry operates. There can be no short-cuts. Very little gas escapes the accounting.

2.   NATURAL GAS LIQUIDS FORECAST

As noted in Chapter XI, natural gas liquids represent a substantial contribution to domestic energy production. In 1979, they accounted for 3.8 percent of the total, almost as great as the contributions of hydroelectric and nuclear electric power. Natural gas liquids will add to the liquid petroleum quantity, but they are a by-product of the natural gas industry. They are identified as natural gas plant liquids when processed by the industry.

The analysis of anticipated natural gas liquids production through the end of the century follows the pattern described for natural gas. Again, the reference is the American Gas Association Reserves Committee as reported at the end of 1978. The analysis on the following pages identifies their figures for the years 1974 through 1978.

Neither a reliable year-by-year production sample nor an independent undiscovered resource analysis is available for natural gas liquids. However, for the last twelve years, natural gas liquids have represented 34.65 million barrels per trillion cubic feet of natural gas production plus or minus 5 percent with the exception of one year. This relationship cannot be relied upon indefinitely, but it provides a guide in anticipating future production.

Four hundred million barrels of natural gas liquids are locked in the Prudhoe Bay reserve, unavailable for production until the gas pipeline is completed. Subtracting this quantity, the proved reserve at the beginning of 1979 is identified as 5.526 billion barrels. Between 1974 and 1978 the rate of withdrawal decreased slightly. A straight-line extrapolation of the 11.87 percent withdrawal rate in 1978 produces a rate of 11.10 percent for the year 2000. This declination fits the physical expectancy and has been accepted.

Additions to the proved reserve of natural gas liquids declined at a constant exponential rate of minus 3.7035 percent using as a base the year 1975 and the average of the next three years identified as 1977. This declination produces a total addition for the 21-year extrapolation which is 5 percent less than the average rate for natural gas liquids production applied to our predicted natural gas revisions, extensions, and additions. On this basis, additions to the natural gas liquids reserve are projected at 532 million barrels in 1979 and 241 million barrels in the year 2000.

Applying the same process, the natural gas liquids proved reserves for the lower 48 states will decline from 5.526 million barrels in 1978 to 3.138 in the year 2000. Production will decline from 694 million barrels in 1979 to 362 in the first year of the new century, 2 percent more than one-half the current supply.

LOWER 48 U.S. NATURAL GAS
PRODUCTION + PROVED RESERVE
(Excludes 31 trillion cubin feet Prudhoe Bay, Alaska Proved Reserves)
1974 through 2000
Trillion Cubin Feet

Year	Total Discoveries + Additions to Proved Reserves	Yearend Proved Reserve	Annual Production	Production Percent of Previous Yearend Proved Reserve
		218.95		
1974	8.68	206.13	21.32	9.74
1975	10.45	197.20	19.72	9.57
1976	7.56	185.03	19.54	9.91
1977	11.85	177.88	19.45	10.51
1978	10.59	169.30	19.31	10.86
1979	11.4	161.74	18.96	11.2
1980	12.0	155.14	18.60	11.5
1981	12.6	149.43	18.31	11.8
1982	13.1	144.45	18.08	12.1
1983	13.6	139.99	18.06	12.5
1984	13.5	135.68	17.92	12.8
1985	13.1	130.87	17.91	13.2
1986	12.8	126.00	17.67	13.5
1987	12.4	121.01	17.39	13.8
1988	12.0	115.83	16.79	14.1
1989	11.7	110.85	16.68	14.4
1990	11.3	105.86	16.30	14.7
1991	11.0	100.98	15.88	15.0
1992	10.7	96.53	15.15	15.0
1993	10.4	92.45	14.48	15.0
1994	10.1	88.68	13.87	15.0
1995	9.8	85.18	13.30	15.0
1996	9.5	81.90	12.78	15.0
1997	9.3	78.92	12.29	15.0
1998	9.0	76.08	11.84	15.0
1999	8.7	73.37	11.41	15.0
2000	8.5	70.86	11.01	15.0

Exhibit D-45

ANNUAL ESTIMATES OF PROVED NATURAL GAS RESERVES IN THE UNITED STATES, 1965 THROUGH 1979 TOTAL ALL TYPES
American Gas Association
(Millions of Cubic Feet – 14.73 psia, at 60°F.)

Year	Revisions	Extensions	New Field Discoveries	New Reservoir Discoveries in Old Fields	Total of Discoveries Revisions and Extensions
1965	14,775,570[a]			6,543,709[a]	21,319,279
1966	4,937,962	9,224,745	2,947,329	3,110,396	20,220,432
1967	6,570,578	9,538,584	3,170,520	2,524,651	21,804,333
1968	3,016,146	7,758,821	1,376,429	1,545,612	13,697,008
1969	(1,238,261)	5,800,489	1,769,557	2,043,219	8,375,004
1970	(99,721)	6,158,168	27,770,223	3,367,689	37,196,359
1971	(1,227,400)	6,374,706	1,317,574	3,360,541	9,825,421
1972	(1,077,791)	6,153,683	1,462,539	3,096,132	9,634,563
1973	(3,474,756)	6,177,286	2,152,151	1,970,368	6,825,049
1974	(1,333,285)	5,847,251	2,013,745	2,151,473	8,679,184
1975	383,449	6,027,433	2,423,382	1,649,424	10,483,688
1976	(1,197,119)	5,337,707	1,421,013	1,993,867	7,555,468
1977	983,551	6,601,229	2,114,505	2,152,639	11,851,924
1978	118,436	6,733,441	1,719,938	2,014,329	10,586,144
1979	2,907,551	7,113,113	2,575,779	1,689,504	14,285,947

Year	Net Change in Underground Storage	Production[b]	Proved Reserves at End of Year	Net Change From Previous Year
1965	150,483	16,252,293	286,468,923	5,217,469
1966	134,523	17,491,073	289,332,805	2,863,882
1967	151,403	18,380,838	292,907,703	3,574,898
1968	118,568[d]	19,373,427[d]	287,349,852	(5,557,851)
1969	107,169	20,723,190	275,108,835	(12,241,017)
1970	402,018	21,960,804	290,746,408	15,637,573
1971	310,301	22,076,512	278,805,618	(11,940,790)
1972	156,563	22,511,898	266,084,846	(12,720,772)
1973	(354,282)[c]	22,605,406	249,950,207	(16,134,639)
1974	(178,424)[c]	21,318,470	237,132,497	(12,817,710)
1975	302,561[c]	19,718,570	228,200,176	(8,932,321)
1976	(187,550)	19,542,020	216,026,074	(12,174,102)
1977	446,930	19,447,050	208,877,878	(7,148,196)
1978	148,733	19,311,048	200,301,707	(8,576,171)
1979	239,323	19,910,353	194,916,624	(5,385,083)

Used by permission of the copyright holder, American Gas Association.

a – Separation of revisions from extensions of new field discoveries from new reservoir discoveries in old field not available prior to 1966

b – Preliminary net production.

c – See footnote e, Table 1.

d – This value has been changed to correct a numerical error made in Volume 23.

( ) – Denotes negative volume.

Exhibit D-46

LOWER 48 U.S. NATURAL GAS LIQUIDS
Proved Reserves and Production
(Excludes 400 million barrels Alaskan Reserve)
Million Barrels

Year	Total Discoveries + Additions to Proved Reserves	Yearend Proved Reserve	Annual Production	Production Percent of Previous Yearend Proved Reserve
		6.06		
1974	619.8	5.95	724	11.96
1975	618.5	5.87	701	11.78
1976	834.8	6.00	701	11.95
1977	291.2	5.59	699	11.65
1978	595.7	5.53	664	11.87
1979	532	5.41	649	11.75
1980	513	5.29	634	11.72
1981	424	5.09	618	11.69
1982	475	4.98	594	11.66
1983	458	4.85	579	11.63
1984	441	4.73	563	11.59
1985	424	4.61	547	11.56
1986	409	4.49	531	11.53
1987	394	4.37	516	11.50
1988	379	4.24	501	11.47
1989	365	4.12	485	11.44
1990	351	4.00	470	11.41
1991	338	3.89	456	11.38
1992	326	3.77	441	11.35
1993	314	3.66	427	11.32
1994	302	3.96	413	11.28
1995	291	3.81	446	11.25
1996	280	3.66	427	11.22
1997	270	3.52	409	11.19
1998	260	3.39	393	11.16
1999	250	3.26	377	11.13
2000	214	3.14	362	11.10

Exhibit D-47

ANNUAL ESTIMATES OF PROVED NATURAL GAS RESERVES IN THE UNITED STATES, 1965 THROUGH 1979
TOTAL ALL TYPES
American Gas Association
(Thousands of Barrels of 42 U.S. Gallons)

Year	Revisions	Extensions	New Field Discoveries	New Reservoir Discoveries in Old Fields
1965[a]	721,605			110,707
1966	634,233	131,583	53,378	74,922
1967	671,112	159,725	57,272	41,649
1968	469,689	155,940	26,642	33,388
1969	106,192	106,815	26,831	41,190
1970	35,446	103,740	34,234	134,159
1971	135,144	93,909	28,513	90,154
1972	38,796	112,537	32,652	54,288
1973	231,460	121,835	19,202	36,482
1974	393,484	149,996	36,095	40,266
1975	345,496	116,810	128,036	28,162
1976	614,356	158,572	20,460	41,378
1977	78,043	152,535	24,950	35,643
1978	365,813	153,181	31,427	45,245
1979	141,727	166,769	38,437	42,872

Year	Total of Discoveries, Revisions and Extensions	Production[c]	Proved Reserves at End of Year	Net Change From Previous Year
1965[a]	832,312	555,410	8,023,534	276,902
1966	894,116	588,684	8,328,966	305,432
1967	929,758	644,493	8,614,231	285,265
1968	685,659	701,782	8,598,108	(16,123)
1969	281,028	735,962	8,143,174	(454,934)
1970	307,579	747,812	7,702,941	(440,233)
1971	347,720	746,434	7,304,227	(398,714)
1972	238,273	755,941	6,786,559	(517,668)
1973	408,979	740,831	6,454,707	(331,852)
1974	619,841	724,099	6,350,449	(104,258)
1975	618,504	701,123	6,267,830	(82,619)
1976	834,766	700,629	6,401,967	134,137
1977	291,171	698,773	5,994,365	(407,602)
1978	595,666	664,179	5,925,852	(68,513)
1979	389,805	660,334	5,655,323	(270,529)

Used by permission of the copyright holder, American Gas Association.

a — Separation of revisions from extensions and of new field discoveries from new reservoir discoverеis not available prior to 1966

b — Preliminary net production.

c — Denotes negative volume.

Exhibit D-48

The Significance
of Soddy's
Physical Economics

Frederick Soddy's attack on Adam Smith's laissez-faire economics is more devastating than that of any of his predecessors including Karl Marx. Soddy was totally concerned with the economic system's potential efficiency, and efficiency will become survival when energy resources are unavailable in the quantities required. Laissez-faire economics violates the physical laws of conservation. Man cannot stand against the laws of nature and survive for long.

Soddy proposed restoring the balance between the physical and political influences on economics, and today the evidence of the necessity for this recognition is mounting. Soddy's physical economics identified the problem and charted a solution. He opened the door for the development of an economic science. His solutions may be too simple or too radical for acceptance by the political and economic communities but his statement of the problem and its parameters must be recognized if economics is to escape from its dependency on myth, political power and psychological machinations.

Economics is in trouble as we enter the 1980s. Perhaps this is the point of beginning. In viewing the economic problem, a clear distinction must be drawn between Soddy's physical economics and the many criticisms and defenses of laissez-faire economics that developed in the first century after Adam Smith. These criticisms targeted the political and humanitarian influences of economic theory. Social justice had been Karl Marx's concern. The laissez-faire system created cycles of excessive production and depression, bankrupting the entrepreneur and reducing labor to intolerable starvation levels that would fuel political rebellion. He attempted to speed the rebellion to clear the way for what became his communist state, but it did not happen the way Marx expected. In the West, the political-economic system adjusted to accommodate the social objectives that political reality dictated.

Soddy developed his physical economic concepts by observing an advanced society. The market is vital to this society to identify relative desires and establish price, the mechanism by which demand becomes effective. A higher price both limits consumption and encourages production of the desired goods and services. But the market and the price mechanism do not produce the materials that the society requires.

Soddy distinguished between real wealth—it includes both consumable food and fuel as well as the relatively permanent wealth represented by homes, farms and factories considered to be the capital stocks of a nation—and the reflection of that wealth which is credit-money. Money can be used in exchange for labor and materials to produce capital, and capital is absolutely necessary, but money is not capital and there is no difference between currency and interest-bearing loan credit in summing up the reflected wealth of the nation. Both should be created by the state as both become claims on the nation's real wealth.

Soddy's theory of economics rests on the necessity of maintaining money with a constant or near constant value. With a reliable means of exchanging value and storing value, the free society can develop its resources and provide food and shelter and entertainment in abundance for all of its citizens. Capital can be created by the state through taxation or by individuals through savings, but those savings must represent the actual giving up of purchasing power (demand on the material resources of the state).

The creation of capital by an expansion of the money supply is the critical element in the economy of a modern state and it is on this function that Soddy concentrates his attention and criticism. When credit-money, created for any purpose, exceeds the increase of the real wealth of a nation, then that created money dilutes and reduces the value of all money. Money must be created to adequately balance the capital stocks that the nation puts in place and support the credit requirements of an expanding population. The economic process requires money-credit to employ energy, labor, and material to increase its capital stocks and advance physical living standards. The problem is the temptation of the delegated authority to create excess money-credit. Soddy cuts through the myths that have been employed to justify the money-creating process.

Money is not capital and money does not beget money. The assumption that money can or should grow exponentially and at any fixed or variable rate of interest is the primary myth that Soddy's analysis targets. Since the earliest times men have been willing to pay for the use of wealth-controlling money. This payment constitutes a contract between the time periods, the present and the future. More will be paid in the future for the use of money in the present. The concept of money value and interest payment develops from this elementary, natural, human characteristic. Money transactions are the means of satisfying this objective. The next step in this natural wealth relationship is the investment of borrowed wealth in a wealth producing endeavor—money invested in wealth producing capital can return a greater sum than was borrowed. Money then appears to be responsible for the increase in wealth and the concept of capital with its magic power of growth develops.

Money becomes capital only when it is invested in wealth producing materials and services. Money does not itself produce wealth and the payment of interest on non-productive money simply inflates the currency and reduces its value.

Before our modern banking system developed with all of its interrelationships with the government central banking authority, money and credit were a private banking affair. The private banker created credit at his own risk and at the risk of his depositors. When he extended credit beyond its wealth-producing and wealth-returning capacity, his bank failed and the banker's depositors lost the real wealth that had been pledged against the loans or the claims on wealth represented by their deposits. Other bankers or merchants with resources would pick up the remaining real wealth at bargain prices, thus reducing the excess money-credit that had been created. The banker's fortune depended on his ability to identify winners in the exchange of credit and real wealth and in the time differential between the present and the future.

Today's banks are only theoretically private. The state is involved and cannot allow more than a token number of bank failures. The state is a representative of the people and the state cannot allow too many of its people to be adversely affected by bank failures. Banks have been caught up in the growth concept, competing not for reputation in protecting its depositors but in demonstrating growing profitability for its investors. Double indemnity charged to the bank stock investor prior to the 1930s is no longer employed to restrain bank expansion. The state has become the banker's partner protecting his growth objectives. The banking system that has developed in the 55 years since Soddy made his observations has grown more subject to his criticism.

Soddy was appalled at his discovery that the expansion of the nation's credit was controlled by private banks for their own profit. He found bankers poorly informed on the physical facts of the nation's real growth potential as well as its growth limitations. Soddy's physical economics attacks private banking's control of the economy. He was a physical scientist. He believed scientists were primarily responsible for the progress of our society in producing the good things that have enriched our lives and for creating the nation's real wealth.

The banker creates money for purposes of producing wealth but when the wealth that is produced does not equal or exceed the value of the money created, then all money loses value. By saving (working to produce wealth without at the same time creating money) men who work can keep the wealth/money ratio in balance and bankers have always wanted a proportion of saved wealth as collateral for the money creating loans they enter into. Conservative banking maintains a safe margin of saved wealth, but conservative banking cannot grow in competition with bankers who use their money producing (lending) power to its maximum potential, and talented business analysts identify the business ventures that can support the banker's loan without savd capital or by finding saved capital collateral in real wealth not otherwise employed, thus maximizing the expansion. Sophisticated business administrators are skilled in credit manipulation and credit expansion.

Inflation reduces the value of money but inflation does not reduce the value of wealth. Real things, useful land and buildings and machinery increase in value as money loses value. The real value of these useful things does not change but their increased money value provides the support for the banker's loan, his collateral requirement; and it is this increased value that fuels inflation. Thus, the process feeds on itself. The builder who has bought land for $300 an acre can obtain three times as large a loan when the value goes to $900 either for reason of inflation or population pressure or the demand for land. He can multiply that collateral by ten times with no inflation if he can demonstrate that the land is now suitable for one-quarter acre building lots at $2,250 a lot after paying all the commissions and fees required in the sales process. No real change has occurred in the real worth of the community, but the money supply can be increased thirty times. Later on, engineers and builders will add real wealth to this land in constructing roads and sewers and homes and factories; then this wealth will be employed in the inflationary process as these structures are influenced by the rising cost of their construction.

To Soddy the solution to the economic problem was obvious. He would control the expansion of money, both credit money and currency money. In 1926 and in 1933 he was concerned with the banker's contraction of the money supply throwing businesses into liquidation and their employees on to breadlines. The nations of the Western world lacked only comprehension of their real wealth and potential productive capacity to keep their economies going and supply their people with both necessities and luxuries. The banker-controlled economy was reducing the money supply when it should have been expanding. The restriction was created by the ignorance of the men who controlled the economy. Economists call it the market. There is no difference. The market is men making decisions to buy or sell, loan money or foreclose loans, increase prices or decrease prices, hire or fire, expand or contract the production of the goods and services that feed the nation. The market is controlled by the wisdom or the ignorance of decision makers. Soddy was not concerned with the political process. He was concerned with the economic mechanism and its potential.

In the 1980s, with natural resource information available to scientists who are not committed to producing a cash flow for a business or political institution, Soddy's scientific economics would have a very different perspective. Consumption of scarce resources must be curtailed until we can identify the means and time schedule for their substitution. The laws of supply and demand in substitution cannot be relied on to translate the immediate present perspective of market economics into forward planning with responsibility for the natural life expectancy of persons being born into the society. Prudent judgments must be made when the lives of millions of persons are at stake and the deciders must be responsible and identifiable. Market theory avoids this responsibility.

Whether in the 1920s and 1930s or the last two decades of the twentieth century, Soddy's scientific economics runs head-on into conflict with our society's concepts of economic freedom. The bankers whom he targeted for undeserved profiting from the nation's real wealth are not a small fraction of the economic community. They are both the leaders of our political-society and the agents of every upwardly motivated adult member of our society. They represent the middle class whose numbers correlate with an advanced nation's economic sophistication. The businessman depends on the banker for the loans that finance the beginning of his business and carry him through periods of stagnation, covering the losses that result from errors in business judgment. The banker finances his mortgage permitting him to build his home and raise his family in accordance with his personal desires and beliefs. Every individual wants to preserve his banker and his banker's prerogative to lend him money.

Soddy's economics did not stop with the identification of the importance of the monetary system. He specified the means of reducing the nation's debt and balancing the budget. Only the public concepts of money and credit stand in the way of reducing or eliminating the national debt. There is no excuse for government ever borrowing money from the banks when the nation's money stocks are low and should be expanded (to stimulate economic activity). Whether money is printed or credit is extended, the government that becomes its own banker need pay no interest in this phase of economic control. Only when the economy is overheated and inflationary tendencies are observed is it necessary for the government to borrow money. Then the money should be borrowed from elements of the economy that represent real wealth producing capacity. These elements must reduce their purchasing power. That "borrowing" can be accomplished most frequently by taxation, directly targeting the activities that must be restricted, shifting the purchasing power of money from the over-expanded economic sector to the sector whose growth must be assisted to serve the nation's purpose.

In another perspective, Soddy's scientific economics was no less charitable to those sturdy conservatives who place their faith in gold. Gold served its purpose during several periods of international economic tranquility, but the limits of an economics based on the value of gold was already apparent in the 1920s. Then the gold standard restricted monetary expansion needed to reduce the effect of the post-World War I depression. Later it was totally ineffective in curtailing the runaway credit expansion which led to the collapse of the world economy in the 1930s. There is not enough gold to support the world's economy today and encouragement of the production and storage of gold is pure economic waste.

So we come to the end of Frederick Soddy's physical economics, the scientist's attempt to bring order and objectivity to the economics we have known. He was an older contemporary of Maynard Keynes and was critical of Keynes' early writings and influence. Keynes did not have to recognize Soddy. The influence of physical economics on the economic discipline is unclear. It would have required too great an educational effort for most economists to learn enough about the physical sciences to appreciate Soddy's perspective. In the 55 years between Soddy's first book and the beginning of the last two decades of this century, economists have retained their political influence. Despite the general recognition that all is not well with economic theory, the barriers to recognition of physical economics have held.

Physical economics drives a wedge between economics and politics, and a scientific economics would not be compatible with the art and mysticism and superstition and compromise methodology that identify the social disciplines. Political science is the art of the possible, finding solutions to today's problems, today's elections, today's rebellion, the war that has erupted and dominates all other considerations. Economics is the handmaiden of political science. Their separation would threaten the nation's social and political fabric. Physical economics spells out change in revolutionary proportions.

Physical economics requires men to employ the tools of science and look into the future and make judgments and carry through with decisions based on this evidence. Physical economics must be independent of political interference in its sphere of responsibility. At the same time, physical economics requires political acceptance and must take its authority from the political community, else it would remain an academic exercise not even recognized in the academic structure itself.

Physical economics implies mandarin political control of primary economic activities. This concept is peculiarly un-American. America's pioneers attacked this virgin continent and showed the world what uninhibited individual initiative could do. American economic power controlled the political community and after World War II that community was the free world. Can it be suggested that this political-economic system must be shorn of its primary source of influence, that the two most important sources of that economic power must be taken out of the political process and removed from the influence of political power? This is precisely what physical economics implies. The control of the money supply and its value on the one hand and the control of energy supply on the other would be placed in the hands of men with great power. Even if their power was most carefully restricted to these functions, their influence would appear to be without precedent in American politics.

But this barrier is more apparent than real. True, America has never come to appreciate its bureaucracy and the performance of that bureaucracy, but America has produced true statesmen and selfless public servants in every generation. When needed, they can be found even though the American political process may have to be altered to find and appoint men to the key jobs that will have a controlling influence on our lives.

Looking back into history, the Chinese gave the name to mandarin administration and produced the society with the longest history of efficient and effective government the world has known. Hjalmar Schacht controlled the money supply in reviving the German economy after its 1922 inflationary collapse. Schacht's economics happened to have been partnered with a disastrous political party that was responsible for World War II, but this does not destroy the validity of the effectiveness of his economic administration. That economy might have set the pattern for the future world if the political society had remained free.

Britain has long developed and experienced a responsible bureaucracy. The line between political decision-making and administration is carefully drawn with centuries of experience. Many deplore the decline in British world influence, affluence, and competitive economic power; but Britain has demonstrated the capacity of a free political system to absorb drastic economic change and reduced physical living standards. Britain has the political base for developing a form of physical economics. Scandinavian countries have made similar contributions to social and political organization of physical economic controls under a free political system that permits the controls to be drastically altered by the political process. Finally, Japan has developed cooperative economic principles that now must be recognized. Today, we have answers for our theoretical economic questions that were not available to Dr. Soddy. They can be employed in developing a new economics within a compatible social and political structure.

Derivation and Development

Section F

The Truth
About War

The French Philosopher, Chartier, a World War I veteran, writing under his pen name, Alain, identifies the dichotomy of peacetime and wartime morality in 93 short essays. Three of these essays are reproduced with permission from his publisher.

Although Chartier draws on his own war experience and the experience of soldiers and writers who observed war in previous centuries, the art of war has not changed with mechanization, air power, and bombs that can annihilate total city populations. The civilian population has been brought into the front line and the practice of war now threatens to destroy an entire civilization, but the organization for war and the winning in war is still governed by the rules discovered in centuries of war experience. They are clearly presented in Chartier's philosophic discussions.

8: ON COMMAND

"There is too much talk. We must find the man who is responsible and punish him." This is what a captain said whose duty it was to be in command of a small town of aviators and workmen. He was not loved, but I do not think he cared.

This method is astonishing, for friendship, confidence, and appreciation of good work can do much with men. I, for my part, belong to those people who believe that a society of men can, with very few exceptions, live and prosper by the good sense of each man; we see that fear and threats do not count for anything in this pleasant order of exchanges and credits, for every calling is respectable. There is then something scandalous in the military power, which always threatens, always makes the man who would resist it openly feel brutal constraint and death. We can invent Utopias, where an army acts solely on the basis of fraternity and by the recognized competence of the commanders, because war is always forgotten. War always brings up the unforeseen and exceeds the possible. When human strength is at its last tether the soldier has to go on marching; at a moment when it is no longer possible to hold a position, it has to be held. Military art strains beyond a man's will. After the last flash of will there are still powerful convulsions in a man crushed by inexorable forces. War is carried through by such convulsions, which are bound, co-ordinated and armed, and this last leap of the collective animal brings about victory. Until then war is a brilliant game and not without risks, but, as we know, the most dashing courage adapts itself to flight or to capitulation as soon as the game seems lost. Now, it is here that military art produces its last effect to the amazement of the free warrior who, from that moment, is regularly beaten. In modern times the famous Frederick of Prussia was the inventor of this mechanical warfare which, apart from utilizing enthusiasm, esprit de corps, anger, and virtue always brought fear into play as an alternative, and he was thereby able to urge on his army a little further. Once this method was rediscovered, every army had to adopt it. There is absolutely no other means of surmounting the highest degree of terror.

Not without fine speeches, however, for it is painful to say to oneself: "How am I to know if goodwill would be sufficient for these sublime actions, when all precautions are taken in case it fails?" Still, tradition remains sufficiently upheld by a spirit of arrogance and laziness; thus everything is ready for the last effort and from the first confusion, which is excusable, but regrettable, every one necessarily again descends to the level of mechanical force. Hence the certitude in councils of war, which seems like the inevitable. And we should not ask what happens to human conscience in those sinister sacrifices, for it is not touched at all, it cannot grasp them. Men have a horror of what they do not understand, but the horror is inexpressible and almost physical. Also, we do not need so much will to be pitiless; on the contrary, we do not need any at all. We only need to be pushed or to push. Such is this terrible calling, and it is so below moral judgment that the most courageous of us speak of it only jokingly, which keeps us from despising military glory, and perhaps also from loving it. "Let's not talk about that," says the hero.

9: THE SYSTEM

I make no attempt to guess what they thought and what men now think who were the hooks, harpoons, or goads to collect, catch, and push men towards that terrible place; those apparently human faces weary the eye by their mechanical seriousness. When I was among the herd of the wretched, I came to know the dumb despair of a man sitting on the edge of his bed, newly equipped and waiting for the bugle call. They were wounded men, half recovered. They had tried to gain an extra day or two and some had succeeded. A day or two of life is something, but even that comes to an end. And so they have to set off, dragging their feet, and with all their baggage on their back. An excess of tiredness suppresses bitter thoughts that aggravate our ills. It is enough to be on the road, that is all they think about. Nevertheless, nearly every one gives way to a strong instinct, which distracts them. The journey is slow, there are unexpected halts, everything happens slowly in war, and time passes quickly. It is easy to miss a train, and the small detachment breaks up on the way. Packs and rifles are left on benches. Still, the System continues with a mechanical patience, the results of which are always astonishing. A sergeant who represents the invisible station-master, an all powerful master, says, when I hand over to him the things that have been abandoned: "Some always run off, but they will be found; where do you think they can go to?" His composure succeeds in taking away all my hope, and that is for the best.

Nevertheless, as the barracks begin to cover a large area, and as civilian clothes become more rare, the soldier is allowed more liberty, and that very fact proves it cannot be used. Like those sweeping ears of corn which every gust of wind drives in the same direction, all the stirrings of imagination are directed in the same sense. The gendarme shows you the way to go; you are free to sit down, to eat and drink, to sleep on a square of grass between those two tracks of mud. I see other men, silent and inert as though the System had forgotten them by the roadside. Just as the second broom picks up the dust left by the first, so there is still a third broom behind it. But here, for these men, there is no visible constraint; only this desert is eloquent enough; it is merely a passage; these muddy tracks grip the attention; their feet soon follow in them. And when they look back they see the rear which is unanimous in saying "No" to these wretches, the relentless rear which waits for them to be gone. When so many human wills and so many human signs enforce the same mute counsel, men hurry sometimes in order to suffer less; and that is the first sign of the return of courage.

Here are the last barracks and here the last gendarme. Here pressure is non-existent. Here the system of the rear closes its last door. All that is beyond this point is for war, and no one has any doubts. The continual action of the enemy which can now be felt puts an end to all thought. A man has only one place in this close game; he looks for it; he cannot be anywhere else. The volcanic line illuminates in vain the clouds in the twilight; here the imaginary fear which incapacitates action seems to be dethroned. Fear at this point seems no more than a brutal emotion, which cannot be foreseen and which leaves no traces. Danger has a shape and the soldier finds his proper calling. Until then all the men that were pushing you presented an abject picture of well-established fear, a spectacle which breeds fear, hatred, and sadness. Now these comrades in distress inspire confidence and fellow-feeling. A little while ago the same question kept recurring: "Why should it be I and not they?" The System exerted its measured pressure against it. Now, on the contrary, every one says to himself: "Why should it be they and not I?" That is why you see the man who went to his post with a firm step returning like Regulus. And that is the second return of courage.

10: THE RULES OF THE GAME

A newspaper reported the story of a private, the father of a family and twice mentioned for bravery, who, when he returned to the trenches with some provisions, took cover to allow a dangerous moment to pass and unfortunately fell asleep, whereupon he was accused of having deserted his post on active service, and finally shot. I take this fact as truth, for I have heard many similar stories. What astonishes me is that the journalist who told this story wanted to make people believe that such condemnations were atrocious and unjustifiable; in which he was mistaken, for it is war that is atrocious and unjustifiable, and if you accept war then you must accept this method of punishment.

The refusal to obey is rare, especially in action. What is more common is the tendency to avoid the most dangerous positions by inventing some such pretext as accompanying a wounded man, especially as it is very easy to lose the way; as for tiredness, there is no need to invent that. For such reasons, even if we presuppose a measure of good faith in the prudent soldier by the power that fear naturally exercises over opinions, we should soon see the troops dissolve and disappear like water into the ground at the very moment when there was an urgent need for all combatants. I add that this is what we should see if the authorities hesitated to carry out punishments that inspire more terror than the battle itself.

Every one has always a good reason to explain why he is not where he should be. If the excuses are accepted, the death penalty, the only one that has any power over fear, is immediately ineffectual, for whether it is good or bad, the excuse will always seem a good one to the coward; he will have some hope of escaping punishment, and that hope, together with fear, is sufficient imperceptibly to turn a man who is always alone away from the strict path of duty. It is therefore necessary that the soldier who is not where he should be, should not be able to invoke either a momentary weakness or fatigue, or a mistake, or even an insurmountable obstacle; hence the need to deal pitilessly with the deed on its face value without taking the reasons into account.

The distant spectator cannot understand these things, because he believes from the tales of the combatants themselves that men have no other thought but to rush against the enemy. I add that the authorities have a very definite interest in making people believe this; for people in the rear would be ashamed to ask for a peace which was merely tolerable, when the combatants were ready to die for it. But the military art very soon sharply reminds those whose duty it is to push the men on to fight of its secular laws, which aim at robbing the combatant of all hope other than the fortunes of war. Moreover, whether we want to make an example or to drive the enemy out of his trenches, man is always the means and the tool. And since the most courageous and the most devoted men are destined for death, it is not astonishing that a few cowards or waverers are sacrificed without hesitation.

But what if a man has proved himself? There are no proofs, and experience shows that a soldier who behaved well when he was surrounded and watched, without counting the excitement of action, is also capable of taking cover a little too quickly when he is alone. I should add that repeated tests accompanied by fatigue often exhaust courage. Even if a man has done marvels, he must often begin again and again, and it is one of the problems of military art to maintain the spirit of the troops well above the limits that the individual combatant fixes for himself. Very often the soldier who has been decorated tries to live henceforth on his reputation without risking too much. Thus ordinary common sense, which later makes him take account of past circumstances, rises again here, sustained by inflexible experience and pressing necessity. That is why hasty executions that are terrifying and even revolting do not affect me more than the war itself, of which they are the inevitable consequence. We should never listen to nor allow ourselves to believe the statement that war can ever be compatible, in any sense whatsoever, with justice and humanity.

Bibliography

1. *American Petroleum Institute, 1980. *Reserves of Crude Oil, Natural Gas Liquids, and Natural Gas in the United States and Canada as of December 23, 1979.* Washington, D.C.: American Petroleum Institute.
2. Bailey, Richard, 1977. *Energy: The Rude Awakening.* London: McGraw-Hill (UK) (North American printing in 1977 by Energy Education Publishers, Grand Rapids, Michigan).
3. Bank for International Settlements, 1974-1980. Monthly and quarterly reports, December 1974 through July 1980. Basle, Switzerland: Bank for International Settlements.
4. Barney, Gerald O., study director, 1980. *The Global 2000 Report to the President,* Volumes I and II. (The Council on Environmental Quality and the Department of State.) Washington, D.C.: United States Government Printing Office.
5. *Brooks, Harvey and Ginzton, Edward L., co-chairmen, 1979. *Energy in Transition 1985-2010.* (National Research Council Committee on Nuclear and Alternative Energy Systems [CONAES].) Washington, D.C.: National Academy of Sciences.
6. Brown, Harrison, 1954. *The Challenge of Man's Future.* New York: Viking Press.
7. *Cook, Earl, 1976. *Man, Energy, Society.* San Francisco: W. H. Freeman and Company.
8. *Cottrell, W. Frederick, 1955. *Energy and Society.* New York: McGraw-Hill. Reprinted in 1970 by Greenwood Press, Westport, Connecticut.
9. Daly, Herman E. 1973. *Toward a Steady-State Economy.* San Francisco: W. H. Freeman and Company.
10. Dix, Samuel M., 1977. *Energy—A Critical Decision for the United States Economy* (Originally printed October 1976, *Last Report to President Ford.*) Grand Rapids, Michigan: Energy Education Publishers.
11. *Duane, John W., 1979. *Energy and the United States.* Jackson, Michigan. Consumers Power Company.
12. Durant, Will and Ariel, 1935-1975. *The Story of Civilization.* Eleven volumes. New York: Simon and Schuster.
13. *Exxon Corporation, 1979. *Energy Outlook 1980-2000.* Houston: Exxon Corporation (Public Affairs Department).

14. Flanigan, James, 1977. "Does Exxon Have a Future?" *Forbes,* v. 120, August 15, 1978, p. 37-42.
15. *Franssen, Herman T., 1978. *Energy: An Uncertain Future–An Analysis of U.S. and World Energy Projections Through 1980.* (Prepared at the request of the Committee on Energy and Natural Resources, United States Senate, Publication #95-157, December 1978.) Washington, D.C.: United States Government Printing Office.
16. *Franssen, Herman T., 1975. *Towards Project Interdependence: Energy in the Coming Decade.* (Prepared for the Joint Committee on Atomic Energy United States Congress, Publication #61-173, December 1975.) Washington, D.C.: United States Government Printing Office.
17. *Franssen, Herman T., 1978. *U.S. Energy Demand and Supply 1976 to 1985, Limited Options, Unlimited Constraints.* Congressional Research Service. Prepared for the Subcommittee on Energy and Power of the Committee on Interstate and Foreign Commerce, House of Representatives, 95th Congress, Publication #21-616, March 1978.) Washington, D.C.: United States Government Printing Office.
18. Georgescu-Roegen, Nicholas 1972. *The Entropy Law & The Economic Process.* Cambridge: Harvard University Press.
19. *Hubbert, M. King, 1974. *U.S. Energy Resources, a Review as of 1972.* United States Congress, Senate Committee on Interior and Insular Affairs, 93rd Congress, 2nd Session, Committee Print Serial 93-40. Washington, D.C.: United States Government Printing Office.
20. *Koenig, Herman E., 1979. *Energy Economics: Foundations of Energy Policy.* East Lansing, Michigan: Michigan State University (Center for Environmental Quality).
21. *Kreinin, Mordechai, 1979. *International Economics,* 3rd edition. New York: Harcourt Brace Jovanovich, Inc.
22. Kuhn, Thomas S., 1962. *The Structure of Scientific Revolutions.* Chicago: The University of Chicago Press.
23. *Levy, Walter J., 1978. "The Years That the Locust Hath Eaten: Oil Policy and OPEC Development Prospects." *Foreign Affairs,* v. 57, winter 1978, p. 287-306.
24. Mason, Stephen F., 1956. *A History of the Sciences.* New York: MacMillan Publishing Co., Inc. (Collier Books).
25. *Meadows, Donella H. and Dennis L., 1972. *The Limits to Growth.* New York: The New American Library, Inc.
26. *Miller, Betty M., and others, 1975. *Geological Estimates of Undiscovered Recoverable Oil and Gas Resources in the United States.* Reston, Va.: United States Geological Survey, Circular 725.
27. Rifkin, Jeremy and Howard, Ted 1980. *Entropy: A New World View.* New York: The Viking Press.
28. Soddy, Frederick, 1933. *Wealth, Virtual Wealth and Debt–The Solution of the Economic Paradox,* 2nd edition. New York: E. P. Dutton and Company, Inc.

29. Stobaugh, Robert and Yergin, Daniel, 1979. *Energy Future.* (Harvard Business School Energy Project.) New York: Random House.
30. Teller, Edward, 1979. *Energy from Heaven and Earth.* San Francisco: W. H. Freeman and Company.
31. Thurow, L. C., 1980. *Zero Sum Society.* New York: Basic Book, Inc.
32. Udall, Stewart, 1974. *The Energy Balloon.* New York: McGraw-Hill.
33. United States Department of Energy, Energy Information Administration. *Monthly Energy Review.* Washington, D.C.: United States Government Printing Office.
34. *Zareski, Gordon K., 1975. *A Realistic View of the United States Natural Gas Supply.* Washington, D.C.: Federal Power Commission (Bureau of Natural Gas).

*Authors or organizations who contributed personally to research or confirmed information.

Index